Praise for *We Should All Be Millionaires*

"Earning a million dollars requires a lot more than just a 'positive mindset.' This book is an honest, realistic, and inspiring look at what it really takes to become an extremely high-earning woman. Rachel Rodgers will give you a million-dollar attitude with a bank account to match."

—Sophia Amoruso,
New York Times Bestselling Author of *#Girlboss*

"As Black women, we are accustomed to the story that we are required to struggle in order to find financial stability or success. This book needs to be read by every woman who is ready for a blueprint for being joyful, finding ease, and growing wealth while standing up for causes that need our voices and attention."

—Rachel Cargle,
Author and Anti-Racism Activist

"*We Should All Be Millionaires* is a must-read, not only to help you become more financially abundant and empowered, but also so that you can become a much-needed agent of change, equality, and equity that our world needs."

—Mastin Kipp,
Bestselling Author of *Claim Your Power*
and Creator of Functional Life Coaching

"There are thousands of books about how to make more money, but *We Should All Be Millionaires* is the book we've been waiting for. Money lessons from a Black woman, mother of four, business owner, and self-made millionaire—an author who understands the specific challenges that women face when it comes to building wealth. A powerful, thought-provoking book about how to create abundance in your life. More money, more options, more possibilities for yourself and your family."

—Farnoosh Torabi,
Author and Personal Finance Expert

"I've personally watched Rachel Rodgers grow her business from the ground up. She delivers a roadmap to go from broke to money-woke in one delicious read. This is for every woman who wants to climb through the hole Rodgers just cracked in the glass ceiling."

—Susan Hyatt,
Author and Master Certified Life and Business Coach

"In passionate and powerful prose, Rachel sets forth a blueprint for determination, liberation, and unapologetic self-love. *We Should All Be Millionaires* is a modern-day money Manifesta for those who are ready to reach for more."

—Rha Goddess,
Founder and CEO of Move The Crowd
and Author of *The Calling: 3 Fundamental Shifts to Stay True, Get Paid, and Do Good*

WE SHOULD ALL BE
MILLIONAIRES

A Woman's Guide to Earning More, Building Wealth, and Gaining Economic Power

RACHEL RODGERS

HarperCollins
Leadership

An Imprint of HarperCollins

Published by HarperCollins Leadership, an imprint of HarperCollins Focus LLC.

Any internet addresses, phone numbers, or company or product information printed in this book are offered as a resource and are not intended in any way to be or to imply an endorsement by HarperCollins Leadership, nor does HarperCollins Leadership vouch for the existence, content, or services of these sites, phone numbers, companies, or products beyond the life of this book.

ISBN 978-1-4002-2163-9 (eBook)
ISBN 978-1-4002-2162-2 (HC)

Library of Congress Control Number: 2021931306

Printed in the United States of America
21 22 23 LSC 10 9 8 7 6 5 4 3 2 1

This book is dedicated to my beloved sister, Angela, whose consistent cheerleading, reminders that I am smart and can figure it out, and occasional loans when I couldn't make payroll have gotten me to where I am today.

Angela, I couldn't have become a millionaire or gained the knowledge to write this book without you. Thank you for being the best big sister in the world. I love you.

"We must overcome the notion that we must be regular. It robs you of the chance to be extraordinary and leads you to the mediocre."

—UTA HAGEN

CONTENTS

INTRODUCTION

"America doesn't respect anything but money.
What our people need is a few millionaires."

—MADAM C. J. WALKER

believe every woman should want to be a millionaire.

If you agree with me, this book is for you.

If you strongly disagree with me, this book is definitely for you.

Every woman needs to see at least seven zeros in her bank account, at the bottom of her own balance sheet, and in her cumulative net worth. Every woman needs to know what it feels like to wield economic power. That's how we make change. That's how we serve our children. That's how we serve the world.

I want you to know what it feels like to be a millionaire. To own a home with no mortgage. To have the freedom to leave a job you don't love. To have more time to spend with your favorite people doing things you enjoy. To have more time to rest.

I want you to know what it feels like to be a millionaire. To have more than you need and be able to put that surplus money to work for your children, my children, and our children's children. I want you to know what it feels like to solve community problems like providing for kids who can't afford school lunch or creating a community garden by simply writing a check. I wrote this book, because that's not the world we're living in right now.

The data is daunting: Women are afraid to ask for the money they deserve and need (and are less likely to get), afraid to make more than their partners, and afraid that having a career means not meeting their family's needs. Screw the thigh gap, let's talk about some other gaps: white women make 79 cents compared to a dollar made by a white man, and Black women make 62 cents.[1] **Sixty-two cents, y'all!** Women also pay more for their debt than men,[2] are less likely to invest than men,[3] and are therefore 80 percent more likely to be impoverished in retirement.[4] When it comes to business, women entrepreneurs raise less money than men,[5] and only 2 percent of women-owned businesses ever hit the seven figure mark.[6] All of this despite the fact that research shows that women are better investors and better leaders than men.[7]

We are going to change all of this, and this book will show you the way. In this book, we are going to cover things you've never seen before, and I am going to teach you how to:

- Build serious wealth.
- Increase your income significantly within one year.
- Get on the path to becoming a millionaire within three years.
- Stop getting in your own way.
- Increase your power, peace, and joy.

And, most important, how to start making Million Dollar Decisions and the exact steps you need to take to get on the path to millionaire status, no matter your current situation or earnings.

Here's what you will not see in this book: me telling you to stop drinking your three dollar latte or to stop being a shopaholic (these are the ridiculous messages women are inundated with by so-called financial gurus on a daily basis). Here's what I will tell you: how to start making a lot more money. You will learn how to add income streams without hustling all the time and start generating an extra $1,000 or $5,000 per month. In this book, you'll learn how to expand your income rather than contract your expenses.

And here's why: whether we like it or not, money is the source of real power in society.

There's very little any of us can do—to get paid for the true value of our work, to make our own decisions, to control our lives, and much less to move women, marginalized communities, and society forward—without the freedom that money can buy. Your options in life are likely to remain limited if your resources are also limited. And, yes, this is a sad state of affairs. I, too, would love to live in a world where that wasn't the case, but that world doesn't exist. And so, sisters, to claim more power in the world, we need more money.

Some of the power money offers us is emotional. When we have money, we are confident that we can build wealth and earn more. When we don't, we always fear not having enough and being judged for it. I learned that lesson at a young age as a kid in New York City, standing in the grocery store checkout line embarrassed about having to pay with food stamps. I remember feeling shame and looking around hoping that none of my friends from school would realize that my family was receiving public assistance.

Many of my schoolmates lived in nice apartment buildings with nice furniture. They went to Kumon, a tutoring program, after school and took art and violin lessons. They had summer passes to the local community pool. I didn't have any of those things, because my parents couldn't afford them. But I went out of my way to pretend that my family's financial struggles didn't exist.

I remember in sixth grade being invited by a group of friends to go on a shopping trip to the outlet stores in Reading, Pennsylvania. I was excited to go but didn't have any money to actually shop. But my mother always found a way. My dad had been doing odd jobs, and one of them was refilling vending machines. He got paid in coins, and that's the only extra money we had. The morning of the trip, my mother and I sat on the floor of our living room rolling quarters. I went on the trip with $33 in rolled coins.

During the trip, I'd browse the stores with my friends and, while they made their purchases of new clothes and sneakers, I'd pretend that I didn't like anything because I didn't have enough money to buy them. Eventually, I did find something I could afford: a wallet. Looking back now, I realize how aspirational to purchase a wallet when I had no money. Even then, I believed that one day I'd have enough cash to fill a wallet. I waited until all my friends left the store, and then I bought my new discounted leather wallet with my rolled coins.

Being financially poor can define who you are and shape what you think you are capable of. When your bank account is empty, you are assumed to be lazy and uneducated, an unproductive member of society incapable of making your own way. My parents were hardworking, smart, and quite productive but I wonder if they knew that? For a time we lived comfortably, but there were other times riddled with layoffs from good jobs, addictions, and all the disadvantages that come with living under constant financial distress. Would money have solved all our problems? Of course not, but it sure as hell would have solved a lot of them.

Money also creates power by giving us autonomy. When we have money, we can make decisions that improve our quality of life and the lives of others without needing anyone else to weigh in. When we have wealth, we can be independent and make our own decisions.

The opposite is true when we're broke. When we don't have money, we can be stuck at a job where we're being sexually harassed (because we need that paycheck, dammit) or with a man who's abusing us (because we need the asshole's financial support). We can't even donate to causes we care about or financially support the political campaigns of people we want to represent us in government. It's harder to advocate for ourselves or others without money, autonomy, and power.

If we as women are truly passionate about improving our lives, making the world a better place for our children, and getting equity for all marginalized people, then we need to step up and make bank. That, in my opinion, is the way we take back the power we deserve from people who underestimate and undermine the contributions women like us make to the world every day.

We've tried using our voices to speak truth to power. We've tried marching. We've tried writing letters to our representatives. We've tried volunteering in our kids' schools. We've tried creating organizations and nonprofits that advocate for the kind of change we want to see in the world. We've begun to raise hell and use our voices, but we need to start playing a different game.

A game we can win. Even though the rules that apply to men don't apply to us.

We all know a wealthy white man who achieved his success by knowing the right people, by easily landing his first great job, by asking for what he was worth. When a man succeeds this way, he is praised. But when a woman tries to assert herself, she's called a bitch—or worse. As women, and especially as women of color, we need to wake up to the fact that our rules for playing and winning the game of success aren't the same as a man's. And that's a good thing, because the rules that work for men don't work for us. The old boys' club that ensures a white man's success is not available to us. And if we think about it, we'll realize we don't even want that version of success. Women need to define success on our own terms and go after our goals in our own ways, even if it seems crazy or risky or unusual at the time.

Because I've seen over and over again that **doing things our own way *as women* works.** When I was a lawyer first starting out, I knew I didn't want a prominent position at a fancy law firm, because I was so over the toxic culture that rules in those institutions: the rigid nine-to-nine schedule, the limited vacation time, and office politics that always resulted in white men winning and a Black woman like me losing. During my limited experience working in corporate firms, I witnessed things like a partner throwing a stapler down the hallway while screaming at the top of his lungs, and being admonished because I got busy doing important research and wasn't there to receive the lunch delivery I had ordered for senior associates (clearly senior associates can't be meeting delivery guys at the elevator to get their own lunch. As if!).

So I decided to open my own virtual law firm, which enabled me to work with clients remotely while wearing a flowy kimono from my kitchen table (I call her my Rich Lady Kimono—she's real cute). And it worked for me, to the tune of $700,000 in annual revenue. Many of my clients, friends, and colleagues asked me how I built such a successful business, and I started teaching them my strategies. Eventually, there was so much demand for business coaching, and I enjoyed it so much that I decided to close my law practice and coach full-time. I transitioned to coaching other women on how to run a business, manage their money, and turn their intellectual property into an empire, which has turned my six-figure business into Hello Seven. (Literally, that's the name of my company.)

I've learned how to play the game of success by my own rules. And in this book, I'm going to help you define your own success and chase after your goals on your terms. It's time for all of us to make a lot more money. And by doing so, we'll literally spread our wealth around, take our power and agency back, and ultimately change the world. So, you know, small things.

This is the part of the book where you start to think, *But, Rachel, there's no way I can earn a million dollars, even with your help.*

And this is where I'm going to tell you that you are absolutely wrong.

You've got kids? Babies at home?

Me, too. I was breastfeeding my youngest when I wrote this.

You've got a husband or partner or life companion?

Same.

You're Black, Asian, gay, trans or member of a systemically oppressed community?

Talk to the Black woman who is writing this book.

Stuck in a job that won't promote you or give you more than a 3 percent raise?

Been there.

You're an entrepreneur who is stuck at $50,000, $100,000, or barely making a profit?

Done that.

The reason you're not a millionaire—yet—isn't because you're not capable. It's not because you're not smart enough or not pretty enough. It's not because you're too loud or too quiet. It's not because you didn't get good grades in college or because you don't have enough experience. It's not because you're too Black or your butt is too big (can a person ever be too Black? Can a butt ever be too big? The answer to those questions is no and no). And it's certainly not because you're not talented enough. It's not because you're a person of color, not because you identify as LGBTQ+, not because you're married, not because you're single, not because you are pregnant, not because you have kids, not because you've chosen not to have children, not because you grew up low income, not because you grew up middle class, not because you live in an expensive city, and not because you live out in the country.

Those are not the reasons you're not wealthy. As I explain in the first half of this book, women, including myself, have learned to make a metric ton of excuses about why we can't earn as much money as men. That's a big reason we aren't winning the game that men have successfully played for years. Most of us aren't even on the game board, because we have been taught—by our well-meaning parents, role models, and systemic racism and sexism—to give away key resources.

Strong women like us routinely forfeit our independence, our time, our power, and ultimately our success. We tolerate bullshit and feel guilty advocating for our own needs in our homes, at work, and in our national politics. Deep down, a lot of us believe that we are somehow at fault for not getting what we deserve, whether that's equal pay or a spouse who does their share of the chores.

But the truth is that we can and should think differently. In the second half of the book, I offer five specific, practical shifts I've made—and helped other women make—that create wealth. The big secret that most men won't tell you is that amassing cash isn't really about the money.

It's about feeling like a million dollars every day.
Because when you feel like a million bucks,
you are far more likely to earn a million bucks.

It's also about daily habits and beliefs. Not hustling for everyone else, never questioning your own instinct and value, not doing every possible thing for anyone who asks, and not being truly all in are the key ways that women like us limit how much we can earn, save, and invest. In this book, I'll show you how doing less can help you earn more, and why investing in yourself is the best choice you can ever make.

WHY SHOULD WE SHOOT FOR $1 MILLION? ISN'T SIX FIGURES ENOUGH?

No, it's not. Here's the problem: While six figures in annual revenue sounds like success, it doesn't feel like success. Fixed expenses are increasing at a faster rate than incomes, making it harder to live a comfortable lifestyle in American cities.[8]

MagnifyMoney (https://www.magnifymoney.com) did an in-depth study in four hundred metro areas across the United States on what it looks like to earn $100,000 and found that most households are spending $25,000 or more every year on their housing alone. These households are spending $10,000 or more each year on childcare as well.

Even in the most affordable metro areas in the United States, $100,000 households are left with 2 percent disposable income (that's only $2,000 per year) after paying their basic expenses. In other words, even when you earn $100,000, you are likely only one emergency away from financial distress.

In 2018, with the economy at its most robust in years, 61 percent of Americans said they could not cover a surprise expense of $400. In 2019, a study by the AARP found that 53 percent of American households did not have an emergency savings account—including a quarter of those who earn more than $150,000 a year.[9]

And remember, the goal isn't just to get by, the goal is to live a comfortable life and to make a big impact on the world. How are we going to back our desired political candidates, contribute to important charitable causes, and help the people around us if we are barely making ends meet?

No, Sis. It's time to shoot for a million.

Okay, but how do you define *millionaire*?

I define a millionaire as a person who has more than $1 million in assets or who generates an income of $1 million or more per year. When you are making this kind of money (trust me, it's possible), you can enjoy your life and make the world a better place.

When I began my career, I was making $41,000 per year as a law clerk for a state judge. Back then, I couldn't have pictured being a millionaire, but I was already on the path to making millions even if I didn't realize it. My only real asset at the time was my ability to earn a living. At the time, I didn't realize how quickly I could increase my earnings so I moved into a cheap basement apartment, lowered my monthly expenses, and began building my law practice with just three clients (who were all friends of mine). I used my one asset (my earning potential as an attorney) to build more significant income. In my first year of business, I made approximately $60,000, more than my previous salary as a law clerk. The following year, I made $300,000, and the business continued to grow year over year until I hit $1 million in revenue. To this day, my business is my most valuable asset.

But that's not the only way to become a millionaire. My friend Emma Pattee is a millionaire. She owns $1 million worth of real estate. When she was just out of college, she decided she wanted to buy her first property. So she rented out the bedrooms in her apartment and slept in the living room so she could live rent free. She didn't buy nice clothing or furniture and lived as frugally as possible. She worked a full-time job, and on the weekends she would find discarded furniture, restore it, and then sell it on Craigslist for a profit. She lived like this until she could afford the down payment on her first property. She rented out that property and earned an income from it. And then she saved up to acquire her next property. She did this for ten years, and now she is a millionaire who doesn't have to work. She spends her days with her son, being an activist, and doing creative writing.

Another friend, Teri Ijeoma, is a millionaire as well. Teri was a schoolteacher. She loved her job, but when some big administrative changes came to her school, she found she no longer enjoyed the work. So she decided to cash out her 401k and use the money to trade stocks and try to earn a living from the stock market. Her first goal was to make $300 per day in the stock market. She met that goal after a few months, and then decided to see if she could earn $1,000 per day. She met that goal, too. Eventually, through day trading, she accumulated $1 million in assets. Teri is now a millionaire.

One of my clients is an attorney named Rosezena Pierce. Rosezena left her law firm job to start her own trademark law practice. When Rosezena and I began working together, she was making about $150,000 annually in her practice. After about eighteen months of working together—during which she worked hard, hired employees, and acquired more clients— Rosezena had her first $100,000 month. She is now the owner of a seven-figure law practice, a million dollar asset. Rosezena is a millionaire.

There are many paths to becoming a millionaire, and you are already on your way. If you have a retirement or savings account, own real estate or stock or have a business that generates income, you have assets that make up your net worth. In this book, you'll learn how to grow those assets to $1 million or more. And if you are starting from scratch like I did, and your only asset is your earning potential, you can turn that into a million dollars too. Stick with me.

At this point, you might be wondering who am I to be telling you all this. Well, for starters, I'm a millionaire. I'm also a mom with three young kids, a bonus daughter, and a loving husband, and I'm the employer of over a dozen people who work for me in my business and my home. My mission is to make as much change and positivity in the world as I can for other women, for Black people and other folks who have been marginalized by our society, and for my children.

But, as I mentioned earlier, I wasn't always wealthy, successful, and confident.

I grew up low income. My dad passed away when I was in seventh grade. My mom was battling an alcohol addiction when I was a teenager, so my older sister and my best friend's family who lived down the street looked out for me. When I had my first child, I was broke. My husband and I were living in a cheap-ass apartment in Phoenix, Arizona. My first business attempt (a T-shirt company) never got off the ground; my second business (a virtual law firm) thrived, but practicing law wore me down; and my third business, Hello Seven, has helped dozens of women, including myself, make bank.

That's me: a Black woman with plenty of kids and a husband and lots of responsibilities, who started with literally nothing but passion. I've made my dreams become my reality. And you can, too.

The American government is gravely disappointing. In the United States, access to education includes becoming saddled with massive student loan debt; we lack universal healthcare and universal childcare (unlike most other Western countries); and systemic racism and sexism abound in all our institutions. I don't spend a lot of time raging against corrupt politicians in Washington. My chosen form of protest is to make money and use it to create the change I want to see in the world.

Martin Luther King Jr. said: "Privileged groups seldom give up their privileges voluntarily. . . . We know through painful experience that freedom is never voluntarily given by the oppressor; it must be demanded by the oppressed."

Demands require capital. It takes money to lobby Congress. It takes money to support protestors who march in the streets. It takes money to bail out activists and fund research that provides evidence of the need for change.

So it's time for us, as women,
to turn toward our money.

To begin to focus on our earning potential and our ability to generate wealth. What works—as I've seen in my own life and in the lives of the women I coach—is focusing on our natural skills and talents, being mindful of how we use our time, and prioritizing the building of generational wealth, because that is how we can make serious change.

And if you're not into dismantling the systems of oppression that exist in our world today, why not? (We should all be participating in our collective freedom.) However, we have a right to build wealth for ourselves as women for no other reason than we want it. We are allowed to make a million dollars because we want to fly first class, carry a Chanel bag, and order fancy champagne whenever we want.

> We are allowed to be ambitious for ambition's sake—unapologetically. This book will show you how to get your money, for whatever reason you want it.

Some of us want a revolution. And some of us simply want to be financially secure enough to take our kids on a beach vacation, pay for college and sleep well at night knowing that our family is cared for. For others, it might be the freedom to live where you want and make your own schedule, or to not just have a seat at the table but to own it. And all those options are just as worthy.

If you picked up this book, you want to be a millionaire. Regardless of your reasons, I am hyped you are here because I am certain that the world is going to be *sooo* much better when more of us have money. In 2018, only 1.7 percent of women-owned businesses made more than a million dollars in revenue.[10] That's insane. Imagine if 10 percent or 20 percent of women earned that much. The potential of women entrepreneurs to spur economic growth has not been fully realized. Imagine what the world would look like if thousands of femme bosses and businesses were hiring, donating, giving back, and creating products that support women and families.

That's the world I want to live in.

I became a millionaire, because I knew what it was like to live without economic well-being. I knew the shame of being poor and the vulnerability of being broke. I never wanted to struggle like that again. I saw how the heavy financial burdens my parents carried affected their health and well-being. I wanted to eliminate that burden both for myself and my parents. I wanted my children to have a financial head start, I wanted to launch the family legacy of building generational wealth. I wanted to live comfortably in a safe neighborhood and not be up late at night stressing about bills. I want the same for you as well.

My mission is to help every person reading this book make a million dollars.

Are you ready?

You may not think that you are but trust me, you are. You have all the ingredients of a millionaire, you just need a better recipe. This book is my own personal recipe. It's worked for me and many of my clients. I know it will produce amazing results for you as well.

Still feeling like making millions is unrealistic? Let me tell you a little story about unrealistic.

The first woman self-made millionaire in America, Madam C. J. Walker, was the most unlikely candidate to become a millionaire. In 1867, just five years after the Emancipation Proclamation, Sarah Breedlove (the future Madam C. J. Walker) was born to former slaves. She was their only child born free. Her parents were someone's property for most of their lives and, once they were freed, continued to work on the same plantation as sharecroppers. And yet, Sarah somehow knew she was valuable.

Despite the many negative messages the world would continuously send Sarah about her worth, she chose not to believe them. Instead, she chose her mission and ambition: to improve her life and the lives of her people. She turned her pain into purpose and got results. Madam C. J. Walker dared to dream of a better world and then got her ass up and created it.

Sarah was forged in fire. She was born at the commencement of the Reconstruction era. Black men had gone from being enslaved to being empowered with the ability to vote and hold office. In counties like Madison Parish in Louisiana, where Sarah was born, newly freed Black people outnumbered white people. This led to a great deal of violence perpetrated by white plantation owners who feared the newly gained political power of their former slaves.

The schools in Madison Parish were torched and teachers were harassed. Southern whites were terrified of what would happen when Black people were formally educated. In this climate, Sarah received only three months of schooling.

The Knights of the White Camelia was born the same year as Sarah. Based in Louisiana, it was a paramilitary organization not unlike the Ku Klux Klan, whose mission was to maintain the supremacy of the white race. During these years, Black people were murdered by the hundreds. Southern whites went to great lengths to undo any gains that the Black community had achieved since being freed, and they experienced no punishment for their actions (sadly, not unlike today).

The Reconstruction era, which took place in the United States from 1867 to 1877, was a period of great economic and social turmoil and resulted in unyielding violence against Black people. Despite the great fear and violence of this time, Reconstruction was also a brief period of civil rights and civil liberties for Black people in the South. If slavery could end, then truly anything was possible.

Sarah's formative years were during a time when a new world was attempting to emerge, a world where Black people could build wealth for themselves instead of having their labor stolen. I believe Sarah's vision for the future was borne from this harsh and yet hopeful time.

Sarah spent years as a breadwinning washerwoman, supporting herself and her daughter, A'Lelia, in harsh conditions. Unlike Sarah, A'Lelia was able to attend elementary school at the St. Louis Colored Orphans Home. The school was established by well-to-do Black women Sarah met through church. Again, when women are wealthy, they provide for the most vulnerable members of society. The support that Sarah received enabled her to do better for herself.

In 1903, Sarah met Annie Malone, a Black woman entrepreneur who offered haircare treatments. Sarah became a salesperson and haircare specialist for Annie, which allowed her to double her wages. Wealthy women open doors for other women.

In 1905, Sarah moved to Denver with $1.50 to her name and every intention of making her fortune. She got a job as a cook and, in her spare time, worked on developing her own haircare formula. Eventually she saved enough money from her main gig to get business cards for her side hustle. She also bought an ad in the local Black newspaper showcasing her haircare products and services. Customers loved her formula, and soon she was seeing clients around the clock.

In 1906, Sarah took on the moniker "Madam C. J. Walker" after marrying Mr. Walker, a newspaper man. This was also her Glow Up year. She went from cooking up hair treatments in her home kitchen to a legitimate operation. Madam formed the Madam C. J. Walker Manufacturing Company and traveled the United States demonstrating what her haircare products could do. At each location, she recruited and trained Black women to become sales representatives for her company. At a time when the majority of Black women were employed as domestic servants earning as little as $100–$240 annually, Madam was offering economic mobility. It wasn't long before Madam had an army of sales reps around the country.

By the end of 1907, Madam had made $3,652 in annual income. That's equivalent to $104,678 in 2020. In other words, in her first full year in business, it can be said that Madam hit the six-figure mark. Prior to creating her company, she had barely made $300 per year. Madam's gift for teaching, deep understanding of her clients' desires, and strong conviction that Black women should be financially independent were her strengths. And she used them to build exponential wealth.

In the years following, Madam moved her business operations to Indianapolis where she built her first factory, a salon, and a training school. She visited Cuba, Panama, Jamaica, Costa Rica, and Haiti to expand her business internationally. She purchased a townhome in Harlem where she established a well-known salon, and built a mansion in Irvington, New York, called Villa Lewaro. At both of these properties, she and her daughter, A'Lelia, hosted Black politicians, activists, and artists.

In 1917, Madam Walker gathered more than two hundred Walker sales agents for their first national convention, one of the first conventions for American businesswomen. During the event, attendees shared their testimonies of how the Madam C. J. Walker Manufacturing Company had changed their lives. On the final day of the convention, Madam Walker's theme was "Women's Duty to Women," and she encouraged her sales representatives to become community leaders and agents of change. She gave prizes to the women who had sold the most products as well as those who had contributed the most to charity. At the end of the convention, attendees sent a telegram to President Woodrow Wilson urging him to support legislation that would make lynching a federal crime.

In sixteen years, Madam C. J. Walker went from struggling washerwoman to notable businesswoman and millionaire. Not only did she build wealth for herself, but she trained more than twenty thousand sales agents who were also able to become wealthy women who gave back. She was politically active, delivering lectures, organizing demonstrations, and even visiting the White House. She made large financial contributions to build a YMCA in a Black community in Indianapolis, to the scholarship fund for the Tuskegee Institute, to the NAACP's anti-lynching fund, and to countless other social, educational, and arts institutions that benefited and advanced the lives of Black people.

Madame Walker left us an inspiring legacy. She taught us that being a millionaire is not just about stuntin' in your new whip with your girls (which Madam definitely enjoyed). It's also about empowering others, charitable giving, and being a politically active citizen.

Madame C. J. Walker had every excuse not to become a millionaire. She was born to slaves. She was poor. She was Black. She was an orphan. She was widowed. She was a single mother. She was abused and cheated on. She lived in an unsafe neighborhood. She had three months of formal education. She experienced racism and sexism and violence. She was the sole breadwinner. She was accused of stealing. Her name was sullied among her peers. She was disenfranchised. The government passed laws to limit her access to success. And despite all these reasons, she still got results.

If Madam C. J. Walker could become a millionaire then, you can certainly become a millionaire now.

You see, we don't need perfect childhoods, fair governments, or lots of money to become millionaires. The only thing we really need is the belief that we can. And some basic blueprints wouldn't hurt either.

I believe Madam's commitment to practicing self-care, her refusal to accept the station to which society had relegated her, and her belief in her own vision, ideas, creativity, and intelligence were the keys to her freedom, power, and wealth. And these are the keys that we will explore together throughout this book.

Let's begin by looking at the stories you tell yourself. Let's replace stories of weakness, unworthiness, and failure with your Million Dollar Story.

PART I

MILLION
DOLLAR
BEHAVIOR

CHAPTER 1

MILLION DOLLAR STORY

"First forget inspiration. Habit is more dependable. Habit will sustain you whether you're inspired or not. Habit will help you finish and polish your stories. Inspiration won't. Habit is persistence in practice."

—OCTAVIA BUTLER

You are living in a financial prison of your own making.

We women are in jail. Our thoughts and beliefs about what our work, time, and energy are worth keep our bank accounts small and our imposter syndrome large. We don't recognize how worthy we are.

Why is that? Why don't women recognize their worth? Why don't more women pursue epic wealth?

Is it because we are the weaker sex? Hell no.

Is it because we're just not good with money? Hogwash.

Is it a part of our womanhood to not pursue wealth with the fervor that men do? Nope.

The answer is that we are all products of our environment. An environment that is uniquely designed to keep money out of our Kate Spade top grain leather wallets.

I remember the moment I decided I was going to become a millionaire. I didn't actually think those words at the time, because I was in high school, and I didn't even know what a millionaire was.

Everyone around me was just trying to survive—moms working their nine-to-five office jobs and trying to keep their cool while working for horrible bosses. Kids trying not to get into a fight on their way to school—they just wanted to graduate from high school on time. Drug addicts walking aimlessly up and down the street, eyes glazed over, looking for their next opportunity to get high.

On 45th Avenue, it felt like everyone around me was just trying to make it, but I believed that my life could be different. I knew I was smart and figured my intelligence and good grades could be the tickets toward a better life. One where our lights didn't go out a couple times a year and I never worried about where my next meal was coming from.

As a biracial Black girl growing up in lower-middle-class Queens, I did not see a lot of examples of wealth, but I did see a few.

AUNT SHELLEY

There was Aunt Shelley on the Black side, my father's sister. The oldest girl of nine children in the Lowery clan. She lived in Bridgeport, Connecticut, and drove a Jaguar. She owned her own home, and it had a formal dining room and a big backyard with what felt like acres of green grass. It was in the nice part of town. My sister and I would visit during brief escapes from the busy, dirty, loud city, and we'd spend time giggling and playing with her two girls, our cousins, René and Jennifer.

I had no idea what Aunt Shelley and Uncle Scrappy, her husband, did for a living, but I knew it must be important. I could tell by the big, fluffy cushions on their gold sectional couch, by the sound system out of which she would play Earth Wind & Fire, and by the amount of food in their fridge.

Aunt Shelley played no games. She used to put us in the tub and scrub us down (I was sheepish about her seeing me naked, but she did not care. I was gonna get a good cleaning. No kid was going to bed filthy in her house!). She would comb and grease and braid our hair, too. So, not only did Aunt Shelley accept no BS, make good money, and own her own home, she also took exceptional care of her girls, including my sister and me when we visited.

When there was a financial crisis in the family—if there were expensive funeral fees to be paid or a family member who needed to go to rehab—my Aunt Shelley got the call and often covered some of the costs. As a kid, I heard her scolding her younger siblings about the financial messes that occurred and that they typically were unable to contribute to cleaning up.

I could tell Aunt Shelley and her husband had a level of financial freedom that my family did not have. It was literally in the air. You can just tell when someone was worrying about the light bill and when they weren't. Financial security is palpable.

Aunt Shelley was a millionaire in my eyes.

AUNT BARBARA

Then there was Aunt Barbara on the white side, my mother's sister. Aunt Barbara used to come to visit us and get us girls in line. I remember her saying I was "as slow as molasses" while she hustled me through the morning routine. She did not tolerate my sister and me fighting and carrying on. Just like Aunt Shelley, she was no nonsense.

(I'm just now realizing that I had some powerful women in my life as a child. Now I know why I'm like this, but I digress).

While Aunt Barbara might have been a bit of a hard ass when it came to our upbringing, she was also kind. She sent us a birthday card with a $50 check enclosed every year, like clockwork. Even when I was thirty-five years old, she still sent me a birthday card and check with "Happy Birthday Rachel" written in the memo. She never forgets about me or my sister.

When my mother was having a really hard time after my father passed, it was my Aunt Barbara that I called for help. She arrived a few days later to take care of us, bring some order to our household, and support my mother.

And when I exhausted all my financial aid options and still had a $6,500 balance of tuition in my junior year of college, it was my Aunt Barbara who wrote me a check and kept the party going. It took me a long time to finally pay that loan back.

I loved visiting Aunt Barbara and Uncle Tommy's house. They lived in a beautiful suburb in Long Island. They had a sparkling clean home with a guest room and a big tree for Christmas. I enjoyed wrapping presents with my Uncle Tommy and laughed when he made crude jokes that embarrassed my aunt. They always brought us beautiful gifts: lambswool sweaters and nice pajamas. The kind of expensive things our parents would not buy us, and we wouldn't think to ask for, but that were lovely to receive.

When my Aunt Barbara and Uncle Tommy retired, they moved farther out on Long Island to the Hamptons and had the beach in their backyard. My jaw dropped the first time I walked into their new home and saw the stunning view of the ocean from their living room. At their house, we ate Death by Chocolate ice cream and talked about life.

Uncle Tommy was a Union worker at Madison Square Garden and got us tickets to quality shows like WrestleMania and Billy Joel concerts. I have no idea what my Aunt Barbara did for a living. But I knew with certainty that they were millionaires.

ALANA

And then there was Alana. Alana was a twelve-year-old Jewish girl who lived in Little Neck, NY. An only child, her parents hired me at age fifteen to be Alana's after-school companion. My job was to pick Alana up from school and walk her home through the tree-lined streets filled with hilltop mansions. Then I would give her a snack and entertain her while her father worked in his home office upstairs. When I met Alana's mother, she told me how beautiful I was and was so incredibly kind. Working for their family was my introduction to nice, rich people.

I remember her mom telling me to eat whatever I wanted. Every day after school, I would open up the fridge, freezer, and pantry and ask Alana which of the snack options she wanted. There were many. I was amazed by how much food they had in their kitchen with only three people living there. They had the frozen pizza bagels and egg rolls that I always wanted to get from the grocery store but my mom wouldn't let me. They had Pop-Tarts, ice cream sandwiches, and those cracker sandwiches with cheese or peanut butter. Alana and I snacked a lot.

Sometimes we would play hide-and-seek to pass the time, and it was very easy to get lost in their house. It had so many rooms. There was a fancy dining room with upholstered chairs and a long polished wood table that no one ever seemed to eat at. The house had two living rooms, and I could barely figure out how to work their complicated TV. The house also had a large playroom in the basement filled with Alana's many toys. Upstairs, Alana's bedroom had a large tent she liked to hide in, a big beautiful dollhouse, and pink ruffles everywhere.

Alana's childhood was basically the opposite of mine. Where my house lacked food, space (I shared a tiny bedroom with my older sister), and toys, this house was teeming. This encounter with such abundance let me know that wealth was possible, and it was a reminder of the abundance we had in my early childhood. You see, we didn't always live a life of struggle. There was a time in my childhood when I thought my parents were rich.

MY MOTHER

One of the most vivid memories of my childhood is going to Macy's on Saturdays with my mother and sister. I was about seven or eight years old, and I remember coming out of the train station and carefully crossing the big boulevard where there were frequent accidents. My mother wore her electric blue leather coat that she had treated herself to a few months earlier, and held our hands tightly as we made our way across the street to Queens Center mall.

Every single Saturday morning, my mom, sister, and I would head to Queens Center to buy clothes or other things the family needed. Every Saturday, my mother would purchase a treat for my sister and me. We would always get new shoes, a new dress, or maybe some new hair bows and earrings from Claire's Accessories. Us girls loved our Saturday shopping trips.

It wasn't so much the new stuff we would buy, although that was nice, but it was the feeling of fun and adventure and having my mom's attention. It was the fact that these shopping dates were our special girls' time. It was the lack of struggle. This was 1989, a short, plentiful chapter for the Lowery family.

This chapter included one of the only family vacations we ever took. We piled into the car and drove eight hours to Virginia Beach. We stayed at the Howard Johnson's right on the water, and my mother and I wore matching green-and-white striped bathing suits. We spent our days in the hotel pool or in the ocean. We spent our evenings walking the boardwalk, browsing shops, and eating at restaurants.

One night we decided to do a haunted funhouse that had masked killers and deranged clowns jumping out at us at every turn. The spooky music and strategically placed mirrors added to the horror. I remember crouching on the floor terrified and screaming for my father to come get me halfway through. I got separated from my family because I was too scared to walk by another threatening character. I'm still scarred from that depraved funhouse, but you know what? We were on vacation and, dammit, we had fun!

This short-lived abundance era included my parents buying their first piece of real estate. We moved from our one-bedroom apartment on Bowne Street—where my sister and I shared the bedroom and my parents slept on a pull-out couch in the living room—to a two-bedroom condo in a nicer building on 45th Avenue. The building was called The Jefferson and, like *The Jeffersons* we were "movin' on up."

We moved to apartment 2M when I was in first grade, and it felt like a palace to me. It had a big living room, an actual dining room, and a ton of natural light. My parents finally had their own bedroom and my sister and I shared a bunk bed in the smaller bedroom off the kitchen. The kitchen was large and all the appliances were brand new. The whole apartment had fresh, beige carpet, and I remember my dad going out to buy a plastic runner that took you from the front door to the living room and bathroom. If you needed to step off the plastic runner, you had better have your shoes off.

We lived next door to the Bellas from Canada who had four kids and were biracial like us. The father worked for the United Nations, and the mom stayed at home. The Bella kids went to private school; we went to public. We had another neighbor who owned a car dealership, and another who was a nurse at the local hospital. It seemed like we were all doing pretty well. And then shit hit the fan.

My mom decided to quit her job after being passed over for a promotion that she felt she had earned. Just a few months later, my father was unexpectedly laid off from his job. We went from owning a condo and Saturday shopping trips to paying for groceries with food stamps and the unemployment line. We lost the condo and the Chevy we lovingly referred to as the "Silver Bullet." We moved to a rental apartment in the same building. I remember the landlord coming to the door to collect rent—it was frequently late, and he was frequently angry.

My parents had many odd jobs and career reinventions after that year, but we never did regain our financial stability. My mother had no idea when she left her job that she would have such a hard time finding another role with similar or better salary and benefits. My mother beat herself up for her "mistake" of leaving her old job, and her self-esteem took a hit. As a result, she didn't feel worthy to pursue the more high-quality jobs for which she might have been qualified.

Then, when I was in sixth grade, my dad was admitted to the hospital for pneumonia and discovered he was really sick. He was in and out of the hospital for more than a year until the summer before I started junior high school, when he suddenly passed away. We were all devastated. My mom was overcome with grief and struggled to get out of bed each day. That's when our financial situation got even worse.

My sister was eighteen years old and took responsibility for the household. She had a full-time job as a receptionist at a spa in Manhattan while going to school full-time. She would come home exhausted and yell at me for not cleaning and yell at my mom for not getting out of bed. During these years, it felt like my mom was in a daze or asleep the whole time. And my sister, tasked with holding the household together, was always working.

At fourteen years old, I got a cashier job at a grocery store and had a shitty boyfriend. I lashed out and drank in the park after dark with my friends. I had dinner at the local pizza shop almost every night. That was back when a good slice of New York pizza only cost

$1.25. I used my paycheck from the grocery store to pay for it and parented myself very poorly.

My grief and sadness from my father's passing and compassion for my mother turned into anger. I was angry at my mother for checking out, and I was angry at God for not saving my dad, and I was angry at my sister for not letting me borrow her clothes so I could look cute in front of the boys I liked at school.

But I was determined not to struggle forever, so I limited being a "bad girl" to the weekends and went to school every day. I always did my homework and studied for tests. I got good grades and convinced the staff at my high school to give me a scholarship for SAT prep classes. I graduated high school and then decided that I was done with watching my mother drink. I packed up a U-Haul truck with two friends and moved onto campus at Stony Brook University on the North Shore of Long Island.

I applied for all the financial aid I could and took out student loans to pay for the dorm and college meal plan. I worked thirty hours per week just like my sister had when she was in college. Then I got an opportunity to move to D.C. for a semester and intern for Senator Hillary Clinton. That's where I learned a lot about my relationship with money.

> "Believe thoroughly in your greater interior self. Know that you have something within you that is greater than any obstacle."
> —CHRISTIAN D. LARSON[1]
>
> · What have you survived?
> · What's an obstacle or ordeal that you got through?
> · How have you advocated for yourself in the past?
>
> That is evidence that you have that unstoppable spirit inside of you. It's proof that you can do hard things.

Just like you, I am a product of my environment. My role models for wealth (my aunties, Alana and her parents, and my mother) showed me that it was possible to make money, live comfortably, and enjoy life. They also showed me different ways of being wealthy. You could be no nonsense and take no shit, you could be the very personification of kindness, or you could be both at the same time.

But the years of financial struggles that my parents, sister, and I experienced made me believe that even if I did achieve financial success, it would all go away some day. I might have money for a time but I could never count on it long term.

And I have to admit that I still, to this very day, carry that fear. I once had a business coach who used to make me repeat "I will never be poor again" on a regular basis. Despite these affirmations, I still worry that all the financial success I've had will one day go away. That I will lose everything and wind up broke like my parents did. Each day, I have to choose to reframe those thoughts that try to steal my peace, and instead tell myself a new story.

I recognize that the fears in my head are just stories that I tell myself. They are a prison that I have created to keep me from experiencing the disappointment of failure. They aren't true unless I continue to believe in them and then act on them and make them true. I can choose to believe something entirely different. I can choose to believe in my ability to make money and provide financial security for my family. I can choose to believe in my ability to make smart financial decisions. I can choose to believe that even if I make a big money mistake or some outside force causes me to lose everything, that I have the skill and ability to make it all back faster than I've ever made it before. This is how we get ourselves out of mental money jail. (See my Quick & Dirty Guide to Thought Work in this chapter to learn how to do this.)

Thinking negative thoughts is a form of self-sabotage that keeps you "safe" and therefore stagnant. Even if the status quo is uncomfortable or makes you unhappy, it feels safer than trying to do something new. The discomfort of being broke used to be very comfortable for me. So much so that whenever I had a surplus of money, I would spend it as fast as possible, because I was accustomed to being broke. Brokeness was a state of being I knew well. I knew how to be broke. I did not know how to be financially stable.

Financial stability scared me. I was subconsciously worried that if I got to a place of financial stability, I would make poor decisions, and lose the money, and look like a failure. If I will only wind up broke in the end anyway, better to just stay broke than try and fail miserably, right? Wrong. This was me sabotaging my own success, because I was afraid of having to become a better version of myself. I was afraid my friends, who were all broke, too, wouldn't like me if I had money. I was afraid of paying taxes and having to be responsible. I was afraid of making a mistake. I was afraid of finding out how powerful I truly am. And I let that fear get in my way time and time again.

How 'bout you? What fears have you inherited from your childhood that are affecting your daily thoughts and actions when it comes to making money and building wealth? How are you sabotaging yourself by committing to thinking negative thoughts? And how will you begin to reframe those thoughts to serve, inspire, and motivate you, rather than make you feel defeated and cause you harm?

LET'S CREATE A NEW MONEY STORY

Before we can start to build wealth, we have to heal our relationship with money.

> *"Create the highest, grandest vision possible for your life, because you become what you believe."*
> —OPRAH WINFREY

The money stories that shaped you may be keeping you broke. In fact, if you are a woman, I would venture to guess that you have a whole lot of money stories in your head that aren't making you feel excited and motivated to go out into the world and get paid. Some of these stories are a result of what you learned about money during childhood. Some of these stories are a result of what our society constantly tells women about their ability to make money (more on this in the next chapter).

Whatever the reason, one of the first steps toward becoming a millionaire is analyzing the money stories that we are constantly playing in our heads. Your thoughts are always a prelude to your actions. So if you want to change your actions (which I presume you do since your actions have not yet led you to millionaire status), then you have to change your thoughts first.

Here are some of the common money stories women regularly tell themselves:

Money is not that important to me. Well, I doubt that. You didn't pick up this book because money is not that important to you. If this is a common belief you hold, the moral high ground may be keeping your coffers empty. You may think it's noble to claim that money is not that important to you. However, we live in a capitalist society where money is a necessity for survival. It may sound nice to say that you are above making money, but unless you are also above paying rent, eating, and clothing yourself, you're full of shit.

When the women I work with tell me that money is not that important to them, more often than not, they are using their supposed lack of concern about money as a defense mechanism. They know they are capable of making a whole lot more money. On some deep level, they know they are seriously limiting their income and choosing not to live up to their full potential. What they don't know is how to fix it. So they declare "it doesn't matter" to feel better. I get it, I've been there and I call bullshit. Money isn't everything, but it absolutely is important. Anyone who says it's not is lying.

But let's say you are one of the few women telling the truth when you say that money is not that important to you. Then my next question is: What *is* important to you? Spending time with family? You need money to go on vacation. Helping others? You can help more people with more money. God? He appreciates donations. Money is not about money, it's about what you are able to do with it.

You have to work really hard to make money. Perhaps your parents came home from work exhausted every day. Maybe you watched them do overtime or work on weekends frequently. You may have watched them work constantly, and yet your family may have still continued to struggle financially. Perhaps you felt neglected as a child, because your parents were constantly working in pursuit of financial well-being. Maybe a family member got sick because he or she was overwhelmed by constant laboring and stress. As a result, you may be telling yourself that making more money is not worth pursuing, because you don't want to risk your health and happiness chasing money like your parents did.

Reject the belief that to pursue your goals and build wealth you have to work yourself to the bone and be miserable about it. The fact is that wealth is built through buying assets. You could acquire an asset (stocks, real estate, a share in a business) and sit back and do nothing all day while your assets accumulate value. Then one day, you can sell the asset and cash in. In fact, this is how many rich people build wealth. So working hard is not a requirement for getting wealthy. There are plenty of ways to get rich that don't involve working yourself into poor health.

I'm just not good with money. This is the one where women take themselves out of the game before it even begins. "I'm just not good with money" is literal foolishness, and it drives me bananas to hear women say this. No one is inherently good or bad with money. You aren't born with an abacus attached to your hand or the natural ability to work a financial spreadsheet. Being "good with money" is an acquired skill. You can learn how to manage your money, make financial decisions, and take calculated risks.

You can also choose not to learn and instead throw up your hands and declare that, sigh, you are just not good with money, and that's why you've bounced another check and don't have your rent money this month. But doesn't that sound weak? Wouldn't you rather be a badass boss bitch running thangs than a woman who gives away her power? You get to decide.

Also, let's take a moment to acknowledge there really aren't any good moves or bad moves when it comes to money. Financial decisions are as varied as the humans making them. Buying a big ass house that comes with a large mortgage may look like a terrible financial decision. But when that big ass house provides a lovely home for my family and offices for my business, makes me feel like a boss, and is a place where I host events that bring in hundreds of thousands of dollars in a matter of days (true story), buying that big ass house turns out to be a great financial decision for me.

Lastly, if you believe the media messages out there that are telling you women are bad with money, don't believe the hype.

There are countless studies that show that women are actually better at investing than men. One such study by investment firm Fidelity found that female investors have been outperforming their male counterparts for more than a decade.[2] So, there you have it: Evidence that girls are not only made of sugar and spice and everything nice, but we can also build a mean investment portfolio. Quote this study the next time your banker asks to speak to your husband (and then bop him over the head with your Chanel purse for being a dumbass).

Don't waste your time beating yourself up if you are guilty of thinking these and other limiting thoughts around money. Nearly every woman has a shitty story she is telling herself about money. This is not a spectacular and unique failure on your part. However, what would be a failure is not actively working to change these thoughts. Replacing your old money stories with new stories that are inspiring, motivating, and exciting will make you feel better about money. And when you feel better about money, you will make decisions from a place of abundance and joy instead of a place of fear and scarcity. This is called *thought work*, and it's very powerful. If you are not familiar with thought work, check out my quick and dirty primer here.

RACHEL'S QUICK AND DIRTY GUIDE TO THOUGHT WORK

When a thought comes into my mind that isn't helping me get to where I want to go, I do thought work, which means I actively work on changing that thought to something that is helpful. This is called thought work, and it is the basis of the practice of life coaching.

Thought work is the act of consciously paying attention to your thoughts and then choosing to entertain different thoughts instead. For example, a thought I used to have all the time is *I look ugly*. All throughout the day, every single day, I would tell myself that I was ugly in different ways. I would be getting undressed to get in the shower, look down at my body and think: *Ugh, look at these ugly stretch marks. You really need to lose weight.* Then I would be getting dressed and go into a tailspin about the way I looked in my clothes. I would tell myself, *Your pants don't fit because all you do is eat cookies all day.* Then I'd be sitting at my desk working on a marketing plan for my business and think: *I should probably do some videos but I need to do something with this hair first. I am a hot mess. I can't let people see me like this.* After work, I'd be playing with my kids and one of them would grab a chunk of my thigh and laugh, and I'd say to myself, *Ugh, when are you gonna get some self-control and lose weight?* Then I'd brush my teeth and wash my face at night, look in the mirror, and be horrified by my eyebrows, my nose, my pimples, my very existence. *Is that what you really look like!?*

In other words, I was a horribly mean bitch to myself. My thoughts were vicious. In fact, I want to punch those thoughts in the face right now for saying all that mean stuff to me back then.

So how did I change the tape that was playing this "you so ugly" song in my head every day? I did thought work.

Thought work is all about remembering that we have a say in the thoughts we are thinking. Our thinking is influenced by many things—our larger society, our particular culture, our families and friends—but it is also, thankfully, something that we ourselves have the power to influence.

Thought work begins when you stop believing everything you think, and start asking questions, like:

What are the facts of this situation?

Where did this thought come from?

How does this thought affect me?

Is there a better way to think about this?

When it comes to me and my too-small pants, it looks like this:

The fact is that the pants do not fit my body.

The idea that it's "because I need to lose weight" is not a fact. It's a thought that comes from messages emanating from pretty much every corner of Western society.

The thought that "the pants don't fit because I need to lose weight" makes me feel terrible. It conjures other torturous thoughts: that there's something wrong with my body, that I'm ugly, that I have no self-control.

There is *definitely* a better way to think about this situation.

Every time I would think some version of *Girl, you ugly*, I reframed that thought into something positive and helpful. So, if I tried on pants and thought, *These pants don't fit because I need to lose weight*, I would reframe that thought into something kinder, helpful, and actually true like "these pants don't fit because they are the wrong size for me. Let me get a different size." Instead of choosing to believe that the pants I was trying on were too small because there is something wrong with my body, I choose to believe that the pants don't fit because they aren't the right size for my body, which is beautiful and deserves proper fitting pants. Same exact scenario but instead of choosing to make tight pants mean that something is wrong with me, I choose to look at the facts and reframe the thought into something neutral or even positive (*The pants don't fit; therefore I need a different size, the end*).

The thoughts you are habitually thinking are a choice and a habit. You can choose to think different thoughts. And the more you reframe your thoughts, the less you will think those repetitive, unhelpful thoughts until one day, you wake up and realize you've stopped being such a mean girl to yourself.

My body is the exact same size it was when I used to be horrible to myself. In fact, I've gained weight and gotten older since I used to think those habitually mean thoughts about how I looked. And yet, I rarely think those thoughts anymore.

Instead, I catch a glimpse of myself in the mirror and think, *Girl, you fine*. And I may even add in a *Look at dem strong legs* and a *Wow, God really gave you a beautiful smile*. Yes, I'm serious. Instead of hatin' ass thoughts, I think loving ass thoughts, and it's a result of thought work.

Thought work is a practice. You can't reframe a negative thought one time and think it's gone forever. No, Sis. You need to practice thought work on a daily basis, and eventually you'll notice that the negative thoughts are drastically reduced, and you're having much more positive thoughts about that particular subject.

Thought work is a life-changing practice, and it has changed my life for the better. When you think more positively about yourself whether it's your body, your work, your intelligence, your financial decisions, or your parenting, you will start taking more positive actions. For example, when I stopped thinking I was ugly, I stopped treating myself like crap. Suddenly, I started to feel worthy of adorning myself with nice clothes, styling my hair and buying new lipstick. I also started moving my body, eating healthier meals, and prioritizing rest. When you think positive thoughts about yourself, you treat yourself better. And when you treat yourself better, you feel better. And when you feel better, you can accomplish anything.

Now that you understand what thought work is, let's talk about what thought work isn't. Thought work is not the only thing we need to do to feel and do better in this world, and it's certainly not a solution to societal ills. For example, I am a Black person who experiences racism as I move through the world. Changing my thoughts is not going to make racism end. I can't think my way to the end of violence against Black people. That's bullshit and, frankly, harmful. Racism is not my fault, and there is nothing wrong with me because I feel angry or hurt when I experience racism. I do not need to do thought work to feel less harmed by racism. Racism is horrific and being upset about it is normal and, I would argue, necessary. Anger can be a powerful fuel for action. That said, I can work with my thoughts so that I choose a more effective and empowering response to the racism I experience in my life.

For example, I might think: *Because of racism, I will never be able to build wealth. My people are systemically discriminated against, and racist practices are built into our banking and other economic policies. Therefore, I will never get ahead and be able to build wealth.*

The facts are these: Racism presents many challenges and obstacles to my ability to build wealth, *and* I have agency.

The thought *Because of racism, I will never be able to build wealth* makes me feel dejected and horrible. So horrible that it is unacceptable to me.

Where does the thought come from? This is complicated. It comes from history, but it also comes from a racist tendency to discount and deny the agency and ability of Black people.

There is a much better way to think about this situation: one that doesn't deny the challenges presented by systemic inequality but also doesn't discount my agency and ability.

I could choose to do thought work on these beliefs and reframe my thoughts to *Because of racism, I must build wealth. My people are systemically discriminated against, and racist practices are built into our banking and other economic policies. Therefore, I will make it a priority to get ahead and build wealth so I can show my people that it's possible for them, too.* Both of these thoughts acknowledge the fact that racism exists and is baked into American economics and politics, but one of them inspires positive action and the other one makes you feel defeated. We get to choose how we respond to the things happening in the world, and our feelings about those things are completely valid. I chose to believe in my ability to build wealth in spite of racism and systemic oppression. You get to choose your response to what is happening in the world, too.

Action step: Find a negative thought that's constantly playing in your head, and take it through thought work:

1. What are the facts of this situation?
2. Where did this thought come from?
3. How does this thought affect me?
4. What's a better way to think about this?

Find a positive or neutral reframe of the negative thought that acknowledges reality, but also asserts your agency. Then, decide to think it on purpose. Every time the old thought pops into your head, pull up the reframe. You can even write down the reframe and place it somewhere you will see it often so that you are frequently reminded to reframe this thought. Commit to this practice and watch your thoughts change. Use the Broke Ass Thought versus Million Dollar Thought chart to find some examples of how to reframe your unhelpful thoughts.

I've also included this handy-dandy chart to help you replace some of your shoddy money thoughts that aren't serving you with thoughts that will. Now, please note that this is not about pretending to be positive or "fake it 'til you make it." You don't have to only think positive thoughts. (Also, have you met me? I am not a bubbly ray of sunshine but a rather keep-it-real, ornery bi-otch, but this shit works even on people like me.) This is about thinking effective thoughts—thoughts that have the effect of making you a millionaire rather than making you broke.

BROKE ASS THOUGHT	MILLION DOLLAR THOUGHT
The world is unfair so I am not going to bother trying.	The world is unfair, and I'm going to be a millionaire to make the world a better place.
I'll never get out of debt.	I am capable of changing my situation.

BROKE ASS THOUGHT	MILLION DOLLAR THOUGHT
Making money is hard.	There are an infinite number of ways to make money. I can find something that feels good to me. It may be challenging but also fun and worthwhile.
Making money is too risky.	I am scrappy as hell, and I will always land on my feet.
I'm not good with money.	Building wealth is a skill that I can learn.
I'll always be broke.	The past has passed, the future is rich. My future can be different from my past.
Rich people are assholes.	Poor and rich people can be assholes, and poor and rich people can be kind. If I'm an asshole, it's not money's fault.
People won't like me if I have money.	There are seven billion people living on planet Earth, it is not possible to be liked by all seven billion. Striving to be universally liked is a game I can't win. My true friends will love me regardless of my income level.
Money changes people.	Yeah, money absolutely changes your life. Now you have a house, a car, and all your needs met without ever having to worry about bills. Holla!
If I get rich, people will only want me for my money.	I can find dope friends who celebrate my success at every income level.
Making more money is gonna make my life more complicated, in other words, mo' money, mo' problems.	Money doesn't solve every problem, but it can solve a lot of them. Let it be easy.

BROKE ASS THOUGHT	MILLION DOLLAR THOUGHT
I don't need more money.	Bish, you lying. Next.
I don't know what I would do with more money.	I trust myself to use my money to do great things for myself and others.
I'm too tired to make more money.	Making money is energizing.
I'm not smart, creative, genius, or entrepreneurial enough to make a lot of money.	There are plenty of stupid people who are super rich, surely I am smarter than those people.
Whenever I get money, I always screw it up.	I've made Broke Ass Decisions in the past, but now I'm making Million Dollar Decisions.
I'll never get out of this hole (I accept defeat).	It might take me a while to reach my goals (or it might not) but either way, it's more fun to try. Many people have hit rock bottom and then have gone on to create amazing things. I can be one of them. My story isn't over yet.

What's a Broke Ass Thought that you have been thinking regularly? What's a Million Dollar Thought that you can replace it with?

Making a practice of doing thought work will change your life and help you break out of "financial prison." But I don't want you to be under the impression that all these crappy money thoughts you have are your fault. The truth is the world we live in has been actively and strategically undermining women's ability to build wealth since the dawn of time (or thereabouts). Let's take a look at the matrix we are living in so we can learn how to win in a society designed for us to lose.

CHAPTER SUMMARY

- Your childhood experiences have caused you to tell yourself stories about money that aren't true.
- You can overcome these childhood stories by analyzing these thoughts, figuring out where they came from and then replacing them with effective Million Dollar Thoughts.
- When you change the stories you are telling yourself about money, you will make financial decisions that serve you well, and you will feel more confident while you do it.
- You have already overcome quite a bit in your life. This serves as evidence that you have an unstoppable spirit that has the ability to become a millionaire and accomplish any other goal you set your mind to as well.

Sometimes when you do this kind of work, heavy stuff comes up. If looking at your money stories feels scary, overwhelming, or sad, know that you do not have to do this work alone. I encourage you to seek support. I, myself, have hired therapists, coaches, and other professionals over the years to help me unpack some of the childhood trauma that was manifesting itself in my life in a negative way. There are even financial therapists who are specifically trained to help you unpack some of these thoughts and stories. Go to helloseven. co/resources for further information. Most of all, know that you are not defeated.

CHAPTER 2

MILLION DOLLAR LIES

"We'll never solve the feminization of power
until we solve the masculinity of wealth."

—GLORIA STEINEM[1]

n 2012, I was about two years into my entrepreneurial journey and had just started my fledgling law practice. I was delighted to have landed my first corporate client. This was my highest paying client ever, and I was so excited. I felt like I was really starting to make strides in my business.

I completed the legal work for this client in October and was waiting for the client to pay my invoice. If you have ever had a corporate client, then you know that corporations can take forever to pay. The holidays came and went, including the New Year's holiday, and still no check. Every day, my face was pressed up against the window, watching the mailbox like a hawk.

Finally the first week of January, my big, fat, juicy corporate check arrived. And so had I, or so I thought. I pulled whatever sweat pants were on the floor of my bedroom over my pregnant belly and headed to the bank feeling like a badass even though I didn't look like it. (Isn't it interesting that money makes us feel powerful even when we don't look the part?)

At the bank I proudly presented my $5,000 check to the teller. That was the largest amount of money I'd ever been paid at one time in my entire life. The teller deposited the check, handed me the receipt and said, "It will be available in two weeks. Have a great day!"

Aw hell naw. Two weeks!? After waiting literally months for that check, I couldn't afford to wait another two weeks. This was a really big deal. My daughter had just come up on the waitlist for the only great childcare in town. This corporate check was the only reason I could afford it. And I desperately needed the childcare so I could take on more clients and improve my financial situation. Everything was hinging on putting the deposit down that day, otherwise she would lose her spot.

So I leaned in real close and whispered so no one else in the bank could hear me. "I really need the money available right away. Is there any way you could remove the hold and make the funds available now?"

The kindly teller said: "I'm sorry, honey. It's an out-of-state check. I can't make the funds available, but you can take it up with the manager if you like."

Sigh.

Insert the old white guy.

So I go stand in a spot out of the way while waiting for the branch manager to come talk to me. While I stand there, I'm getting my story together, while also deeply regretting looking less like a trustworthy professional and more like a broke college student who definitely bounces checks.

After what felt like an eternity, the branch manager comes over and I explain my plight. I tell him how I waited for that corporate check for a long time, I tell him about my daughter's childcare, and how badly I needed that money today. My face is red with embarrassment, and I feel like such a loser for not being more financially secure. I'm a lawyer, for God's sake. I should be doing better than this.

The branch manager nods as I tell my story and then walks over to one of the other bankers. They huddle over the banker's computer screen obviously looking at my account and talking about whether they think my check will bounce. I was horrified that they were analyzing all my purchasing decisions over the last few months. I really wished I hadn't purchased that Shake Weight last week.

As I sat there mortified and fighting back the hot tears that wanted to stream down my face, watching myself be judged by two old white guys, something shifted in me. A new level of determination. I was pissed at myself for letting this happen. I said to myself, *Sis, this will never ever happen again.*

Never again will my financial situation be so precarious. Never again will my daughter's needs be at risk. Never again will I let the future of my family be decided by anyone other than me and maybe my husband, but mostly me. *Never, ever, again.*

The branch manager did release the hold on my big ol' corporate check that day, bless his soul. I left the bank and went directly to my daughter's new childcare to pay the deposit. Then I got back in my car and sobbed like a baby. I was ashamed of my financial choices and my lack of stability. But I knew I had the power to change my situation, so I went home and got to work.

That year, my business revenue went from $60,000 to $300,000, and I did it by focusing on building wealth and fully capitalizing on my sellable experience and expertise. (More on how to do that in Part II of this book.) After that day, there was one thing I knew for sure: I would never put my fate in the hands of an old white guy ever again.

The media wants you to think you're a shopaholic with a bankruptcy-inducing coffee habit.

It's not surprising that I felt judged and sheepish having the bank manager review my bank accounts. A study by Starling Bank found that the messages about women and money in media largely assume that women are excessive spenders, and men are financially successful.[2] They found that 65 percent of money articles in women's magazines define women as loose with the cash. Women are advised to limit, restrict, and take better control of shopping "splurges." To seek discounts, cut coupons, and save their money. We women apparently need to reign it in and stop buying all those goddamn lattes.

"Women are then encouraged to maximize their economic contributions through forms of thrift like saving small sums, earning small amounts, or finding a means of financial support, like a parent. Or a husband."[3] Anyone else ready to throw a shoe? The key word here is *small*. The media thinks women are small and their money should be small and their spending should be small. To this I say, *hell naw*. I am not small. My money isn't small. My saving isn't small. And my spending isn't small, either. Everything about me is Notorious B.I.G.

Now let's explore what men are told to do with their money. In media geared toward men, the messages assume financial success and encourage men to invest, spend, and take financial risks in order to achieve power. It's no wonder that 58 percent of women let their male partners make the important financial decisions.[4] And many of us feel like we are "not good with money." That is the lie the world is selling to us every single day.

Sallie Krawcheck, the CEO and cofounder of the digital financial platform for women, Ellevest, and former CEO of Merrill Lynch Wealth Management and Smith Barney, talked about the difference between the way we talk to boys versus girls about money in her *Fast Company* op-ed:

> From childhood, we as a society send girls messages that they are bad with numbers, relative to their brothers. Still today, parents talk to boys about making money and investing and to girls about saving money and being careful with it. Girls get lower grades in math than boys for the same answers at school. And girls get lower allowances at home than boys for the same chores.
>
> As we get older, we women are told that we're bad with money in a thousand small ways: Women's magazines—on the rare occasions that they have written about money—have presented it as a challenge, describing financial planning as "difficult" so "you'd better buckle your seat belt," and showering us with money quizzes to find out whether we're a "Carrie" or "Miranda" money personality. In fact, Carrie herself was a tough, savvy, modern New Yorker in every

way–except when it came to money. There, she bought too many Manolo Blahniks and so couldn't afford to buy her apartment. Seriously . . .

Women have effectively internalized the messages that our society sends them about money, and the result is that the primary emotion so many of us feel about money is shame. We feel shame when we are in debt; we feel shame because we spend too much, certainly; we feel shame because we earn too little–and we even feel shame because we earn too much. This is particularly so if women earn more than their male partners– which even today is a such a taboo that both parties will lie to the federal government about their incomes.[5]

Sallie is right. In a recent survey to my community of thousands of women entrepreneurs, I asked if they feel confident in their ability to manage their money and make financial decisions, and 90 percent of these women answered no. Ninety percent! And this is a diverse group of professional women, most of whom have advanced degrees and own their own businesses. The median income among these women is more than $100,000.

Many of my clients come to me with relatively modest financial goals. They want to make another $1,000 per month, for example. That is equivalent to only 1–3 new clients per month for most professionals, or a relatively reasonable request for a raise or one creative new revenue stream (like renting a room in your apartment, selling your famous pies on the weekend or offering tutoring on the side), and they think it is an insurmountable goal.

We are taught that our financial goals are too big and that we are inadequate to accomplish them. We are taught that we are asking for too much and we are not worth that amount of money. And then on top of that, we are taught that we are not good with managing money. These constant messages from our families, the media, and popular culture keep us undervaluing our work and underestimating our ability to make beaucoup bucks. The scariest part is that these messages are reiterated by our government in the form of laws.

YOUR GOVERNMENT HAS BEEN
KEEPING YOU BROKE

Systemically, women have been disempowered to manage money. Women's rights to earn an income, own and manage property and open a bank account are relatively new in the United States and around the world. In 1769, seven years before the United States was officially formed, the colonies adopted an English law that made women one with their husbands upon marriage. This law meant that women became the property of their husbands and only the husband was a citizen with full legal rights. This also meant that any inheritance or property owned or income earned by a woman was her husband's property.

This law remained in effect for almost one hundred years. In the mid-1800s, various states began passing laws that expanded women's rights to own property or to receive an inheritance, but in many cases it was in effect only when their husbands were incapacitated. Even in cases where women were allowed to own property, they weren't allowed to manage it and direct its use. As time went on, states began passing laws enabling single, divorced, and widowed women to have economic rights, but married women's rights continued to be extremely limited.

The Married Women's Property Act was passed in New York State in 1848. This law granted each woman the right to receive an inheritance in her own name, own and manage property, enter contracts, and file lawsuits on her own behalf. For the first time, women were granted separate economy, which meant that they could maintain and control their own economic lives and were no longer treated like juveniles financially. This was only in New York State. It took approximately fifty years for each state to pass their own version of the Married Women's Property Act.

While white women were legally the property of their husbands, 90 percent of Black women in the United States were legally the property of slave owners[6] and therefore excluded from all economic life (except, that is, to ensure the financial well-being of slave owners through her stolen labor). Upon emancipation, Black people did not have financial means. The Freedmen's Bureau was created by the US government in March 1865 to address the financial, health, and social needs of four million newly freed men and women. However, due to a lack of funding and widespread opposition by President Andrew Johnson and white Southerners, the Freedmen's Bureau failed to ensure the economic well-being of the Black population in the United States.

The Freedman's Savings and Trust Company was established at the same time as the Freedmen's Bureau to provide a place for Black Union soldiers and other Black folks to deposit their pay and receive a basic financial education. At this time, unlike most white women, Black women were well represented in the workforce. Black people deposited millions of dollars into the bank, though each deposit was small, ranging from $5 to $50. As a result of ongoing political opposition, lack of oversight, and corruption, the bank failed less than a decade after its founding.

The bank was shut down in June 1873, leaving 61,000 Black depositors, both working men and women, with losses of nearly $3 million. About half of those depositors eventually received some portion of their deposits back while others received nothing. Some depositors and their descendants spent more than thirty years petitioning Congress for reimbursement for losses.[7] The failure of the Freedman's Savings and Trust Company created justified feelings of betrayal, abandonment, and distrust of the American banking system among Black people that would remain in the Black community for decades.

Of course, when laws are passed, custom is not instantly changed. So even when women are granted additional rights under the law, in most cases it takes years for widespread adoption. For example, in 1920, it became unconstitutional to deny women the right to vote on the basis of sex. However, women still had to navigate a variety of state voting laws that could keep them from voting based upon age, citizenship, residency, mental competence, and more.[8] And most women of color remained unable to vote.

For Black women, the same poll taxes, literacy tests, and grandfather clauses that had kept Black men from voting prevented Black women from doing so as well. Add to that the intimidation, threats of violence, and lynching that Black people experienced when they attempted to vote. The result is that it took the passing of the 24th Amendment, ratified in 1964, and the Voting Rights Act in 1965 to see large numbers of Black women finally able to vote.[9]

Similarly, Native Americans weren't granted the right to vote until 1924 with the passage of the Snyder Act, which ironically granted them full US citizenship (prior to that they were not deemed citizens under the 14th Amendment). Yet Native Americans were still prevented from participating in elections, because the Constitution left it up to each state to decide who has the right to vote. Similar to Black people, it took more than forty years for all fifty states to allow Native Americans to vote. Native Americans also experienced the same intimidation and strategic limitation of their voting rights at the state level until the passing of the Voting Rights Act.

For citizens of Asian descent, it wasn't until 1952 that they were all granted the right to vote. The Chinese Exclusion Act passed in 1882 barred people of Chinese ancestry from becoming US citizens. And in 1922, the Supreme Court ruled that people of Japanese heritage were ineligible to become citizens, preventing them from gaining the right to vote. In 1923, the court found that "Asian Indians" were also not eligible to become citizens.[10] It was nearly thirty years before the McCarran-Walter Act granted all Asian Americans the right to become citizens and vote. And it took two decades more for the Voting Rights Act to accommodate voters with limited English, finally making voting more accessible for Americans of Asian descent.

Separate economy isn't only determined by one's ability to own property and vote. In 1963, the United States passed the Equal Pay Act requiring equal pay for equal work. But as we know, sixty years later, Latina and Native American women still make only 54 cents and 57 cents, respectively, on a white man's dollar. Black women make 62 cents on a white man's dollar, and white women make 79 cents on a white man's dollar. And not only has women's earning capability been unequal for so long, but women's ability to manage money and take out loans is also incredibly new.[11]

It wasn't until the 1960s that it was common for a woman to have her own bank account without her husband, father, or brother involved. And even then, many women did not have access to credit. Women were unable to get a credit card without a male cosigner and when applying for mortgages, banks would discount a married woman's income especially when she was of childbearing age. This meant that when married women were given access to credit, they were granted only 50 percent of what a male applicant making the same amount of money would be granted. Single, widowed, and divorced women were denied credit altogether without a male co-signer, regardless of their income.

The Equal Credit Opportunity Act was passed in 1974 and prohibited lending discrimination based on sex or marital status. Two years later, Congress amended the law to further prohibit lending discrimination based on race, color, religion, national origin, age, the receipt of public assistance income, or exercising one's rights under certain consumer protection laws.[12] Therefore, women have only had equal access to mortgages, credit cards, loans, and the wealth these financial instruments can help generate for less than fifty years.

This means that our mothers and grandmothers were unable to have their own bank accounts, acquire their own credit cards, or buy a home with a mortgage. Before 1974, women couldn't do things like start their own businesses, access higher education, or make large purchases like a car, without the approval and cosign of a man. Think about how little control women had over their own lives during this time. The twin challenges of being paid less for the same work as a man and being denied access to banking and credit until very recently had the effect of robbing women of agency.

Hey, you just read a whole bunch of depressing shit, and it might be sending you into a spiral of despair. Or perhaps a fit of rage. Why not take a moment for some Million Dollar Self-Care? Here are few fun things you can do:

- Have a glass of rosé or a square of dark chocolate
- Have a dance break to "Soulmate" by Lizzo

- Watch a five-minute clip on YouTube of RuPaul doing literally anything
- Pet a cat
- Snuggle a baby
- Take a twenty dollar bill and fold it into an origami heart
- Smash the patriarchy (just kidding, that's gonna take a while)

When it comes to women and money, the US government (and other governments around the world) have only very recently granted women the right and access to build wealth that white men have had for two thousand years. Yes, Virginia, white men have had a two-thousand-year head start when it comes to building wealth.

Not only have they had a massive head start, but the collective labor of women and people of color, most of all Black people, has been absorbed by white men as wealth, under the law, for centuries. And that wealth has been passed through generations of white men's families via inheritances, creating the wealth gap that exists to this day between men and women and whites and people of color.

And we're still not done.

Something that has always affected women's ability to build wealth is the job of birthing the next generation of our species. Up until 1978, women could be legally fired from their jobs for becoming pregnant and routinely were, thus causing significant interruption in a woman's ability to generate wealth. And while the Pregnancy Discrimination Act has since made it illegal, in practice, women are still denied promotions and even illegally fired when they become pregnant in the midst of building their careers. There have also been studies that show mothers are less likely to be invited for an interview when applying for jobs and are given lower starting salaries than childless women.[13]

Women also face a discriminatory financial penalty if they are not thin. A landmark study conducted in 2004 found that a sixty-five-pound increase in a woman's weight is associated with a

9-percent drop in her earnings. The "obesity penalty" amounted to losing three years of experience in the workplace in terms of wages.[14] The worst part about wage discrimination against fat women is that there are little to no explicit laws preventing it. Only one state (Michigan) and nine cities have laws prohibiting workplace discrimination based on weight. For all other jurisdictions, obese women might be able to sue their employers based on sex discrimination[15] under Title VII of the Civil Rights Act, but no one has successfully done it to date.

Let's not forget our queer sisters. Employers were 30 percent less likely to request an interview or further information from a woman perceived as LGBTQIA+ compared to one perceived as heterosexual.[16] And for trans women, it is so difficult to maintain full-time employment due to widespread discrimination that one in eight trans persons become involved in underground economies—such as sex and drug work—in order to survive. One Boston study found that fewer than 25 percent of trans women are employed full-time. And trans women of color and Black trans women, in particular, face disproportionate rates of unemployment, harassment, and lethal violence.[17]

> *"There is no such thing as a single-issue struggle because we do not live single-issue lives."*
>
> —AUDRE LORDE[18]

Okay, so that is a boatload of evidence that suggests that we are fucked. Whether we are fat, Black, trans, pregnant, Native American, or all the above, there is widespread, government-sanctioned discrimination of women of every shape, size, ethnic background, and sexual orientation, and it's keeping us all broke. You may be feeling a bit pissed off or maybe even sad and defeated after reading all that (I had steam coming out of my ears the entire time I researched and wrote this chapter). And for good reason. However, there is some good news.

Cisgender straight white men have had centuries to build wealth, businesses, political power, and so on.

Women have only had fifty years, and already we have women millionaires and billionaires and presidential candidates.

It goes to show how powerful we are in spite of the many ways that our government has been complicit in holding us back.

Now let's use our anger to continue the work of burning down the societal constructs that do not work for us. But we're going to need capital to do it. Activism requires fuel in the form of finances.

Women as a collective have been systematically disadvantaged and discriminated against when it comes to their ability to build wealth, and that discrimination and disadvantage continue to this day. Having economic power is going to enable us to change the law, change the world, and make it a better place for all.

So, what's our next move?

Our next move is forgiveness.

I'm not talking about forgiving the media or the government (funk that!). I'm talking about ourselves.

It's time to forgive ourselves for thinking, *We're not good with money*. These thoughts are not manifesting out of thin air. No. These thoughts are the result of millennia of conditioning that makes us believe building wealth and becoming a millionaire is out of reach for us.

So, I want to invite you to forgive yourself for every financial misstep or mistake that you feel you've made. Forgive yourself for letting that narcissistic boyfriend get away with not paying rent for six months. Forgive yourself for the thousands of dollars in student loan debt (Sis, you invested in yourself—celebrate that). Forgive yourself for the credit card debt and late payments. Forgive yourself for the underemployment and lack of negotiating for a higher salary. Forgive yourself for your FICO score.

Be gentle with yourself, because you are the product of centuries of practices that have made it difficult for you to earn money, have money, and manage money. The system is literally rigged against us.

Being angry at yourself and belittling yourself are ineffective. It will only weigh you down and make it much harder to make money and win. So, take a moment to pat yourself on the back for coming this far, for surviving in a financially messed-up world, and for picking up this book. You are doing the work to level up your financial life. As Maya Angelou says, "when you know better, you do better."[19]

Now it's time to move away from what you've been taught about scrimping and saving and not buying lattes, and instead recognize your ability to earn a whole hell of a lot more. Regardless of your background, experience, degrees or lack thereof, I would bet money that you have far more earning potential than you recognize.

Jerrold Mundis, the author of the book *Earn What You Deserve*, defines underearning as: "to repeatedly gain less income than you need, or than would be beneficial, usually for no apparent reason and despite your desire to do otherwise." You are an underearner if you are earning less than you have the potential to earn, and your potential to earn is solely determined by you. Barbara Stanny, the author of *The Secrets of Six-Figure Women*, estimates that one out of every three workers is an underearner, most of whom are women.

So, how do we overcome underearning?

To answer that, let's take a look at how we become underearners in the first place. According to Stanny, women are underearners because we routinely accept less money for our work, give away our skills for free, or don't believe we are worth more. We put other people's needs before our own. And we fear the discomfort of disappointing people, saying no, and putting up boundaries.[20]

In summary, we women have been making some Broke Ass Decisions that have led to chronic underearning. Ladies, it's time to start making Million Dollar Decisions, and I am going to show you exactly how to do it in the next chapter. (Quick, turn the page!)

CHAPTER SUMMARY

- For decades, the media has told women that we are bad with money. We are inundated with messages that we are shopaholics buying way too many lattes and making poor financial decisions.
- The government has reinforced these messages with actual laws designed to discriminate against women's earning potential. Only in the last hundred years have laws been passed to stop widespread discrimination against women's economic lives.
- Even though laws have been passed, our culture continues to discriminate against women in ways that limit our ability to build wealth. This especially affects the wealth accumulation of women of color, queer women, fat women, and pregnant women.
- It's time to forgive ourselves for believing that we are "bad with money," because it's not our fault. We need to heal our relationship with money so that we can stop underearning and become millionaires.

CHAPTER 3

MILLION DOLLAR DECISIONS

"Nothing happens until you decide.
Make a decision and watch your life move forward."

—OPRAH WINFREY

A TALE OF TWO BOOS

One of my favorite clients is a fun, energetic woman in her early forties. Let's call her Broke Boo. Broke Boo is a senior analyst at a tech company making about $80,000 per year. She has two kids: a twelve-year-old boy who excels at every sport and a studious sixteen-year-old girl who gets excellent grades and travels the country with her high school band. Her ex-husband lives nearby, and they have a solid co-parenting relationship with little to no drama.

Broke Boo lives in a suburb of Chicago. She's always dressed to the nines with the perfect blowout. I imagine her strutting down the hallways of her company office looking stunning in pencil pants, blazer, heels, and a chunky ring. She charms her coworkers, neighbors, and fellow parents at her kids' schools. She's got lots of friends and many invitations to parties and other gatherings. Too bad that doesn't extend to her boss.

Broke Boo's boss offered her a promotion six months ago. She immediately started doing the work required for this new role, however, she has yet to receive the raise that was supposed to go with this new workload. She worked up the nerve to ask her boss when she will see the pay increase go into effect, and her boss told her "soon." She hasn't heard another word about it since.

Broke Boo also sells real estate on the side. This is her real passion, and she hopes to one day do real estate full-time. She loves selling, marketing, and staging property, and she really loves real estate investing. She's created a custom spreadsheet to analyze real estate deals and has $50,000 saved to buy her first investment property, but she hasn't pulled the trigger yet.

Broke Boo is dating a lovely gentleman named Josh. Josh is fun and is always taking her into Chicago for a night on the town. He knows the hot spots for young Black professionals like themselves. They have been dating for three years and spend a lot of time together, though they do not live together. Josh has even met her kids, and he's really good with them. Josh is currently underearning in his administrative role at a hospital. He'd like to earn more and has put in for a promotion, but it just hasn't happened.

When Josh's grandmother dies, he comes into a small inheritance. Broke Boo advises him on how to invest in real estate. She then finds the perfect investment property for him and runs it through her spreadsheet. The property will net Josh an extra $2,000 per month. Josh buys the property with Broke Boo's help and makes the additional money he was looking to earn at his job.

When Broke Boo isn't working at her day job or showing a house, she can usually be found running her son around to his various sports activities and taking her daughter shopping, to the hairdresser, and to visit with friends. She spends about twelve hours per week in her car driving the kids to their various activities. Even though she is a very busy woman, she makes sure she walks the dog every morning at 6:00 a.m. and has a cooked meal on the dinner table for her kids and Josh every single night.

One might say that Broke Boo is superwoman.

Or one might say that Broke Boo is making a whole lot of Broke Ass Decisions.

At first glance, this Broke Queen is doing quite well for herself. She's got a great relationship with her family, a fun boyfriend, and lots of friends at work. She has a good job making decent money, and she has a side hustle that she's passionate about. She's got a beautiful, full life.

However, beneath the perfectly put together outfits and the shiny hair worthy of a Pantene commercial is a woman who is putting everyone before herself and her wealth. Broke Boo has shared with me that she is exhausted by the end of the day, but she stays up into the wee hours of the morning just to have a few minutes to herself. She would love to hire a personal trainer, but she can't afford it right now.

Broke Boo just moved into a new place and is saving up to buy nice furniture that will fit her new space better. She has put off her dream of doing real estate full-time and buying an investment property because something always comes up. She's afraid to spend the money in her savings account because it's her safety net, which she feels she needs as a single mom. Her boss drives her nuts, and she's gotten into arguments with him a few times in the past but she holds it together because she doesn't want to lose her job.

Let's take a look at some of the decisions Broke Boo is making:

- She gets along with her ex-husband because she requires practically nothing of him. Why doesn't he get off his ass and drive these kids around some of the time?
- She let her boss give her more work without increasing her pay. She's been waiting for a raise to match her workload for more than six months and hasn't raised the issue with her boss again or put a boundary in place.
- She has incredible knowledge around real estate investing and instead of taking a risk and using it for her own benefit, she helped her boyfriend invest instead. Now he is making extra money and benefiting from Broke Boo's knowledge, and she did not get paid for her labor and expertise.
- She is taking care of everyone and no one is taking care of her. Her daughter is old enough to get herself around without being driven. And both her kids and Josh could take turns making dinner so she doesn't have to do it every single night. Also, why can't someone else walk the damn dog at least some of the time?

- The worst part is that Broke Boo isn't making time for her own self-care. She is running herself ragged and puts off her own happiness and pleasures. She can't pursue her dreams when she is running on empty every day.
- Even though she has a good income, savings, a boyfriend, great kids, nice clothes, and overall good life, she is constantly stressed about money. It's the number one source of stress in her life. She doesn't trust herself to make smart spending decisions, so she hoards cash in her bank account. This lack of self-trust also prevents her from hiring help, demanding more from her family members, and investing in her own self-care, like a personal trainer, which she definitely can afford but believes she can't.
- All of this is leading to very little free time, low energy, and high anxiety, evidenced by the fact that she has trouble sleeping. The saddest piece of Broke Boo's story is that she is not pursuing her dreams, feels broke rather than feeling abundant and is not reaching the full potential of her life.

Broke Boo's thoughts—that she can't trust herself to make smart financial decisions, that she has to do everything herself, that she's not allowed to invest in herself because she has to put the well-being of her children first (why do we mothers believe that taking care of ourselves equals disadvantaging our children? In reality, the opposite is true), and that she can't even have time to herself until all her loved ones are sleeping, let alone have her own dreams and desires be prioritized—can be psychologically damaging when they persist over time.

For many of us, these unchecked and unchallenged beliefs become self-fulfilling prophecies, a never-ending cycle in which bad self-esteem begets bad decisions begets no money begets low joy. If you want to end the cycle, you have to dare to believe something different for yourself and begin to act on those beliefs, despite your fears that the whole world will far apart if you are carrying it all on your shoulders every day.

Broke Boo's life isn't awful, and she's not impoverished, but there is an undercurrent of anxiety about money that is preventing her from experiencing the fullness of joy that is possible for her life.

With just some small changes, Broke Boo would no longer be Broke Boo. To see what I am talking about here, let's look at my other client, Rich Boo.

Rich Boo is also a fun, energetic woman in her early forties. Like Broke Boo, Rich Boo has two kids, ages ten and thirteen, and an ex-husband with whom she co-parents her daughters. She and her ex-husband get along well enough.

Rich Boo works as the marketing director at an executive training company. She absolutely loves her job. When she joined the company, they offered her a salary of $80,000, and she negotiated for several weeks until the company agreed to pay her $120,000 plus commission. Now she's working her dream job and making the kind of money she wants to be making. She also gets to work from home, which eliminates having to commute and gives her the flexibility to be there for her daughters when they need her.

In addition to working at the executive training company, Rich Boo is a life coach on the side, coaching a handful of clients to negotiate higher pay for themselves and go after what they want. The side hustle brings her income up to $175,000 per year, because this Rich Queen charges top dollar for her coaching.

She lives in a fabulous loft in downtown Chicago. She's always wanted to live downtown, and when she decided to leave her husband, she took the opportunity to live out this dream.

Rich Boo's arrangement with her ex-husband is that she has the kids one week, and he has the kids the next. On the weeks she doesn't have her girls, she goes on dates with the various men she meets on a dating app. She's having a great time dating, and it's very low pressure.

Rich Mama taught her kids how to pack their own lunch so she doesn't always have to do it. She makes dinner two or three nights per week, and the other nights they get takeout or eat leftovers. They have two dogs whom she and her kids love. Rich Boo has a dog walker who comes over and walks the dogs every day. This gives her time to do personal training three times per week. She feels like a badass when she lifts weights.

Her father passed away recently, and she came into a small inheritance. She is actively looking for an investment opportunity for this money and has talked to a few of her wealthy friends for advice.

Rich Boo is not trying to be superwoman. She's something way better: a Million Dollar Decision maker.

Here are some of the Million Dollar Decisions Rich Boo has made that allow her to be happier and, basically, a rich boo:

- She didn't accept the first offer but negotiated a salary that she felt was commensurate with her experience and the progress and profit she would bring to the company.
- She has a side hustle that she loves and where she gets to empower women. She charges top dollar for her valuable services, allowing her to increase her income significantly.
- She is willing to take risks to reach her goals and fulfill her desires. As a result she has her dream job, dream apartment, and is having fun dating.
- She is focused on increasing her earning potential and becoming a millionaire. She negotiated for commission, which gives her an income that isn't fixed and one in which her work can increase her income.
- She's also looking for an investment opportunity and is seeking advice from friends who have the kind of wealth she wants to have. Notice that she has the kinds of friends who can advise her on making Million Dollar Decisions. That's not an accident, Rich Boo vibes attract other Rich Boos.
- She does not try to do everything herself. She outsources to her kids, her ex-husband, and her dogwalker, which gives her the space in her life to pursue her personal goals and engage in self-care. It also has the added benefit of teaching her kids and other loved ones how to be independent and self-sufficient. She knows she doesn't need to do everything for the people in her life in order to express her love.

Broke Boo might be well liked by others, but Rich Boo is getting what she wants.

MILLION DOLLAR DECISIONS (MDD) VERSUS BROKE ASS DECISIONS (BAD)

A Million Dollar Decision is one that:

- creates time and energy,
- frees up mental space,
- reduces piddly shit and creates space for the stuff that matters to you,
- allows you to feel strong, secure, and free,
- creates options instead of eliminating options.

It's that feeling that your life is expanding instead of contracting. As you can imagine, a Broke Ass Decision is one that does the opposite. A BAD is one that:

- steals your time and energy,
- depletes mental space,
- increases piddly shit and prioritizes it above your greatest desires,
- makes you feel weak, insecure, and trapped,
- eliminates options rather than creating them.

The road to becoming a millionaire is paved with Million Dollar Decisions. Courageous, invigorating, delightful decisions that prioritize your well-being and your wealth. When you prioritize your well-being and wealth, it benefits everyone around you and is actually the opposite of selfish.

Most of us are smart women who understand the difference between a Broke Ass Decision and a Million Dollar Decision, but we keep making BAD moves anyway.

Why is that?

BROKE ASS DECISIONS	MILLION DOLLAR DECISIONS
Letting a house guest stay with you for a week, even though you know it will disrupt your work, peace, and well-being.	Telling your guest they can stay with you for two nights and giving them a list of hotels where they can stay for the remainder of their trip.
Walking the dog yourself every morning and night even though you don't enjoy it and you're always tired.	Hiring a dogwalker or delegating it to a family member.
Your car broke down and you take it to the mechanic to fix for the third time this year.	You head to the dealer and trade in your broken down car for a reliable, certified, pre-owned car because time is money.
You make dinner for your spouse and kids every night even though you work hard just like everyone else in your household.	You make dinner once or twice per week, and invite your spouse and children to make dinner the other nights while you put your feet up and relax. Resentment is instantly gone.
Your childhood trauma is getting in the way of your happiness, but you think you can't afford therapy so you do nothing about it.	You understand that your mental health is essential to your well-being and wealth so you do some research and find a local therapist that offers a sliding scale. You also borrow a few books on trauma from the library.
You don't want to hire help in your business, so you spend twenty hours per week doing admin work.	You recognize the value of your work, so you hire a part-time assistant for twenty hours per week, and you spend your freed-up time acquiring more clients and making more money.
You do your own laundry because you can't imagine having a stranger handle your underwear.	You use a laundry drop-off service because you can't imagine spending hours doing laundry this weekend when you need to rest and recuperate so you are ready to slay on Monday.

BROKE ASS DECISIONS	MILLION DOLLAR DECISIONS
Your boss compliments you and says you did excellent work. You reply that it was really a team effort even though it totally wasn't and downplay your hard work.	Your boss compliments you and says you did excellent work. You say thank you and place a diamond tiara on your head like the goddamn Queen that you are. And then add that to your list of receipts for your upcoming salary negotiation.
A friend owes you money but you don't ask for it back even though she tells you she just booked an expensive vacation to Tahiti.	No one owes you money because you have a policy not to lend money. You either give it away or don't because it's cleaner that way.
A friend owes you money but you don't ask for it back even though she tells you she just booked an expensive vacation to Tahiti.	You call, email, or text your friend and ask her to pay you back.
There is a course you want to take to further your training, but you are afraid to invest in yourself so you don't sign up.	There is a course you want to take to further your training so you sign up immediately because you know you can trust yourself to do the work and get results.
You want to make more money but it feels too overwhelming so you never begin.	You do some research, make a decision, and then take step one toward making more money immediately because a Rich Boo is a decisive boo.
You help your romantic partner with his or her business by handling the marketing, responding to emails and giving them a daily pep talk. Partner realizes their dreams and you don't.	You prioritize your own dreams and handle your own action around it. You give yourself a pep talk every morning. When you have time and energy for it, you offer your partner a pep talk as well.

BROKE ASS DECISIONS	MILLION DOLLAR DECISIONS
You compete daily for the title of Supermom by volunteering at your kids' school, making their lunch, cleaning their clothes, driving them to every activity, staying up until 10:00 p.m. doing their science project and (sobbing with exhaustion into the hand-sculpted clay volcano you just built), overall burning yourself out.	You compete daily for the title of Happy Woman by taking time for your own self-care, including massages, reading a novel, hot bubble baths, workout classes, orgasms, and tranquil walks in nature with the wind blowing through your hair.
Your phone is always by your side so you never miss a demand of your significant other, kids, mom, sister, boss, coworkers, friends, clients, neighbors, dog, cousin, that guy who claims he's your cousin, and aunties.	You put your phone on silent and take a breath of fresh air.
You apply for a job. They make you a lowball offer, and you immediately accept.	You apply for a job, and you let them know your salary requirements before they even make you a lowball offer. Once you receive an offer, you negotiate because you know you're worth it and you've got options.
You spend five hours looking for ways to cut your expenses. You clip coupons, spend an hour on the phone with the cable company, and skip those two lattes that you really wanted. You save a grand total of $82.	You spend five hours researching ways to make more money. You dig into different side hustles, choose one, and get your first client. You made a grand total of $782.

The key thing I want you to understand is that whether you make a Broke Ass Decision or a Million Dollar Decision is entirely up to you. You have a choice. And the sum of your choices is your life. So, if you are not satisfied with your life right now, know that a certain set of choices you made have led you to this life. Simply start making different choices, and you will start living a different life. Choice has led you into this life, and choice will lead you out of this life.

WHY WOMEN MAKE BAD MOVES

There are three main reasons we make a Broke Ass Decision when we have the opportunity to make a Million Dollar Decision.

The first BAD move is that we want to be liked by everyone.

First, **we want to be liked.** Belonging is essential to survival. According to Maslow's hierarchy of needs, once our needs for sustenance, sleep, homeostasis, and physical safety are met, our next greatest need is to belong. This biological need is built into our DNA, and for good reason. As a species, humans have depended on small groups for reproductive and survival needs. If you were ostracized from the group as an early human, you would die.

This explains our intense need to be liked. According to Matthew Lieberman, one of the founders of social cognitive neuroscience, "The importance of social connection is so strong that when we are rejected or experience other social 'pain,' our brains 'hurt' in the same way they do when we feel physical pain."[1] The consequences for social exclusion have been found to influence many negative behavioral, cognitive, and emotional outcomes. As a species, we have developed traits that are designed to prevent rejection and encourage acceptance.[2] As women, there are serious consequences for us when we are not liked, even today.

Marianne Cooper, the lead researcher for Sheryl Sandberg's book *Lean In: Women, Work, and the Will to Lead*, cited many peer-reviewed studies, which found that

high-achieving women experience social backlash because their very success—and specifically the behaviors that created that success—violates our expectations about how women are supposed to behave. Women are expected to be nice, warm, friendly, and nurturing. Thus, if a woman acts assertively or competitively, if she pushes her team to perform, if she exhibits decisive and forceful leadership, she is deviating from the social script that dictates how she "should" behave. By violating beliefs about what women are like, successful women elicit pushback from others for being insufficiently feminine and too masculine. As descriptions like "Ice Queen," and "Ballbuster" can attest, we are deeply uncomfortable with powerful women. In fact, we often don't really like them.[3]

So, if women's likeability is both an innate human need and comes with serious monetary consequences, isn't it right that we are willing to give up almost anything to be liked?

The answer is no.

Because if we want to have the kind of power, agency, and financial freedom enjoyed by men at a much greater rate, then we need to stop watering down our skills, talents, leadership, and money-making abilities for the sake of being liked.

The answer is being liked by a group of people of your choosing. A group of people who support you and accept you and love you for exactly who you are. A group of people who believe in you, want more for you, and inspire you to go get it. Not the watered-down polite version.

WHAT WOULD YOU DO IF YOU WERE A "BAD GIRL"?

My friend Nina had been feeling unhappy. She wasn't quite sure why. She had a successful business, a beautiful family, great friends, and several fun hobbies. She had it all, but she could not understand why she felt so unfulfilled. She hired a life coach to help her sort through her feelings.

During their first session, the coach said, "Here's a question I want you to ask yourself every single morning: What would you do if you were a 'bad girl'?"

Nina was shocked, but she immediately understood why. As women, we are trained to be nice. We prioritize being a "good girl" (whatever that means) over being happy, satisfied, and even safe. This desire to please others is so ingrained in us that we must ask ourselves this question every day so that we can practice listening to our own desires.

Go ahead, answer the question. You might be surprised at what comes up for you.

For Nina, when she thought about what she would do if she was a bad girl, her first thought was to get her own place. Nina lived with her husband and two daughters, and she wanted her own apartment. Clearly this is only something bad girls do! A mother and wife with her own place? Pearls will be clutched! Well, guess what? With some additional coaching, Nina did go and get her own apartment. It was a small studio apartment, and she went there whenever she wanted to get away from her family. It wasn't long before Nina realized she actually wanted to leave her husband. And so she did.

Now Nina lives in a beautiful house with her two girls and her feminist boyfriend who treats her the way she wants to be treated. She also closed her business and landed her dream job. She's happy and fulfilled, all because she was willing to be "bad."

What does being a bad girl even mean? It means following your own heart's desires instead of following the standard blueprint laid out for "good girls" by society. And if that's the case, I'm proud to be a bad girl.

Action step: Grab a journal and write at the top of the page "What would you do if you were a bad girl?" Write down whatever comes to mind, no matter how "bad" it is. Allow yourself to explore your true desires and not just what society has trained you to want, say, and be.

The second BAD move we make is that we hang out with people who are making Broke Ass Decisions.

A few years ago, I had a VIP Day with my client, Yolanda. Yolanda and I spent the day reviewing her business model and updating her offers, marketing, team, and systems to streamline the business and help her achieve her goals. During our lunch break, I asked Yolanda what obstacles did she think might get in the way of reaching her goals. I mentioned that sometimes it's the people around us, like friends and family members who are naysayers, who slow us down. Yolanda immediately started shaking her head.

"I don't have that problem," she said.

I said: "You don't? I'm surprised. Almost all my clients have to rethink who they are spending time with when they are ready for their next level of success."

Yolanda just kept on shaking her head. "Not me. This is something I handle on an annual basis."

"Really? How so?" I asked.

That's when Yolanda proceeded to tell me about her Annual Friend Review. Every year just before the holidays, Yolanda spends time evaluating her circle of friends. She gets out a pen and paper, writes down a list of the people she spends the most time with and then evaluates how the friendship has gone that year.

Things that she might evaluate include: Was this friend there for me this year? Did we have fun bonding times this year? Does this friend frequently use our time together to complain about her life but then do nothing about it? Do we still have similar interests? Do I look forward to spending time with her? Do I feel energized or drained after spending time with her?

Yolanda said that every year, after evaluating her friendships, several friends do not make the cut. And so she unapologetically cuts the cord on that friendship and instead invests that time and energy into mutually beneficial relationships. She said this year, her boyfriend might not make the cut. His review was coming up soon!

Folks, Yolanda is a damn genius.

This Annual Friend Review is a brilliant idea, and here's why: According to research by social psychologist Dr. David McClelland of Harvard, the people you habitually associate with determine as much as 95 percent of your success or failure in life.

That's right. When you spend time with people who are making Broke Ass Decisions in their own lives, it's very likely that you will begin making Broke Ass Decisions in your life as well. This plays out with a variety of life and financial decisions. For example, when people are choosing where to invest, they won't systematically think about all the options. Instead, they will consider what people they know are investing in.[4]

As a business coach, I've come up against this problem frequently. I will work with a client to create a plan of action for her business. The client is excited about her plan and all in. The following week, she messages me to say it's all wrong and will never work. My first question is: Who have you been talking to? Usually it's an unsupportive, if not pessimistic, spouse/parent/friend who has convinced the client that the plan will never work. I wish I could tell you that usually the client gets refocused and executes the plan and accomplishes her dreams. Unfortunately, that is often not the case. More often than not, clients who have a negative influence in their ear on a daily basis spend years spinning their wheels, too afraid to take the leap. Negative influences can rob you of your dreams.

The people with whom you frequently spend time heavily influence your decisions. Think about the group texts you participate in daily, the Facebook Groups you frequent, and the people you spend time with every weekend. Are these the kind of people who are making Million Dollar Decisions? If not, you may need to cut the cord (or at the very least, buy that friend a copy of this book!). Another option, particularly if it's a close relationship, is to have a heartfelt conversation with your loved one about how much you need their support in order to make the moves you want to make.

We'll talk more about building your Million Dollar Squad in chapter 5. For now, grab a sheet of paper and conduct your very first Annual Friend Review.

The third BAD move is that we are living in a broke ass environment.

In chapter 2, we talked about the barrage of media messages that we receive on a daily basis as women. Whether you are scrolling Instagram or watching a show on Netflix, you are surely taking in negative messages about your abilities to make, manage, and invest your money. This constant barrage burrows into your headspace and convinces you that you are gonna be a #brokebitch4life.

These media messages are reinforced when you apply for a credit card, loan, or mortgage and get denied, which is more likely to happen to you because you are a woman and banks don't trust you.[5] (Working women are a third more likely to be refused a loan than men.) It is also reinforced when an emergency comes up, and you realize you don't have enough money to handle that emergency. And when you see friends, family, and social media acquaintances having to raise money via GoFundMe for the various hardships that come up in life. These messages accumulate into a fear that is so constant it's likely to grab a beer and settle in on your favorite spot on the couch.

So, what's a Sister to do?

In order to go from feeling broke and therefore making Broke Ass Decisions to feeling worthy of the Million Dollar Life you want, you need to detox your environment.

I first learned about environmental detoxes from my friend, Susan Hyatt. Susan is an author and coach, and she describes an environmental detox as simply taking a look at your environment and assessing how it's making you feel. It's much easier to make Million Dollar Decisions when your life space is clear of scarcity signals. You want to notice your physical surroundings, the media messages you are taking in, your home, your wardrobe, your work life, your daily habits, and your possessions, and notice whether these things are sending you messages of abundance or messages like "never enough," "shabbiness," "financial anxiety," "existential anxiety," "settling or making do" or "do more with less."

For example, I have a client named Kristen who has a cute little house in Nashville. She fixed it up for her and her son (she is a single mama) and was super proud of the space that she created with her own money and creativity. However, when she did this environmental detox exercise, her first thought was one cabinet in her kitchen that banged into a vent on the wall when it was opened.

She couldn't fully open the cabinet, which meant she couldn't fully utilize that cabinet space. As a result, all her dishes, spices, and kitchen appliances were shoved into three smaller cabinets. Every time she opened one of those cabinets, things would fall down onto the counter and floor. One day, as she was preparing coffee before an important work call, she broke one of her favorite mugs trying to rummage through the cabinet. She was late to the call because she had to clean up the broken mug off the floor and it totally killed the positive vibes she had woken up with.

Every day she worked around that annoying cabinet while she made coffee, prepared lunch, or washed dishes. She realized that one stupid cabinet was stealing precious minutes of her valuable time on a daily basis and making her feel broke. Finally, after conducting this detox, she called a contractor to come take a look at it and, $500 later, the vent was relocated, the cabinet was fixed and working properly, and she was feeling like a boss. That $500 investment was a Million Dollar Decision saving her space, time, and energy.

Now it's time for you to conduct your own environmental detox. Think about the people and brands you follow on social media, your home environment, your clothing, your work life, your various possessions, and your daily habits. Ask yourself: *How does this thing make me feel? How is it influencing my mood? Is it giving me energy or making me feel drained? If this thing in my environment could talk, what would it be saying to me?* If it's saying "you are broke," toss it, donate it, or otherwise make it disappear, and replace it with something that makes you feel rich.

For example, are you always flying economy for work travel even though you are too tall to fit in the cramped economy seats? You arrive at your work events feeling cranky, exhausted, and not on your A game when a first-class ticket would give you the space to feel comfortable, be relaxed, and get some work done so that you land at your destination feeling refreshed and ready to slay your meetings.

Or do you own a bunch of clothing that doesn't fit quite right, is bland and boring, and makes you feel hidden in plain sight? Why not donate or discard your janky undergarments, ill-fitting blazers, and boring tops, and replace them with clothes that fit perfectly, made of fabrics that drape beautifully and make you feel ready to be seen and heard?

Note that your clothing, your home and other aspects of your environment don't have to be expensive in order to make them feel rich for you. I used to be the queen of Craigslist, finding great second-hand furniture for a steal to make my home feel nicer. I also used to shop at thrift stores in fancy neighborhoods (you can find some real quality clothing donated by wealthy women there!). Even things like purchasing flowers for yourself, sitting outside in the sun, eliminating clutter, taking a nap, lighting an aromatic candle, reading a really good book and taking a bubble bath can make you feel rich even though they don't cost much. Upgrading your environment is about making choices that make you feel amazing.

According to Susan, an environmental detox can take 10,000 pounds of emotional weight off your shoulders. Detoxing your environment will make you feel better, sleep better, and boss up. When you look around your home and your workspace and feel cared for, and even when you scroll Instagram and see uplifting positive messages that reinforce the notion that you are worthy, it will become easier to make Million Dollar Decisions in every area of your life.

A FORMULA FOR
MILLION DOLLAR DECISIONS

By now you understand what a Million Dollar Decision is and the common reasons women don't make them more often. But you may still be wondering, *How do I make a Million Dollar Decision?* Well, there's a formula for that.

My coaching team and I know how challenging it is to make Million Dollar Decisions in a world that constantly tells you that you are only worthy of brokeness. So, we've created a formula and an acronym to help you evaluate the important decisions you make and determine what a Million Dollar Decision looks like for you.

The acronym WSABM is the same as the initials for We Should All Be Millionaires, the title of this book. I hope this helps you remember the formula, even when you don't have a pen and paper handy.

Here is the formula for evaluating the various scenarios in which you want to make a Million Dollar Decision:

W is for Want. What do you want to do? Check in with your innate desires rather than crowdsourcing. Seeking wise counsel is a good choice, but before doing that, check in with what you actually want. If you knew for sure that any decision could yield your desired outcome, what would you most want to do?

S is for Shoulds. What are the shoulds operating here? Identify all the shoulds that come up when you think about this situation. What shoulds are coming up in your mind as you consider this decision? Is your want a *should* in disguise? Which shoulds do you agree with, and which are not yours?

A is for Action. What precise action will you take to move you in the direction of what you want? Identify the first thing—or two or three—you will need to do to begin executing this decision. This may need to be broken into several smaller action steps.

B is for Body. What does your body feel about taking that action? Imagine yourself taking this desired action. When you envision yourself taking this action, how does it make you feel? Do you feel alive, excited, is your heart all aflutter? Or is there a sense of impending doom? Or something in between? Check in with your body, because she doesn't lie.

M is for More. How will this decision or direction lead to *more* for you? What will you have *more* of when you go this way? This becomes an important why to sustain you while executing your decision. Remember to focus on the *more*, rather than the cost. There will, of course, be costs in any Million Dollar Decision you make (such as time, money, and effort), but you especially want to pay attention to what you will gain from making this decision.

Use this formula the next time you need to analyze a decision and determine what a Million Dollar Decision would look like for you. Remember that a Million Dollar Decision is one that creates time and energy, frees up mental space, reduces piddly nonsense and creates space for the stuff that matters to you, allows you to feel strong, secure, and free, and creates options instead of eliminating options. There is no right or wrong answer here, only what's right for you right now in this particular moment in time.

Broke ass thinking leads to Broke Ass Decisions, which lead to broke ass bank accounts. In other words, BADs beget more BADs. Likewise, MDDs beget more MDDs. So, start by making one Million Dollar Decision, and it will become easier to make the next MDD. Over time, you will find that you've created a Million Dollar Life paved in Million Dollar Decisions. Eventually it will become a habit that you don't even have to think about.

Making Million Dollar Decisions means choosing yourself, betting on yourself, and declaring that you are worth it. Madam C. J. Walker was a master at this. She said, "I am a woman who came from the cotton fields of the South. From there I got promoted to the washtub. From there I was promoted to the cook kitchen. And from there **I promoted myself** into the business of manufacturing hair goods and preparations. I have built my own factory on my own ground." Regardless of your current environment, friend circle or desire to be liked, you can start making better decisions. You can promote yourself to a better life.

CHAPTER SUMMARY

- If you want to be wealthy, you have to start making Million Dollar Decisions instead of Broke Ass Decisions.
- Million Dollar Decisions create time and energy, free up mental space, reduce piddly nonsense and create space for the stuff that matters to you. MDDs make you feel strong, secure and free and create options instead of eliminating options.

- Broke Ass Decisions have the opposite effect. BADs steal your time and energy, deplete your mental space, increase piddly crap and leave little room for your greatest desires. BADs make you feel weak, insecure and trapped and eliminate options rather than creating them.
- The top reasons women tend to make Broke Ass Decisions is because of their desire to be liked, the influence of Broke Ass Decisionmakers in their life, and living in a Broke Ass environment.
- Use the WSABM formula to evaluate your decisions. Use it to make more Million Dollar Decisions, expand your life, and build a phat bank account.

CHAPTER 4

MILLION DOLLAR BOUNDARIES

"A girl should be two things: who and what she wants."

—COCO CHANEL

My daughter is a master negotiator. She gets it from her mama.

Unfortunately, her preferred negotiation tactic is The Guilt Trip. She'll stop by my home office while I am knee-deep in a pile of work, intensely focused on my laptop, and say: "Are you *still* working? I wish you had time to play with me." What an adorable pain in the ass.

Of course, this used to work very well on me. I would immediately be riddled with the guilt the patriarchy has taught every mother to feel from the moment she becomes pregnant. And this guilt was exacerbated every time I saw the "charcuterie board" level snacks that other moms were sending their kids to school with (seriously, how did they find the time?). If I continued working, I'd feel like a terrible mother for not spending enough quality time with my daughter. And if I stopped working before I had completed my tasks for the day, I'd feel unproductive and like I was disappointing my clients and my team.

This is the trap that so many women are caught in every day. We bobble between other people's needs like the tiny pinball in an arcade machine. You get whacked around all day long and end the day frustrated that the things that are actually important to *you* never got done. After decades of this, you wake up to a life that you feel you never got to live. *Hell naw, my friends!*

As a species, we women must stop giving away our power. To our spouses, to our bosses, and, yes, even to our children. When we allow other people's desires to take precedence over our own, it creates a situation like the one we have today where many women have no idea what they actually want. We become so accustomed to the world telling us what to do that we can no longer hear our own voices. That ends now.

This chapter is called "Million Dollar Boundaries." When we talk about boundaries, we are really talking about power. By the end of this chapter, you will understand how to stop giving away your power, how to reclaim your power for your own purposes, and how to invest in your power to build everything you want for yourself, including wealth. This is not only for yourself but for each young woman and girl who is watching and learning from you.

As a society, our environment is riddled with messages that tell working women they are never doing enough and tell men and children that it's their job to make sure we women feel as bad as possible about it. In damn near every book, TV show, and Instagram feed, there is a storyline that tells us that women exist for the benefit of others.

What my daughter now knows is that her mom has spent a lot of time thinking about and coaching around this topic and has come to this conclusion: My children are not entitled to my attention all day every day. I work because I *want* to work. I find joy in helping other women and other mothers, and I frankly don't want to set a precedent for my children that how an adult spends her time should be dictated by first graders. Where did my daughter learn that she is entitled to every moment of my time? From me feeling guilt-ridden, from books she reads and TV shows, and from the same messages that we are all getting from all forms of media, from the people around us, from our employers, and even directly from our government by failing to provide us with adequate parental support (the message is clear: do more with less).

So, what do I say to my beloved daughter when she tries to lay this learned guilt trip on me?

I usually say something like: "Most other moms have to get in their car and commute for an hour, go to work, be gone eight hours, and then commute back. So they're gone ten or twelve hours out of the day, and some can't make it home for dinner. How lucky are you that Mommy gets to work from home, so I am here with you in the morning, and I'm here when you get home from school? I even get to see you whenever I take a break from my workday. Isn't that awesome?" She's not moved.

Then, as she's standing there, I continue: "This is a family, and we all get to benefit from Mommy's work. You get to go to a great school, we live in a nice house, we eat good food, and we do fun things together like kayaking and traveling. But we all have to contribute, too. So, go entertain yourself while I take this call. That's your contribution to our family today. Can you make that contribution?"

At this point, my daughter is on board if not particularly pleased. She says, "Okay, Mommy. But after you're done with work you have to play Candyland with me."

"Deal," I say, and we have an accord.

By talking to my daughter about the realities of life and my own desire to work as well as be a mom, I am respecting her enough to be honest with her. I am also setting expectations for our relationship. I am letting her know that even as my beloved daughter, she is not entitled to my every waking moment, and I don't exist solely to meet her needs. This is incredibly important because not only does this benefit me, it sets an example for her. I don't want her to grow up into an adult woman who thinks that her desires don't matter and that everyone's needs are more important than her own.

Would most moms you know negotiate with their children? Would you? Or would you be manipulated by a seven year old? Would you try to make excuses about why you can't spend every moment with her? Would you not expect your child to understand that you need to work in order to support the family?

BITCH, YOU NEED
BOUNDARIES AT HOME

Whether you are a mom or not, the women I know tolerate a great deal of manipulation. My friend Maryam is a great example. She'll say to me that she can't leave work on time to pick up her son, but that's not really true. Maryam could negotiate getting out of work earlier. But she doesn't, even though picking up her son on time after school is really important to her (and she gets charged a $1 for every minute she's late!). Instead, Maryam tolerates the boss keeping her late despite knowing she's got somewhere to be. By doing so, she gives him power over her schedule. Night after night, Maryam is running to her car and driving like a bat out of Hades trying to get to her son's school on time, rather than setting a boundary with her boss.

Why does Maryam do this? Again, because the patriarchal society we all exist in has taught us to prioritize others over ourselves. It's also taught us not to use our voice to speak up and ask for what we want.

I implore you to stop letting people dump all over you, whether that's a boss emailing you at night or a partner who expects you to do all the housework. When I was growing up, both of my parents had full-time jobs. But only my mom was hustling home to make dinner. She was the only one doing laundry and cleaning. But there was no reason that my father didn't have to do household work, except that she was a woman and he was a man. And this unfair division of labor persists today.

A perfect example is my client Kendra. She lives with her boyfriend, Jack. Both Kendra and Jack have full-time jobs, but Kendra has a substantially longer commute, like two hours each way. She leaves at 6:00 a.m. for work and comes back at 8:00 p.m. But guess who is making dinner? Jack literally comes home at 6:00 p.m. and sits on the couch doing nothing, waiting for Kendra to arrive home and start making dinner at 8:00 p.m. Dinner's not done until 9:00 p.m. every night, so all Kendra has time to do is eat and crash. Then she does it all again the next day. And she spends every weekend running errands and doing the housework she didn't have a chance to do during the week.

That's ridiculous. But it's not unusual.

I can't count the number of times a client has said something like: "My partner is great—he cooks once or twice a week." As if that's something to write home about. We are so accustomed to doing everything that if a male partner does *any one domestic thing*, we're impressed. We women need to wholly reject the idea that our household won't run unless we do everything. That outdated belief, along with the idea that we're not a "good mom" or a "good wife" unless we do *all* the domestic labor related to our children and our household, is a lie. It's simply not true.

So, my question for you is: What are you tolerating at home? Are you letting your children run a nightly guilt trip on you when you work the same hours as your husband (who somehow escapes ever getting a guilt trip from the kids)? Are your housemates watching the dishes pile up as if dishwashing is a science only you are capable of doing? Are you the one arranging all the playdates, fielding all the emails from your children's school, doing the laundry, the dishes, the cleaning, *and* managing to make sure the toothpaste magically never runs out? Yet your partner never so much as offers to make you a cup of coffee? Are you everybody's Domestic Bitch delivering a plethora of snacks, cold beverages, and a variety of sandwiches (some with wheat bread, some gluten free, some with crusts trimmed off, one with precisely three slices of turkey) to suit every family member's exacting specifications while they lay on the couch and relax—something you never have time to do?

It is well documented that working women handle the vast majority of the "second shift," the work that greets women when we come home from work. A study of more than 8,500 heterosexual couples conducted by the University College of London found that women did the bulk of domestic work in 93 percent of the couples surveyed. When both parties worked full-time, women were five times more likely to spend at least twenty hours per week doing household chores.[1] Even in the case of women breadwinners, things do not improve.

A study of the effects of earning inequality on household chores among American dual-earner couples found that in cases where the wife's income is higher than her male partner's, the men did *even less* housework than male breadwinners.[2] *The fuq?!*

The visible household work (cooking dinner, washing dishes, folding laundry, lint-rollering dog hair off the sofa cushions) is not the only problem. There is also an invisible workload that is placed on women. According to sociologist Susan Walzer, the invisible workload includes

> the intellectual, mental, and emotional work of childcare and household maintenance. Women do more of the learning and information processing (like researching pediatricians). Women do more worrying (like wondering if their child is hitting his developmental milestones). And they do more organizing and delegating (like deciding when the mattress needs to be flipped or what to cook for dinner). Even when their male partners "helped out" by doing their fair share of chores and errands, it was the women who noticed what needed to be done.[3]

In other words, women do all the thinking about the household and its management. A joint study by Arizona State University and Oklahoma State University found that 90 percent of the women they surveyed felt solely responsible for management of the household.[4] House managers who run the households of high-net-worth individuals routinely make $100,000 or more. So, when you serve as de facto house manager for your household, know that you are performing a second full-time job in which people who do this professionally are paid six figures. And we're not done.

(Are you tired yet? I'm exhausted, and frankly pissed, just thinking about all the work and responsibility women take on nowadays.)

Women not only manage their households but most are also solely responsible for the emotional well-being of their children. Mothers are often the first responders to their children's distress. It's no wonder that so many women are underearning. We are burned out and exhausted from all the multitasking, context-switching (which costs you twenty-three minutes every time you are interrupted[5]) and sheer volume of responsibility our society expects us to accomplish every day. According to the ASU/OSU joint study, the women they surveyed felt "overwhelmed with their role as parents, had little time for themselves and felt exhausted." No shit.

And this issue isn't limited to domestic life. It happens in the workplace, too.

YOU ALSO NEED
BOUNDARIES AT WORK

As a young law student, I was selected to work in a prestigious law clinic representing elderly and disabled clients in housing and social services cases. The clinic was overseen by a professor named Paul whom I really liked. On the first day of orientation, Paul introduced himself as a "typical old gay man who loves Broadway." I was a fan.

In the clinic, Paul paired us with a partner and then assigned cases to us. I had several partners throughout the year, all of whom were white men (at the time, my law school as a whole was mostly white men; no surprise there). Paul was a good professor and really cared about our clients, but I noticed he would always give me a hard time and would let my white male counterparts get away with murder. Even when my team would win a case, he would still critique me and say that I could have done better.

One day, I went to court to argue for an elderly woman whose landlord wanted to evict her. The facts were on our side, and I had done my due diligence. I had been working on the case for weeks with little to no help from my partner on the assignment. Still I was confident that we would win the case for our client. But when I showed up, the opposing attorney representing the landlord, with his stack of files, fancy suit, and Ferragamo loafers, looked me up and down as if I were not a worthy opponent.

He refused to speak to me and demanded, instead, to confer with my supervisor. When Paul arrived at court, instead of standing up for me, he excluded me from further discussions regarding my client. Paul then went before the judge and delivered my winning argument, robbing me of the opportunity to represent the client that I had worked so hard for. After we won the case—using the argument I had put together—Paul had the audacity to say that I could have been better prepared. He said I needed to incorporate more "thinking time" into my argument preparation. In other words, Paul felt that in addition to doing all the work, I needed to spend time just sitting and pondering my client's case. (Perhaps this is what my white male colleagues were doing while I hustled my heart out for our client. They were very busy sitting and "thinking," something they had time to do because I did all the freaking work.) There was no pat on the back, no "good job, Rachel." Instead, Paul decided to use this massive victory for our client as a time to tell me about all the ways in which I remained inadequate.

I was fuming. I worked so hard in that clinic and carried the lion's share of the load while my various partners used the time to study for other classes—a luxury they could only afford, because they knew they could rely on me to get the job done. I remember walking out of Paul's office afterward, hot tears burning in my eyes because I was so angry. Not only was I angry, but I felt misused and maybe even betrayed by a man I trusted and for whom I had worked hard.

As I fiercely stomped down the hallway in a rage, I passed a large photo of me that hung in the hallway of this institution. As one of the few women of color on campus, I was asked to pose for a few photos as a new student. I didn't realize at the time that I was being asked to be the literal poster child for diversity at this school. My photos were in every brochure and featured on the law school website to serve as evidence that "brown people go here."

As I angrily walked passed that blown up photo of me hanging on the wall, I finally realized the extent to which I had been misused by my school. The institution was gaining power by draining mine. I realized in my senior year the exact reason I had thought about transferring to a different law school so many times. I was tolerating a school that recruited brown people and wanted us here as a show of diversity but then didn't actually put the effort in to make our experience here equitable. That moment of clarity was worth the feelings of betrayal. Right there in that hallway I made a promise to myself: *There will never be another old white guy who tells me what to do again. Never.* I'm proud to say that I kept that promise. That promise is what led me to build my own company and become a wealthy, badass woman.

> **Million Dollar Boundary:** (noun) a declaration to yourself and others (friends, family, boss, and so on) where you clearly state what you will do, and won't do, in a given situation. The purpose of setting a Million Dollar Boundary is to set reasonable limits, protect your energy and sanity, and therefore feel more joyful, more powerful, and more moneyfull. Million Dollar Boundaries help you become rich in money, joy, time and peace, however, in order for boundaries to work, you have to actually enforce them. Every time.

WOMEN ARE COMPLICIT

So, what about you? What are you tolerating at work? Are you allowing your boss to call you early in the morning, late at night, and every weekend? Are you sleeping with your smartphone under your pillow in case your supervisor has a new idea he wants to share at 3:00 a.m.? Have you taken on a whole host of new responsibilities without the promised raise that was supposed to accompany that pile of additional work? Are you allowing your coworker to keep dumping work on you that he should be doing himself? Are you raising your hand (or being "picked") to handle ordering the mint chocolate ice cream cake for Ronald's birthday celebration at the office, just because you're a woman and therefore responsible for "womanly office duties" like party planning and cake ordering and gift coordination and napkin selecting? A male colleague couldn't possibly be asked to handle such a task—after all, he's got important work to do.

In summary, society has some destructive notions about women. We are not treated as equals at home or at work. We are treated as a dumping ground for all the work that men are taught not to do.

And that absolutely includes systemic sexism built into our politics, our laws, and our institutions.

And yet, women are complicit.

We are participating in our own oppression. We allow others to fritter away our time, to make their priorities more important than our priorities, to access our unending labor without proper remuneration or respect. This is excellent news for you. Because if you have been a willing participant in the constant gender inequality that gets in the way of your goals and dreams, then you also have the power to stop doing that. You have the power to say no. You have the power to stop participating. You have the power to reclaim your time, attention, and labor for your own benefit.

BOUNDARIES
ARE THE SOLUTION

There are a lot of misconceptions about boundaries. Many people think a boundary is about controlling what other people do to you and around you. That is not true. Boundaries are not about controlling other people in any way. Try as I might to tell my toddler to stop whacking the spoon full of mashed potatoes out of my hand when I am trying to feed him, he just keeps doing it. I can't control him anymore than you can control your boss, your romantic partner, or your bestie who insists on going back to her shitty ex for the seventh time. *Sigh.*

But what you can do is decide how you are going to behave and what you are going to do in response to any given situation. You do not set a boundary to control other people's behavior. Boundaries aren't about saying no to other people. Boundaries are about saying yes to yourself.

That's where my boundary comes in with my toddler: When he whacks the spoon full of food out of my hand, and it winds up all over my clothes and floor, I get to decide what my reaction will be. I get to decide what I will do when he does that. And my decision is to tell him no, stop feeding him, and take him out of his high chair. Mealtime over. Now he understands that when he whacks food out of my hand, I am going to assume he doesn't want to eat and immediately end mealtime. Because I do this consistently, he has stopped whacking food out of my hand when I am trying to feed him, because he wants to actually eat. He understands that if he wants to eat, he needs to eat the food on the spoon and stop covering me in mashed potatoes. In this situation, I use a boundary to say yes to my sanity and no to wearing mashed potatoes every time my kid has a meal.

The same goes for your boss, your honey, and your best friend. If you stop answering the phone when your boss calls late at night, your boss will probably stop calling you after hours. And even if he doesn't, who cares? You are no longer pulled into nonemergency work situations at 9:00 p.m. Problem solved. If you and your honey agree that you will cook and they will clean but you keep winding up cleaning the disastrous kitchen every night before bed, then you can choose to stop cooking for them or stop cleaning up after dinner. You can't make them clean, but you can stop doing the cooking you never wanted to do in the first place. No anger, no fighting, no attempt to control others. Just a boundary and your own freedom from a situation that isn't working for you.

Same with your girlfriend who calls you every time her ex breaks her heart again, but who keeps getting back with said heartbreaking ex. You can't make her stop seeing this guy, but you can stop being the person she vents to every time he does something crappy. You pick up the phone, and she flies into yet another story about how he did her wrong. You gently interrupt and say, "Hey Sis, I am sorry that happened but unfortunately I can't talk about that right now. Let's talk another time. Bye."

This is what it looks like to be a woman with boundaries. You don't need to be controlling, you don't need to get angry (although you can), and screaming and crying are totally optional. All you need is an enforced boundary to protect your heart, your time, your joy, your labor, your sanity, and your money. You know why? Because it's not anyone else's job to protect you.

No one else could possibly know all the ways in which you might need protecting. Your boss, your partner, and your best friend can't read your mind. They don't necessarily know what you want, what you need, or what is making you unhappy. You are the only one who knows that with certainty.

Maybe your boss thinks you will be excited about his new ideas and want to hear about them right away, even after work hours.

Maybe your partner got the impression that you love cleaning the kitchen, because they saw you play music and dance while you did dishes and wiped down the counters. (They didn't realize that this was your coping mechanism for not murdering them.)

Maybe your bestie thinks you find her relationship drama entertaining and you enjoy listening to her never-ending saga. And maybe you used to but have lost patience for it lately.

Hell. Maybe my toddler is trying to make me laugh when he swats a spoonful of mashed potatoes out of my hand. Who knows?

Honestly? It doesn't matter. What matters is that you have Million Dollar Boundaries to protect your time, your money, your effort, your labor, your love, your happiness, and your overall well-being.

It's also important to note that when you set a boundary, don't do it to piss someone off, to get even, or to make someone else suffer. Set a boundary because it serves you, not because it hurts someone else. For example, the wrong way to set a boundary in the scenario where you cook and your partner is supposed to clean, would be to refuse to go to the concert that your partner has been looking forward to just to make them suffer. You really wanted to go to the concert, but you are setting this "boundary" to teach them a lesson.

Can we not?

This is not a boundary. This is petty rubbish. This kind of behavior will not protect you or serve you. It will cause you and your partner to suffer. Nobody wins. Also, it's just plain childish, and you are a grown ass woman. Don't set boundaries to make someone else suffer. Set boundaries to prevent your own suffering.

BROKE ASS BOUNDARY	MILLION DOLLAR BOUNDARY
You tell colleagues "I don't check email after 5:00 p.m.," but you're lying to them and yourself because, actually, you do—your phone notifications ding all night long, pulling your attention away from family time and self-care, and you often reply to emails right up until bedtime.	You do not log into your work email after 5:00 p.m. on weekdays. Ever. Period. You've clearly stated this to your colleagues, so they know the dealio.
You continue to divulge your ideas and goals to those with a history of "that idea ain't worth a dime" mentality, just to put way too much energy into arguing against their feedback even though they aren't making any growth in their own life.	You have a select group of Squad members to whom you turn for support and advice, and with whom you share your dreams and ideas. You know they have your back. Everyone else can wait to see your plans as they happen.
You keep a mental scoreboard of everything you've done in the house, like a bad round of *Family Feud*, while making your loved ones guess why you're so pissed. "We'll go with she's mad no one is picking up the damn dishes, Steve."	You have a real and vulnerable conversation about sharing the responsibilities in your household, outlining clear outcomes if needs aren't met.
You send a laundry list of demands including "a bag of peanut M&M'S, only the green ones" to send a message that you're special, and they're lucky to have you. And then settle for a water bottle in the closet that's supposed to be "the green room" anyway.	You let publications and media events know ahead of time what you are and aren't willing to discuss during your interview.

BROKE ASS BOUNDARY	MILLION DOLLAR BOUNDARY
Your employee routinely is late for work, consistently misses deadlines, and when he does complete the work, it's not meeting your standards. You hint at these problems for months but fail to have a conversation with him clearly communicating your expectations. And then you work late every night finishing work you are paying him to do.	Your employee isn't meeting your standards for his role. You immediately have an honest conversation with the employee, let him know that there will be a probationary period and what you need to see for him to keep his job. When he doesn't rise to the occasion by the end of the probationary period, you fire him.
Your family member asks to borrow money from you. You are not comfortable lending money, but you do it anyway. She doesn't pay you back at the agreed time and you are irate but say nothing.	Your family member asks to borrow money. You are not comfortable lending money so you say no. The end.
You tell your children that you have to focus on work during work hours. While sitting in your home office, they interrupt you twenty-three times. You entertain their requests and interruptions every time.	You tell your children that you have to focus on work during work hours and not to interrupt you unless someone is bleeding. While sitting in your home office, you work with the door locked. There are little to no interruptions. You finish work early and give your kids your undivided attention.
You tell your boyfriend if he mistreats you one more time you are leaving him. He mistreats you again, and you stay.	You tell your boyfriend he has mistreated you, which you've clearly told him before not to do, so you are leaving him. Now. #boybye.
A client demands a refund for services rendered because he changed his mind about it and doesn't want to pay. Instead of enforcing your contract, you give him a refund to avoid a confrontation and hope he doesn't bad mouth you on the internet.	A client demands a refund for services rendered because he changed his mind about it and doesn't want to pay. You tell him no and to go ahead and tell whoever will listen that you enforce your contracts and are not having it.

BROKE ASS BOUNDARY	MILLION DOLLAR BOUNDARY
You decide to take charge of your health by waking up early to workout. You put on your workout clothes and your partner stops you on your way out the door because she wants you to spend that time making her breakfast instead. You cave and make her breakfast. Then it's too late to workout. This happens almost daily.	You decide to take charge of your health by waking up early to workout. You put on your workout clothes and your partner stops you on your way out the door because she wants you to spend that time making her breakfast instead. You say no and ask her if she would consider making breakfast for the both of you, for a change, so that it's ready when you get back from your run. Then you go on your run.
An old client decides to launch a competing business and steals your intellectual property and tries to pass it off as his own. He even goes so far as to file a trademark application for it. Afraid of fighting a legal battle, you change your company name and let him steal your work.	An old client decides to launch a competing business and steals your intellectual property and tries to pass it off as his own. He even goes so far as to file a trademark application for it. You hire a lawyer, send him a cease-and-desist letter and suit up for a whole lot of "not having it." He immediately withdraws the trademark application and issues an apology.
You know that the "money is bad" narrative is a myth that keeps people of color and particularly women suppressed and controlled. Yet, you still consume it through media, religion, people in your circle, and so on, and it leaves you feeling guilty about your ambition, subconsciously sabotaging your goals.	You question every common narrative that potentially diverts you from your goals. Who said it and why? You educate yourself on the patriarchal history of subjugation and refuse to live under it any longer. You educate others by your example and messaging. It's so insidious, you may not always realize it, and you become intentionally vigilant to weed it out.

ENFORCING YOUR
MILLION DOLLAR BOUNDARIES

Now that you understand what Million Dollar Boundaries are and the important role they play in your life, let's discuss how to enforce them. This is where women often experience challenges with setting boundaries. Many of us are happy to set a boundary and can even handle the communication of that boundary, but struggle when it comes time to enforce that boundary.

I used to see this in my law practice all the time. When I was practicing law, I regularly represented women business owners who had been stiffed by a client. In most of these cases, the business owner had performed many, many hours of work and then their client failed to pay them. They would ask me if I could help them collect the money they were owed, and I told them I could. But I always had a few questions for them to answer before I began.

My first question was always, "When was the last time you reached out to your client and asked them to pay you?"

When asked this question, 80 percent of my clients would say, "I haven't."

I'd stare at the phone blankly, thinking I must have heard them wrong. I'd ask again, "So you never reached out to your clients to let them know the payment is late and request payment?"

And they would shock me by confirming their previous answer, "No, I have not."

I had this conversation with enough business owners to know that a lot of women struggle with having hard conversations. (It's not just my clients. When it comes to negative feedback, one study found that 69 percent of women opted not to share.[6]) Many of my clients, who were brave enough to build successful businesses, would rather pay a lawyer than have to call or email their customer and request payment for services rendered. In at least some of these cases, their customers may not have even realized that their payment was late. A clear, direct conversation could have resolved at least 50 percent of these late payments (and subsequent cashflow problems) for my clients, but the mere idea of having that conversation was too terrifying.

All these business owners had a clear boundary with their clients in the form of payment terms included in their contracts. When they worked with a new customer, the customer would agree and sign the contract, which told them when and how much to pay and what would happen if they didn't (like late fees, being reported to credit bureaus, work not being delivered, and so on). So, the boundary line was set, but it was not enforced.

When these business owners did not receive payment on time, they didn't do any of the things that they said they would do. They didn't enforce late fees, they didn't stop delivering the work, and they didn't report the client to credit bureaus. They didn't even make a phone call or send an email reminding the client to pay. As a result, the boundary did not accomplish its goal, and these business owners were not protected by it.

The sad truth is that you are better off not communicating a boundary at all than stating a boundary and not enforcing it. An unenforced boundary sends a message to the person that you are a pushover, a doormat, or otherwise somebody whose boundaries they don't have to bother respecting, because there will be no consequences. They know that you won't keep the promises you made to yourself. This is why it is incredibly important to always enforce your boundaries even when it's scary.

Why is boundary setting challenging for some women? Why did so many of my female business owner clients refuse to enforce their payment terms with their customers? Because women are socialized to be nice, and being nice often gets interpreted as being responsible for everyone else's feelings, even at our own expense.

To enforce your boundaries, there are a few mindset shifts you have to undergo. Clearly, you will have to learn to be less nice. Nice is not going to help you accomplish your life's purpose.

If you are being nice when you don't want to be, you're really just lying.

In order to enforce your boundaries, you may also have to be less generous. It's important to acknowledge the difference between being generous and being taken advantage of. I use my own feelings as a guidepost. If I am enjoying being generous, I keep doing it. If I'm not enjoying it, I don't. Being generous should feel energizing and empowering. If it feels exhausting and oppressive, stop. Be a joyful giver or don't give.

As a wealthy woman, I am asked for my money, time, and resources every day. I have had to get very comfortable with saying no. Otherwise, I would spend all my time making other people's goals and priorities happen at the expense of my own. At first it was uncomfortable to have to tell people no all the time. I used to explain all the reasons I couldn't. Sometimes I would exaggerate so that my reasons for saying no sounded really solid. What a waste of energy! The truth is that I just didn't want to do it in most cases, and while I may have had many reasons for saying no, I was not obligated to explain myself. *No* is a complete sentence.

And that brings me to the last consequence of enforcing your boundaries: You have to be okay with disappointing others. Sometimes people won't like your boundary. They may even be offended or hurt by it. That's okay. It's not your job to make everyone comfortable, and you aren't responsible for everyone's feelings. Let other people be responsible for their own feelings just as you are being responsible for your own feelings by setting and maintaining clearly communicated boundaries.

Here's what I know for sure: You can't be an economic powerhouse and be liked by everyone. It's not gonna happen. In fact, it's probably impossible in our patriarchal society. Make no mistake, prioritizing niceness and therefore failing to enforce your boundaries is costing you money. A research study led by professors from the University of Notre Dame, Cornell University, and the University of Western Ontario found that agreeable women earn less than those who are disagreeable. On average, the study found that agreeable women made $3,213 less per year than disagreeable ones. In addition, the study also found that disagreeable people are seen as more competent.[7] Enforce your Million Dollar Boundaries, and you will find that you are more respected, more powerful, and more wealthy.

CHAPTER SUMMARY

- Women do the lion's share of both visible and invisible domestic labor, and this gets in the way of our ability to build wealth.
- Women also get the short end of the stick in the workplace, causing our labor to not be properly remunerated and respected.
- These widespread societal issues related to women's labor lead to exhaustion, depression, and feelings of inadequacy in women.
- The solution is to set clearly communicated boundaries to protect ourselves from other people's actions and mistreatments by saying *yes* to what we do want and *no* to what we don't want.
- Once communicated, boundaries must be enforced to properly serve their purpose.

Action step: Choose one thing you are done tolerating, set a boundary, and then communicate that boundary to whoever needs to know. If you want an extra challenge, review areas of your life where your boundaries may be lacking. Calculate the cost of this lack of boundaries in actual dollars using your effective hourly rate to calculate it. Then add it up to see what it's costing you annually.

Your effective hourly rate tells you the monetary value of your time. To calculate your EHR, you divide the total amount of money you are making each month from all sources (salary, side hustle, rental income, dividends, and so on) by the approximate number of hours you are working each month (for most people, that will be 160 hours based on a forty-hour workweek).

Here's the formula to calculate your effective hourly rate: (total amount of money you make each month) / (the number hours you work each month) = EHR

Example: Let's say you make $5,000 in gross salary per month, and you work a forty-hour workweek. You would divide $5,000 by 160 hours, which equals $31.25. Your EHR is $31.25 per hour.

Let's say your sister frequently drops her children off to be babysat by you while she goes out for a night on the town. You love your nephews, but that five hours of unpaid babysitting every week is costing you $156.25 per week (your EHR times five hours) and $625 per month. Maybe it's time for a boundary.

CHAPTER 5

MILLION DOLLAR SQUAD

"Find a group of people who challenge and inspire you, spend a lot of time with them, and it will change your life."

—AMY POEHLER[1]

Who you spend time with can predict your success with great accuracy. That is why building a community of ambitious, intentional humans around you who are also on the journey to building wealth and success is crucial. This is not optional. No one ever reached Mount Everest alone.

Ascending Mount Everest requires a year of training, equipment, licenses, and most important, Sherpas. Sherpa people are an ethnic group native to the most mountainous regions of Nepal and Tibet. They are known for incredible mountaineering skill and experience. In fact, the term *Sherpa* has been used to describe mountain guides of all backgrounds. Wouldn't it be amazing to have a *Sherpa* guiding you toward wealth?

Sherpas "prepare the route for foreign climbers to follow, fix ropes in place, and carry the necessary climbing kit up the mountain."[2] Sherpas also know the local people, the local culture and have "phenomenal energy and power on the mountain." They have been described as the backbone of any Everest expedition. Even the few who ascended the final summit alone had guides for the majority of the climb and only went the very last day of the journey alone. Most climbers are with a team of fellow climbers whom they've trained with and who ascend the mountain together with their guides. It is so dangerous to climb Mount Everest alone that in 2018 Nepal banned solo climbers.[3] (Likewise, I'd love to ban solo wealth travelers. This journey is so much harder and so much riskier when going it alone.)

This is how I want you to think of your own journey to success: not something you want to attempt without a community. When you are building something (a business, a wildly successful career, an organization, wealth) out of nothing, it is similar to climbing Mount Everest. You are attempting a feat that few people believe they are capable of and therefore don't even try. Like Mount Everest climbers, you will need to make many important decisions on the journey. You will need knowledgeable guides (you have me via this book, so that is a very good start), you will need the right equipment, you will need someone to set down the ice ladder and to encourage you to keep climbing.

While building wealth is unlikely to be physically dangerous, it requires mental toughness like the kind required to even attempt to scale Everest. It is so much harder to reach your full potential when you are hanging out with people who are not interested in personal development and reaching their own definition of success. You've gotta have a squad if you want to climb the peak of Millionaire Mountain!

YOUR SUCCESS IS IN YOUR SQUAD

We've all heard that Jim Rohn quote: "You are the average of the five people you spend the most time with."[4] Don't believe me? Let me drop some science.

Dr. David McClelland, renowned social psychologist, Harvard professor, and author, studied human motivation for more than thirty years. As discussed in chapter 3, he found that "95 percent of your success or failure in life is determined by the people with whom you habitually associate." Ninety-five percent, my friend.

If you literally do nothing but join a success squad, you will make more money by osmosis. Just by spending time connecting with successful people on a regular basis, you will find more success for yourself.

This is why I feel comfortable telling potential clients "hang out with me, my team, and clients, and you'll make more money." It sounds obnoxious, but it is 100 percent true. Over the years, even the least active people in my coaching programs who don't show up to the live training sessions and don't do most of the work still wind up making thousands more dollars than they were making before they joined the program. Just being a member of my community of go-getters naturally led to client referrals, media interviews, raised prices, and, as a result, more money. One of my friends recently told me, "I feel like you literally sneeze on me and I get wealthier." Accurate.

So if you want to get better grades, earn that next promotion, or make more money, hang out with people who are already doing those things. A 2015 study conducted by researchers at the HSE Centre for Institutional Studies found that the academic performance of more than a hundred Russian university students was similar to that of their friends. Based on a 2013–2014 examination of the students' social network data, researchers concluded that while the students didn't choose their friends because of their friends' grades, those who hung out with high achievers improved their own performance. And what about those who hung out with underachievers? You guessed it—their grades dropped.

According to LinkedIn, 70 percent of professionals get hired at companies where they already have a connection.[5] And 80 percent of jobs are never posted online—it's the "hidden job market"—to find out about these jobs, you gotta know someone and get an inside tip or referral.[6] Likewise, in his extensive study of social networks, Ronald Burt, a professor at the University of Chicago's Booth School of Business, discovered that the most successful people—labeled "brokers"—move between different networks, passing information and building bridges between groups. This makes brokers invaluable to the people around them. These well-connected brokers reap the most rewards: They get promoted more quickly, earn more money, and receive more recognition.

Being a part of a social network of successful people enables you to get access to information not readily available from a Google search. This has been one of the greatest advantages for me in my entrepreneurial journey: Being in a room of accomplished people where folks are freely sharing their specific strategies, resources, and referrals for success. These are the conversations happening in private communities and at events with your high-achieving peers.

To quote the musical *Hamilton*—you wanna be "in the room where it happens." But how do you get into these rooms in the first place?

Become a joiner.

MY MILLION DOLLAR SQUAD

There are moments in life where you make one decision—a Million Dollar Decision—that forever alters the trajectory of your career and your income. You make millions, and you can trace it all back to that one important decision. The choice that launched it all. For me, that decision was deciding to join and commit to a new community.

My very first investment in community was a program called Lift Off created by authors and coaches, Pamela Slim and Charlie Gilkey. Just a few months into starting my business, I discovered Pam from an interview she did online and knew immediately that I wanted to work with her. I learned about her Lift Off program, which involved a retreat in Arizona followed by several months of coaching in a community of fellow entrepreneurs. The program cost $2,500. I could afford the initial $500 deposit. I had no idea how I would make the four additional monthly $500 payments, but I believed I would find a way. And I did.

Ten years later, I can't tell you how crucial the Lift Off network has been to my success and really affected every aspect of my life. One of the women I met at the retreat, Liz Dennery Sanders, not only became my client but also referred many clients to me after the retreat. She remains a dear friend and adviser. She is the one who taught me to hire household help (including the life-changing advice to hire a night nurse for the first few months after my son was born) and has advised me countless times on branding, managing employees, and even the topics covered in this book. We have traveled the world and the entrepreneurial journey together.

Other Lift Off alumni also became colleagues, friends, and clients. One, Arash Haile aka DJ Shammy Dee, DJs all the live events I host. Another, Jennifer Lyle, not only became a client but when my kids and I were driving across the country she allowed us to stay a night at her home in Ohio even though she wouldn't be home. Another friend, André Blackman, gave me a tour of Raleigh when my husband and I were thinking of moving out of New York. Not only was his support the reason I felt comfortable moving to North Carolina, he became the emergency contact for my kids' school. Pam herself recommended me for my very first paid speaking gig, and Charlie was the one who helped me realize that a business partner I wound up suing was cheating me out of thousands of dollars.

Not only has the Lift Off alumni community (lovingly referred to as The Pamily with Pam Slim as the "broker" between us all) been crucial to my success, but so many of the additional connections I have made over the years came from members of that community. For example, one of my closest friends today was referred to me as a legal client by Pam Slim.

That $2,500 investment I made ten years ago has literally resulted in millions of dollars in revenue, amazing friendships, new career directions, physical relocations, and more. These fellow sojourners have made the journey so much more fun and so much less lonely. They have also made the journey faster as we share resources, referrals, and specialized knowledge with one another to lift each other up. Your squad is crucial to your success, and it might be the main ingredient you are missing right now.

MANY WOMEN LACK A STRONG NETWORK

So, who are the homies that you're rolling with on a daily basis? Are you spending time with friends and family members who aren't supportive of your ambitions? Or are you spending time with the kinds of people who motivate you to greatness?

Now you know exactly how much it matters when you spend hours on the phone every week with your friend Brenda, who spends a lot of time complaining about her job, her boyfriend, and her overall life but takes no action to improve any of those things. Imagine how much closer you could get to your goals if that time with Brenda were instead spent brainstorming exciting new ideas, making introductions to key connections, and encouraging each other?

To be clear, I am not suggesting you stop being friends with Brenda and you only choose to connect with people based on what they can do for you and your career. But I am suggesting that in addition to hanging out with your friend, Brenda, you find folks to connect with who have similar interests as you. It will make you feel less alone, give you someone to talk to about the challenges along the way and enable you to accomplish your goals faster.

If your squad is not quite where you want it to be, and the homies are not matching your ambition, you are not alone. Forty-eight percent of female founders report that a lack of available advisers and mentors limits their professional growth.[7] And women in the United States are 28 percent less likely than men to have a strong network, according to LinkedIn. Sadly, this "gender network gap" holds true across virtually every country in the world.[8] Most women don't have a community of badasses on whom they can rely, and the result is a continued massive pay gap and way fewer women business owners reaching seven figures in revenue. As annoying as it is, that tired old saying is true: Your net worth is, in fact, in your network.

But don't start beating yourself up, because your lack of a network is not your fault. There are three indicators of a strong professional network: where you live, where you work, and where you went to school. If you live in an area where the median income is $100,000 or more, you are three times more likely to have a strong network than someone who grew up in a less affluent area. Likewise, if you attended a highly ranked university, you are two times more likely to have a strong network than someone who didn't. And last, if you work at one of the top companies in your country, you are two times more likely to have a strong network compared to others. "Where you grow up, where you go to school, and where you work can give you a 12x advantage in gaining access to opportunity."[9]

No surprise there, am I right?

As we have come to expect in these United States, this adversely affects women and people of color. As a Black woman, I had none of these advantages: I didn't grow up in an affluent neighborhood, attend a top school, or work at a Fortune 500 company. People of color are far less likely to have grown up in an affluent neighborhood. And women and people of color are less likely to have attended a top school and to work at a top company. The result is that most women and people of color have less powerful networks and therefore less access to professional and wealth-building opportunities. Systemic racial and gender disparities are always at play when it comes to women building wealth, especially women of color and even more especially, Black women. However, that does not mean that it has to stop us. Building your trusted community of ambitious peers is key to closing gender and racial pay gaps. So go get you some new friends and you will be contributing to economic equality.

YOU DON'T NEED A WHITE MAN TO GET AHEAD

Now you know just how important building a solid network is for your success. You also know that, as a woman or woman of color, you are at a disadvantage when it comes to building a strong network. As a Black woman who did not grow up in an affluent neighborhood, attend top schools, or work at top companies, building a network was one of the first things that I set out to do when I began my career as an attorney. I did not have a strong network then. Now, as the owner of a multimillion-dollar company ten years later, I enjoy a strong professional and social network of dear friends that regularly opens doors and creates additional opportunities for me. And I, in turn, am able to open doors and create opportunities for those in my community as well. You can create a robust community for yourself, and you don't have to do it the way men do.

A recent study conducted by professors at Northwestern University's Kellogg School of Management[10] found that both men and women benefit from an open, diverse network in which network members have varied contacts that do not overlap. However, in addition to an open, diverse network, women also need a close inner circle of women to help them advance their career. Women in the inner circle provide support and gender-specific job advice.

This study analyzed the networks of graduate students from a prominent business school. After controlling for grades and work experience, the study found that the more influential connections a male student had in his network, the higher the leadership position he would acquire. For women, 77 percent of the highest-achieving women had a close inner circle of two to three other women.[11] But women who had a male-dominated network and lacked strong ties with other women, were less likely to acquire a high-paying position.

The results are clear: Women need other women to get ahead.

When I was in college, I took a course called Women in Leadership. We read a book with an entire chapter dedicated to the idea that all women needed to find white men to be our allies, open doors for us, and advocate for our careers. Much to my dismay, my professor was in support of this theory. I was disappointed but thought, *Maybe she's right*, and took that advice to heart. In reality, though, white men usually only support other white men. So relying on them to open doors for us is a fool's errand. Furthermore, there are lots of women out there who are fantastic mentors, teachers, and coaches and can help you get where you want to go. We don't need to wait on white men to let us on to the elevator.

So, let's rethink this whole "I need a white man on my side" strategy. The idea that women can't get ahead or build wealth without a white male ally is damaging and automatically requires women to play small. And yet, this advice is repeatedly doled out to this day.

When women rely on white male allies, it requires us to make ourselves palatable to white men in positions to open doors. The moment we begin to shrink ourselves to fit a mold that, let's face it, we don't fit nor should we want to fit, we lose. We stop being our authentic selves and are now pretending to be someone we are not, which is not going to serve us as we work to step into leadership positions and build wealth long term. White men are afforded the freedom to be themselves at work. Women deserve the same freedom.

Most of all, relying on white male allies is futile. White men are going to continue to open doors for other white men before they open a door for any woman. And they're definitely going to open that door for a white woman before they open a door for a Black woman or a Hispanic woman or an Asian woman. That is the sad truth.

The perfect illustration of this is the world of venture capital where only 8 percent of the investors are women, 2 percent of investors are Latinx, and fewer than 1 percent of investors are Black.[12] Most venture capital firms do not have a single woman or person of color on their investing team, evidence that their "diversity initiatives" are just lip service. And what do these white men who get to choose which ideas have a chance at becoming the next big company do? Exactly what we would expect. They overwhelmingly choose to fund white men.

Imagine what it must be like to go into a room full of white dudes to pitch your idea, as a woman, and have them viciously poke holes in your concept. Women pitching venture capitalists (VCs) are routinely asked inappropriate questions, like "Do you plan to have children?" that they would never ask a man and that would be illegal in a traditional job interview. This happens all the time in these pitch sessions. The environment itself distrusts women and prevents them from showing up as their best and having a real shot at funding. They are dismissed early on and have to prove themselves worthy. Unlike white men who can waltz in full of piss and vinegar, knowing that their whiteness and maleness give them a great shot at funding out the gate.

In 2018, out of the $130.9 billion in VC funding that was awarded to entrepreneurs, women only got 2.2 percent of the pie.[13] Two percent = crumbs. Only 4 percent of the few female founders who raised equity financing were Black and 2 percent were Latinx. White male VCs make these investment decisions despite the fact that it's against their own interests. Companies with a female founder perform 63 percent better than investments with all-male founding teams[14] and businesses founded by women deliver twice as much per dollar invested than those founded by men.[15] And yet VCs would still rather fund founders who look like them. What a bunch of dumbasses!

Waiting for a white man to be your ally and open doors for you is like waiting for your period to show up when you know you forgot to take your birth control. Bish, you are pregnant. Stop checking your undies because she's not coming.

WHEN WHITE MALE ALLIES
SLAM THE DOOR IN YOUR FACE

Several years ago, when I was trying to figure out how to scale my law firm, I joined a private coaching program where I got to learn from an experienced entrepreneur who happened to be a white man. Let's call him Dave. I was the star student in Dave's program, because I did the work and got results.

I developed a good relationship with Dave and, much to my surprise, he offered to open doors for me. He referred a client to me and introduced me to the founder of an exclusive community of high-performing entrepreneurs. Because of Dave's referral, I received an invitation to this community, which hosted a sought-after annual event.

Upon my arrival at the first annual event, I realized that I was not like most of the people in the room. In terms of revenue, I had one of the smallest businesses. The lowest revenue of the attendees was $1 million, and the highest was $200 million. The community included *New York Times* bestselling authors, CEOs of well-known tech companies, and almost zero diversity.

Out of a group of 150 people, there were only three Black people, and one of them was me. There were very few women in attendance and almost no people of color. There were many speakers on the roster, unfortunately only one was a woman and one was a person of color. Every other speaker was a white male. The worst part about it was that the few women in the room were incredibly accomplished and could have delivered amazing keynotes.

The lack of diversity bothered me and the few other women members of the community, and we spoke to the founder about it. He quickly dismissed our concerns and let us know that he did not care.

The lack of diversity meant that there were many microaggressions throughout the event. On the final day, a man at my dinner table felt comfortable enough to make an inappropriate sexual comment to me and a fellow woman attendee. When any organization or company creates an environment where participants feel they can get away with making inappropriate sexual advances, that is a giant red flag.

Despite the challenges, I remained a member of the community for two years. I felt it was important to be "in the room" and get the information that women of color do not typically have access to. I told myself that I could put up with the challenges for the sake of bringing back the business knowledge to my peers. It turned out that one homogeneous white male community leads to another.

During the second year's event, I met a smart business coach. Let's call him Tim. After attending his workshop and talking with him over lunch, I decided to join his mastermind. My previous coach, Dave, was already a member of his mastermind. Once inside, I realized that Tim's mastermind was also very white. However, Tim told me that he wanted his mastermind to have more diversity and wondered if I knew any women or people of color who wanted to join. I referred several friends (none of them white and male) to the mastermind.

In Tim's mastermind, I again became the star student. I had many successes, and other members regularly looked to me for advice. I was asked to speak before the group multiple times. My business revenue grew significantly as well during this period, and I decided it was time for me to step up into the higher level, the Inner Circle, of Tim's mastermind that included only businesses making $1 million or more in revenue. Dave, my previous coach, was a member of this Inner Circle.

However, when I requested access to the $1 million-plus level, I was met with strange excuses and calculated delays. Even though I had been an asset to this mastermind for a year and a half and despite meeting all the qualifications for membership, Tim did not want me in the higher level network, and he didn't want to tell me why.

It came to a head when I attended another annual meeting. During this meeting, I was again asked to speak and teach a particular marketing technique that I had successfully executed. I agreed to speak.

I knew that there would be Inner Circle meetings during the event, and I asked if I could attend. Tim started stuttering. He mumbled something about not knowing if he had enough tables in the room where the Inner Circle would meet. This was obviously bogus. Something was up.

I asked a good friend who was also in attendance about the Inner Circle meeting and why Tim would be acting all weird when he knew that I was a valued member of the community and met all the qualifications for membership in the Inner Circle. This friend told me that she had no idea what was up but that she, too, had asked to attend the Inner Circle meeting and was told no due to space issues. Despite this, it still didn't sit right with me.

Having been told that I would not be allowed in the Inner Circle meeting and also knowing in my gut that I was being lied to, I went home before the Inner Circle meetings began. I cried in the taxi on the way to the airport and hid my tears when I reached my seat on my red-eye flight home. I was being ostracized from a business community in which I had invested so much time, and for the life of me I couldn't understand why.

The next day, after spending the day at a book fair with my kids, I got a text from my friend. Guess where she was? You guessed it: at the Inner Circle meeting. She had been invited after all. Somehow, on the morning of the event, they miraculously found room for her in a meeting I was told I couldn't attend due to space issues. Now I knew I was being purposefully pushed out and that it wasn't about space issues or any other silly excuse.

A few days later, I got a call from Dave, my former mentor. He confessed that he was the one who did not want me in the Inner Circle. He had told Tim that if I joined, he would leave. Naturally Tim gave in to Dave's threat. They all attempted to cover it up, rather poorly. Tim was afraid that I was going to share this story publicly and convinced Dave to confess that it was him all along.

It turned out that Dave, my former mentor and friend who had initially opened doors for me, did not want me in the Inner Circle, because he said I "lacked integrity." He claimed that other entrepreneurs who were mutual connections had told him that I don't pay my bills, that my business dealings are shady and that I can't be trusted—all lies and inconsistent with my many years in business with plenty of long-term business relationships. Dave would not tell me who told him this. After this, I reached out to every mutual connection we had and asked directly if they were the ones saying that I lacked integrity and didn't pay my bills. Everyone who responded claimed not to have said anything of the sort. So, for all I know this was a made-up lie to prevent me from joining the Inner Circle.

Perhaps it was because I had previously asked the leader of the community for high-performing entrepreneurs to make his event more diverse and put women on the stage. Maybe Dave didn't want me in the Inner Circle holding its members accountable. Or perhaps Dave was cool with me as long as he was my mentor, but once I became a peer, he no longer wanted to see me succeed. I will never know the true reasons this whole gaslighting masquerade took place. But what I do know is that I would have been the only Black person in the Inner Circle and one of the very few women, and they deemed me not worthy.

Everyone involved was a person I considered a friend. I vacationed with them, shared resources with them and talked to them about my biggest business challenges. It was a betrayal, and I was deeply hurt by it. I was also ashamed for not seeing it coming and for allowing myself to be hurt by them. Looking back, there were many red flags that I ignored along the way. I thought tolerating this kind of mess was what was required to make millions.

Through this experience I learned a valuable lesson: White men are (almost) always going to choose other white men, and they are more than willing to harm women and people of color in the process. Even the ones who joke and laugh with you, even the ones you consider your friends.

Since that day, I have chosen not to be a part of communities that lack diversity. My network had become too white and too male. When I got more successful than they were comfortable with these white men slammed the door to the network in my face and spread lies that damaged my reputation. This incident, as painful as it was, made me realize that though the white male networks are more visible, there were plenty of amazing women and people of color who were ready and willing to be powerful allies and coconspirators toward our mutual success.

I refuse to allow my career to be beholden to a group of people who historically have not respected people like me, have held women and people of color to a standard that they don't hold themselves to, and who have withheld opportunities from women like me. I don't recommend that you do either.

You don't need a white male ally to open doors for you. You need a tight-knit community of badass women who will welcome you into their circle with open arms, support you, and refer you. Let's talk about how you find such a community if you don't already have one.

HOW TO BUILD YOUR MILLION DOLLAR SQUAD

As that cautionary tale teaches, we need to have some criteria for folks to join our Million Dollar Squad. Consider the following:

- Does this person bring wealth, energy, power, peace, and/or joy into my life consistently?
- Does this person bring financial riches into my life (client referrals, job leads, genius money-making ideas)?
- Does this person bring emotional riches into my life (boost my mood, make me believe I can do anything, inspire me to take better care of myself, make me laugh like a hyena)?
- Does this person help me climb that Million Dollar Mountain, moving ever closer to the peak, like a trusted Sherpa, or are they dragging me down to the depths?

- Conversely, do I feel confident I can add something magical to this person's life—elevate them, too?

The journey to your million dollar empire does not have to be lonely. With clear intentions and key action steps, you can build a supportive, resourceful network of women to connect and consult with every day. Here are some of the things you can do to start building your robust community of business besties.

Become a joiner. You may not be comfortable joining new communities, attending events, and being a part of social gatherings. Maybe you are an introvert or maybe you've been to one too many terrible networking events. You have no desire to get stuck in the corner with a guy named Bob who goes on and on about something you care nothing about while you awkwardly smile and nod, trying to balance a glass of wine and a miniature plate of cheese and plotting an escape route in your head. Ugh. I'd rather have a root canal.

Joining does not have to feel like this. There are many incredible communities out there with a cool woman who has also been caught by a Bob and would so much rather talk to someone like you. I encourage you to rethink networking and community and find your people. Research new communities to join. There is likely an awesome community of diverse professional women who curse and maybe smoke weed and are 100 percent your people.

I am a member of several diverse communities, including: a group of lawyer moms who tell all their secrets, a group of millennial feminists sharing career advice, a group of women looking to increase their pay, a group of life coaches working on their limiting beliefs, a group of women looking to fall in love with their bodies regardless of size, and a group of Black entrepreneurs making seven figures and more. And that's just my Facebook Groups. No matter what you are into, there is a group out there for you.

And it does not have to be a strictly professional community. There are running groups, cycling communities, knitters, Muslim business owner moms, moms of young children, homeschoolers, lesbians who love gardening, and more.

Rethink what it means to build a network. Do your research and find local and online communities that fit your beliefs, your lifestyle, and your personality. Attend live events where the kind of people you want to connect with will be in attendance. Join communities that allow you to be you. Once you find such a community, be sure to invest your time in building real relationships with fellow members.

Reconnect with the community you already have. As busy women, we have every excuse not to invest in our nonfamilial relationships. We are busy. We are tired. We are Netflixing. However, if you want to have meaningful relationships to call on in both good times and bad, you are going to have to reconnect and recommit to building those relationships. And it doesn't need to take all your time.

A great way to reconnect with old friends and colleagues is to communicate. As the saying goes, "to get a friend, be a friend." Rather than just reaching out to say, "Hey, thinking of you," reach out to say, "I mentioned you on my podcast," "I nominated you for an award," "I referred a client to you, hope that's cool," "I popped something into the mail for you." Be generous and create small miracles for people, and they'll become loyal friends for life. A little generosity can go a very long way.

In the first few months of starting my business, I found entrepreneurship to be very lonely. So, I decided to send a holiday card to everyone I knew. I made a list of all my friends, family, former coworkers, law school classmates, and more. Then I spent two weeks gathering their mailing addresses. I ordered inexpensive cards from VistaPrint, wrote a special note in each one, and then dropped it in the mail.

It took me a few weeks to get all those cards out. But over the next couple weeks and months, I reconnected with so many old friends and colleagues who responded to my card with an update about their lives. In some cases, friendships were reignited, clients were referred, and reunions were planned. It felt good to share my life with others and to have them share their life with me. I felt supported and no longer lonely.

For the communities you are a member of, consider stepping up your game. Stop being a lurker and actually attend events, lend your support to other members, and participate in group discussions. Create time for your community. No point joining a dope book club if you skip every meeting and never attend. Set aside time to strengthen relationships and make it fun! Rooftop party. Workout date. Brunch and biz talk. Or a group text with four of your besties that's fire every day.

Create your own community. If the community you want to be part of doesn't yet exist, create it! Choose a name, decide what your community will be about and then start inviting the kind of people you want to connect with into the community. Be sure to let people know what's in it for them. Will they get to connect with other people who are obsessed with houseplants, Marvel comics, and social justice? Will they be able to share their questions, ideas, and wins with the community? Will there be Zoom sessions and live events? How will you bring this group of people together?

You can create a group for this community on social media or find another home for this group online or offline. Then start spreading the word. Share it with your friends, colleagues, and Instagram followers. Ask each of your first members to invite two people who would be a great fit for the community. Run an ad or alert the media. It may start off small, but before you know it, you could be the leader of a thriving, diverse community of 10,000 people who are into the same things you are.

Here's a fun exercise: Take action on building your community by writing a Squad Description. It's like a job description except it's about your dream squad and way more fun. Use it to describe your fantasy squad. In it, share the kind of people you are looking for and what you hope to do together. Here's an example to get your creativity flowing:

Wanted! 7 Badass Broads Who Are Interested in Making Millions, Sipping Rosé, Sharing Genius Ideas, and Next-Leveling Every Part Of Our Lives!

We will text each other daily to hype each other up. We will meet monthly to discuss dreams and goals. We will refer clients to each other and unlock doors. We will vacation together and occasionally be available for that "Hey, can you read this real quick?" super important email proof. Who's in?

Writing a fantasy Squad Description helps you clarify exactly what you want, and, if desired, you could post this somewhere and attract your dream peeps. My clients have done it and it works. There is a fabulous, ambitious woman out there who is looking for someone like you to be a part of her squad. Get out there and find her, because we are stronger together.

WHO'S IN MY MILLION DOLLAR SQUAD TODAY?

It's only right to end this chapter with an ode to my Million Dollar Squad, without whom I would not be making millions and would not have finished this book. Here's how each member of my squad helps me up-level my life:

D: My reliable rock. Reminds me what I am capable of daily, never lets me question my talents, but will tell me when I play myself and will stay up with me all night as moral support while I get an important project done.

A: My practical supporter. Tells me, "You are a smart girl, you will figure it out," and then lends me some money. She will also watch my kids when I'm having a rough day and just need a break.

R: My biggest cheerleader! Always reminds me that I am a boss, shows up with a word whenever I need him and makes me laugh hysterically daily. Also gives reliable financial advice.

S: My life coach. Challenges my limiting beliefs and won't let me stew in negative thoughts. She's my "Let's go to Paris!"

and "Definitely buy those expensive shoes" friend, and I love her for it.

A: Is the grounded model of zen that I want to be when I grow up. Always positive, always calm, always delightful. Has believed in me so much that I believe in myself more, and if you visit her she'll leave a loving note by the bed and cut up fruit in the fridge.

L: My "This is how to live" friend. Has taught me to hire help, take good care of myself, and guided me through hard conversations I had to have. Will also plan a fabulous trip for us, send stunning care packages and quality referrals.

L: My "sensitive soldier" friend. A model of self-care and loving yourself. Hilarious and will march with you in the street if you ask her. Also great at untangling complex relationship issues.

That's a few members of my squad. And there are many more beloved friends and family members who are there for me as well. They make my life better, help me to live in abundance, and that makes me richer every single day.

CHAPTER SUMMARY

- Ninety-five percent of your success or failure can be predicted based on the kind of people you regularly spend time with. Build your squad and next-level your success.
- Many women lack a powerful network, and this contributes to the gender and racial pay gaps and continued inequality when it comes to access to opportunity.
- Women are taught that having white male allies is essential to our success. I call bullshit. White-male-dominated networks can be harmful to women. Research shows that white men gonna help white men. Women should seek to create an inner circle of close women friends.
- Despite disparities, you can create your own amazing network by becoming a joiner, connecting more deeply with communities you are already a member of, and by creating your own community.

CHAPTER 6

MILLION DOLLAR VISION

"If one is lucky, a solitary fantasy can totally transform one million realities."

—MAYA ANGELOU

The doorbell rang . . . again. This was the fifth interruption since I had started working that day.

If it wasn't a FedEx delivery man, it was a Jehovah's Witness. And if it wasn't a Jehovah's Witness, it was my husband wanting to talk to me every time he went in or out the front door (which was frequent).

All day long, I sat at my desk, which was positioned exactly six inches from the front door, trying to build my business with incessant interruptions.

I had purchased this house with my husband in 2008. Instead of having a wedding or a fancy diamond ring, we chose to elope in Napa and came home to our new little cottage. Ours was the tiniest house in an affluent neighborhood. The house had two bedrooms, one bathroom, and 1,100 total square feet across two floors. When we moved in, it was just my husband and me and my bonus daughter who lived with us part-time. It was plenty of space for our little family.

Fast forward to 2014, and the walls were closing in. By that time, I had three kids (a teenager and two toddlers), and my husband and

I both worked in the home. I was focused on growing my law practice, and my husband was a busy stay-at-home dad.

I worked in the foyer of our little house because it was the only spot where I could fit a desk and a bookcase. The master bedroom was occupied by our three kids, and my husband and I had exactly one queen-size bed and two nightstands in the tiny second bedroom.

My desk faced out into the front yard and was right next to the front door. People would see me working there at my desk and knock on the window glass to get my attention if I tried to ignore them (which I often did!). It was so frustrating.

Here I was, a supposedly Boss Ass Bitch growing her six-figure business, serving clients, and managing a team all from a tiny home office in which everyone and their damn mama interrupted me every single day. Recording video or hosting a webinar was a nightmare. I couldn't review a contract or get through a written email with any level of focus. It was so bad that at one point I started getting up at 4:00 a.m. just so I could have a few hours of uninterrupted work before the cacophony of daily life began.

Did I mention the part about sharing the one and only bathroom in the house with a teenage girl? *How did I survive, y'all?!*

Anywho, living in a dollhouse with a family of five meant that I often needed to escape to maintain my sanity. One of my favorite things to do was go for a run (more like a jog/walk/run-a-smidge) around the neighborhood. I would run up the hill where all the big, fancy houses were. One day I noticed a new house being built on my favorite street in the neighborhood. It was enormous and beautiful; the kind of house that I dreamed of living in with my gaggle of children. One where I would call to them from the other side of the house and they literally couldn't hear me because that's how much living space there was between us.

The house had big beautiful windows with lots of light, a beautiful front yard, and a three-car garage. I could tell there was a big yard out back and imagined the two stories full of pretty tile, fireplaces, and gorgeous hardwoods. #idreaminrealestate

One day the house was close to complete, and a sign had been placed out front: It was officially for sale. I noted the address and ran home to check realtor.com to see just how much this dream house cost. I figured it was out of my price range, but maybe somehow some way I could make it happen. Big beautiful houses are very motivating. I would find a way!

The moment I saw the listing, however, my heart sank. The house was listed for $2.7 million. That was only about $2.3 million out of my price range. *Sigh.* I was so disappointed. I felt defeated. My tiny little house with my teenager shoved in with the toddlers and my husband and I without any privacy and my so-called empire crammed into a corner by the front door . . . none of that made me feel like a badass. It made me feel like no matter how hard I worked I would always be struggling and uncomfortable and unable to afford the lifestyle I wanted for my family.

I let myself mope around the house for a full forty-eight hours.

Then, after a tough love pep talk from my husband, I dusted myself off and allowed myself to dream.

So what if I couldn't afford that mansion on the hill right now? It didn't mean that I would never be able to afford a mansion on a hill. It was up to me to make it happen. But how would I ever make it happen if I judged myself foolish for even daring to dream?

So I decided to make it real by calculating the actual costs of my dream lifestyle. I got out my laptop and a calculator and looked up what a monthly mortgage on a $2.7 million house would cost ($12,000 per month, if you are wondering). I decided that I actually don't want a $12,000 per month mortgage, even if I could afford it, so I decided to set my home budget at $1 million with a mortgage of around $5,000 per month. That sounded dreamy and doable.

I looked up the costs of the extracurricular activities I wanted to be able to invest in for my kids ($500 per month), private school tuition ($3,500 per month), the Mercedes SUV I wanted ($1,200 per month), and the four family vacations I wanted to do each year ($2,000 per month). I also added in the costs for a full-time nanny/housekeeper ($4,000 per month) and a personal trainer ($800 per month). I wanted to be able to save or invest a significant amount of money every month ($5,000 per month) and to pay my mom's rent every month ($1,300 per month).

When I added up my various lifestyle upgrades, they amounted to approximately $23,000 per month. I rounded up and set a goal for personal salary at $25,000 per month or $300,000 per year. That meant I needed to triple my current salary at the time to achieve my desired lifestyle. Not an easy task but also not insurmountable.

Then I got to work brainstorming ideas to increase my income significantly. I looked at how many more legal clients I could take on if I hired a paralegal. I looked at different products or services that I could offer. I looked at how much I could earn if I purchased a small rental property. I was open to any and all ways I could use my skills and experience to generate more income.

But that's not the only thing I did. It's not even the most important thing I did.

HOW YOU FEEL MAKES YOU MONEY

The move I made that really helped me to next-level into the woman I wanted to become came in the form of a coaching question. Around this time, a coach I know asked me, "How can you start to embody the woman you want to become right now?" She suggested that I not wait for that $300,000 annual salary to start treating myself well.

You see, feeling states are better determinants of our success outcomes than the numbers. Emotions like compassion, gratitude, and a healthy degree of pride in yourself lead to success.[1] So, if you feel like a Million Dollar Badass every day, then you will likely become a Million Dollar Badass relatively quickly, even if you are only making $40,000 per year right now. However, if you feel broke and defeated every day, then you will likely stay broke and defeated. This is such a simple concept, but it's quite revolutionary. Like one of my dear friends says all the time, "You gotta feel rich to get rich."

So, what I did next was get regular haircuts. What do regular haircuts have to do with getting your dream house? Quite a lot. I had been managing my thick, long, and curly natural hair on my own for years. I rarely ever went to the salon and only got haircuts once every two years. So, I found an amazing natural hair salon in Harlem and got a fabulous new haircut. And I started to go every few months for a wash, style, and trim.

Every time I left the salon, I felt like a million bucks. I noticed that when my hair was freshly cut, styled, and looking fabulous, I was more likely to reach out to potential clients. I found myself recording marketing videos, setting up coffee dates with colleagues who could refer clients to me, and overall put myself and my business out there a lot more, all because of a fresh haircut.

Then I started treating myself to other things like meeting with a personal stylist who helped me pick out some new clothes that fit my new post-baby body and looked great. I had been walking around in old maternity clothes more than a year after giving birth. No more rags for me! I invested in a wardrobe that made me feel fabulous and didn't cost a fortune.

I started to experiment with other ways to feel like a Million Dollar Badass every day. Simple things like taking a real lunch break, sitting on the patio in the sun for a few minutes, and walking to my favorite neighborhood coffee shop for a latte and croissant while I worked made a real difference. I bought a new novel to enjoy and actually gave myself time to read it, and I started getting up early to go to the gym. I even Marie Kondo'd my closet (her book *The Life-Changing Magic of Tidying Up* had just come out). These inexpensive or free lifestyle upgrades made me feel good, and when I felt good I was more likely to take on tasks that would help me to make more money.

Just three years after calculating my dream lifestyle, I achieved my dream. I was earning $300,000 per year in personal salary, my kids attended a great private school, and I was able to pay my mom's rent every month.

It took a little longer to acquire my dream house, because we decided to move to North Carolina and build a house from scratch. But now I live in a house not very different from that mansion on the hill. It has big, beautiful windows with lots of light, a beautiful front yard, and a three-car garage. It has a big backyard, a fireplace, pretty tile, and gorgeous hardwoods. I call my children from my fancy home office (which has its own door!), and they literally can't hear me because that's how much living space there is between us when I'm working.

I am living my Million Dollar Vision, and it's even more amazing than I imagined.

Now it's time for you to create your vision for the life you want. Maybe that includes a big house, monthly facial appointments, and private school for your kids. Or maybe it includes a tiny house, zero debt, and the freedom to travel whenever you want. Maybe your dream is to become an Iowan goat farmer or a French baker or a Chilean winemaker. It doesn't matter how outlandish, outrageous, and downright insane it seems, as long as it's your dream. Not the one society tells you to have, but the one your heart desires.

YOUR VISION SHOULD BE BIG, HAIRY, AUDACIOUS, AND MINDFUL

Jim Collins and Jerry Porras coined the phrase BHAG, which stands for Big, Hairy, Audacious Goal. They defined a BHAG (pronounced bee-hag) as a "clear and compelling" goal that "serves as a unifying focal point of effort, and acts as a clear catalyst for team spirit." It's a goal that has a clear finish line so you know when you have achieved the goal. And it's one that you have a 50 percent to 70 percent chance of achieving.[2] It's not something so outlandish that it's highly unlikely that you will ever achieve it, but it's definitely something you'll have to stretch yourself to make happen.

BHAG has become part of our business lexicon and is a common practice among large corporations. But BHAG makes sense for us as individuals as well.

Scientifically speaking, Edwin Locke and Gary Latham synthesized more than four hundred research studies on goal theory. They explain that "there is a linear relationship between the degree of goal difficulty and performance. . . . Specific, difficult goals lead to higher performance than no goals as well as vague, abstract goals such as 'do your best.'"[3]

It makes sense right? Think about it: A clear compelling goal that feels out of reach is exciting. It floods your body with feelings of possibility and gets your creativity flowing with ideas of how you could possibly make this goal happen. Those positive feelings lead you to positive actions. Whereas ho-hum goals that feel really attainable (like you have 100 percent chance of achieving it with little to no effort) are a bit of a snooze fest. Ho-hum goals don't get you hopping out of bed in the morning. They are the type of goals that you forget about and never revisit, and ironically, still don't achieve because they are not motivating even though they are attainable.

If having a big hairy goal scares you, know that the risk and fear factor are part of what is motivating about these goals. So being, what I like to call, *scared-cited* about your Million Dollar Vision is not only a good thing but important.

Harvard psychologist and author of the book *Mindfulness*, Dr. Ellen J. Langer believes that most people are much more capable than they think they are, and she has done many studies to prove it. For example, she did a popular "counterclockwise" study where she took senior citizens on retreat in an environment that was set up like 1959. She made the participants carry their own luggage up the stairs and otherwise treated them like they were in the prime of physical health. The results were remarkable. "At the end of the retreat, members of the group showed demonstrable improvement, on average, in objective tests of memory, height, weight gain, posture, vision, and hearing. They even looked noticeably younger."[4] They literally began acting the age they were in 1959.

The point? Your thoughts about what you are capable of can hold back your capabilities. When you set a big goal, you jolt yourself out of your self-imposed limitations and become more mindful. Mindfulness requires you to be present and gives you a fresh, positive perspective on the world.[5] You are back to being a bright-eyed child who is not afraid to share her big dreams out loud and fully believes in their possibility. You're not worried about the future, you're excited about it.

When we set a big exciting vision for our lives we are making a mindful choice to stop living on auto-pilot and go after exactly what we want. This makes us more present, more focused and more joyful as we work toward our vision on a daily basis. Not only are we more likely to arrive at our vision with this approach but we are likely to find meaning, excitement and happiness every day of the journey toward this vision.

"Ninety-nine percent of people in the world are convinced they are incapable of achieving great things, so they aim for the mediocre. The level of competition is thus fiercest for 'realistic' goals, paradoxically making them the most time and energy-consuming."

—TIM FERRISS

Here's another reason to make your goals big and seemingly ridiculous: There will be fewer competitors, since most people aim for average rather than greatness. There is plenty of room for you at the top.

YOUR MILLION DOLLAR VISION

Now it's time for you to create your Million Dollar Vision. What does your million dollar life look like? What kind of work do you want to do? How much money do you want to earn? Where do you want to live and what do you want to do with your free time? What will your daily life look like once you are making more money?

Just like that fateful day when I sat down and totaled up what my dream life would cost ($25,000 per month or $300,000 per year), I want you to do the same thing, right now. Because once you have that monthly number, then you've got a specific BHAG to aim for.

HOW TO LIVE LIKE A MILLIONAIRE

STEP 1: MENTALLY UPGRADE YOUR EVERYDAY LIFE

Here, you'll identify the upgrades that will help you to practice more Million Dollar Behavior. Ask yourself: In each of the following arenas, what upgrades would help give me more time, energy, joy, power, and peace?

- Home/Physical Space
- Recreation/Travel

- Transportation
- Education (Self/Partner/Kids)
- Wardrobe
- Savings/Investments
- Self-Care/Daily Habits
- Giving/Community Contributions
- Household Work/Hired Help
- Other

STEP 2: RUN THE NUMBERS

Revisit each category above and estimate how much money per month it would cost you to make these upgrades. For example: To move to a larger house in a nicer neighborhood might cost $1,500 per month more than you are currently paying in mortgage payments.

- Home/Physical Space
- Recreation/Travel
- Transportation
- Education (Self/Partner/Kids)
- Wardrobe
- Savings/Investments
- Self-Care/Daily Habits
- Giving/Community Contributions
- Household Work/Hired Help
- Other

Now use this to create a new target income for yourself.

Current Monthly Income + Total Cost of Monthly Upgrades = Targeted Monthly Income

STEP 3: BRAINSTORM MONEYMAKERS

Now that you know how much you need to earn in order to make all the upgrades you want, find twenty-five—yes, twenty-five!!—ideas for bringing in extra cash. Go!

Here are a few ideas to get you started:

- Create a side hustle doing something you enjoy and your neighbors need like tutoring, babysitting, organizing, tax planning, lawnmowing, and so on.
- Rent out a room in your house.
- Have a garage sale.
- Sell your designer goods that you no longer use.
- Create a new offer (an art piece, your professional services, or delicious cupcakes) and email everyone you know asking if they are interested (this is how I launched my law practice).
- Call the people who owe you money and ask them to pay up.

STEP 4: COMMIT TO YOUR FIRST UPGRADE

What's one upgrade you can make *now*? One thing you can change that will really up-level your power and peace and give you some time and energy for Million Dollar Behaviors? Commit to that one upgrade right now, and set a deadline by which the upgrade will be executed.

Many of the women I coach have a big vision for their lives that includes wealth and success, but they can't define what that life looks like on a daily level. Instead, many get caught up in the practical details of how to do the work, or they get stuck focusing on what path they should take to get to the big vision. In other words, they get so overwhelmed by the *how*, they don't allow themselves to really dream up the *what*.

It's crucial we give ourselves permission to dream big first. Forget all the details of your life. Forget all the chores, responsibilities, and tasks in your life as it is right now. Don't limit your dreams because you are not exactly sure how you'll get there. No one knows how they will get there on Day One of the journey. You only have to be willing to dream big and then take the very first step.

If you don't know exactly what you want or are having trouble getting clear on the details, follow your jealousy. The word *jealousy* derives from the Latin word *zelosus,* which means "full of zeal." In many old languages, the root word for *jealousy* had a positive connotation and referred to emulation, devotion, or watchfulness.[6] I, too, believe jealousy is a positive thing; it can be a signal of what we want for ourselves.

For example, when I babysat Alana (see more in chapter 1) and went to her big house in a beautiful, safe neighborhood, I was jealous because I wanted those feelings of safety and security that she enjoyed. I wanted to be surrounded by beauty and have a pantry full of snacks, just like her family had.

Likewise, when I saw one of my clients going on international vacations three times per year, I was jealous. I wanted to have enough disposable income to afford multiple lovely vacations each year. And when a friend showed me his bank statement and how much he had earned in a single month ($90,000), I wanted that for myself. And when another friend wrote a book and became a best-selling author, I knew I wanted that, too.

When you do not grow up with different examples of what success can look like, it can be hard to dream. It's hard to envision things that you don't even know are possible for regular people. When you see things in a movie, read them in a book or see one of your friends or colleagues accomplish something and it makes you feel jealous, follow that inkling. Explore that desire. Your desires will help you birth your ideal life.

> *"Urge and urge and urge,*
> *Always the procreant urge of the world."*
> —WALT WHITMAN, *Leaves of Grass*

Desire is powerful. Desire is what creates the world. Your children were created out of desire. The bees pollinating and the birds singing, this is all borne of desire. Our culture says that women's desire is very dangerous. Historically, women have been punished for their desires. Wanting sex, wanting food, wanting money, these are all things for which our society has punished women. We shame women for gaining weight, we shame mothers for working too much and caring "too much" about their careers, and the worst thing that we think could happen to a woman is that she should become a stripper and use her powerful body to make money.

This ongoing punishment for our desires has trained us not to want. It has dulled our appetites and our ambition. It has made us afraid to dream. The result is that many of us dream too small or not at all. If you are struggling to create your Million Dollar Vision, practice wanting. Every morning when you wake up, before you jump in the shower, make breakfast, or start meeting the needs of other people, ask yourself: *What do I want most right now?* And then listen for the honest answer. Take the time to pause and notice what you are craving. The more you listen to that inner voice, the more clear your Million Dollar Vision will become.

ONCE YOU CREATE THAT MILLION DOLLAR VISION, YOU GET TO BE HER NOW

Once you have nailed down your vision, you must begin to Be Her Now.

Does the woman who is the CEO of a multimillion dollar corporation wear janky, old underwear and never get enough sleep?

Does the woman who owns a million dollars in assets let people waste her time and violate her boundaries?

Does the woman with the big house and the beautiful career never allow herself to have fun?

Imagine how the woman whose dreams are fully realized and who has accomplished everything she wants to accomplish approaches her work, her relationships, her time, and her self-care. How does she treat herself and how does she treat others?

Ask yourself authentically: *Who is she?*

Who is this woman that you want to become? Who is this woman who has everything that you want in life?

What is she like? How does she spend her time? How does she feel when she wakes up in the morning? What are her daily habits? How does she adorn herself? Who does she spend time with? What is she creating?

Envision the kind of woman you want to become and then start to Be Her Now.

If the woman you want to become takes good care of herself, how can you begin to take good care of yourself now? If the woman you want to become has strong boundaries, how can you begin to express and enforce your boundaries now? If the woman you want to become is a highly sought-after expert, how can you take steps to be that expert right now?

This is what it means to Be Her Now. To begin to take the action steps that will lead you to the life you want. Maybe you can't quit your job right now, but you can create a side hustle that can begin to replace the income from your salary. Maybe you can't hire a house-keeper right now, but you can use a drop-off service and save the time it takes to do the laundry. Maybe you can't hire an assistant to protect your schedule right now, but you can start saying no to the things you don't want to do.

The more you step into the shoes of the powerful woman you want to become, the faster you will actually become her. There is scientific evidence to back this up.

A 2015 study found that wearing formal business attire increased big-picture and abstract thinking, essentially thinking like a CEO, because the subjects felt more powerful when they were dressed in business attire.[7]

Another study conducted by Yale in 2014 had some participants in sweats and some in suits conduct mock negotiations.[8] Those dressed in sweatpants averaged a theoretical profit of $680,000, while the group dressed in suits amassed an average profit of $2.1 million. The study concluded that the poorly dressed participants would often defer to the suited ones, and these suited participants could sense this heightened respect, which caused them to back down less than they might have otherwise.

Does this mean you need to wear a suit every day? Of course not. However, this research shows that when you adorn yourself in a way that makes you feel powerful, your thinking sharpens, you feel more confident, and thus you are more likely to do powerful things. So take off those broke-ass sweats! Dress so you feel like a million bucks.

Your attire certainly isn't the only way to take steps right now toward the life you want. Do other things that make you feel powerful, like saying no to an invitation to an event that you don't want to attend, taking a hot bubble bath with fancy bath salts and your favorite playlist in the background, or taking up a new hobby just because you want to. When you treat yourself well and grant yourself permission to heed your own desires, you will feel powerful. And when you feel powerful, you will do powerful things that lead you toward the life you want.

You are responsible for the results you are getting. If people mistreat you, if you constantly feel overworked, if you never have enough money—those results are on you to change. There are absolutely systemic issues at play, but we aren't powerless to address the things in our lives that aren't working for us. This is very exciting, because it means you are fully capable of making different choices that lead to different results. The power is in your hands.

The results you have now are at least partially based on how you treat yourself, the thoughts you think, and what you choose to do with your time. If you want different results, you need to change the way you care for yourself, your thoughts, and how you spend your time. The kinds of changes you will want to make to your daily habits depend on the woman you want to become, not what society says you should be doing.

"BE HER NOW" IS NOT ABOUT ACCUMULATING DEBT

When I introduce the concept of "Be Her Now," sometimes my clients are a wee bit confused.

"Okay, Rachel, so you're saying I should go out and buy a new Mercedes, upgrade to a bigger house, hire three full-time employees, and get a private tutor for my kids . . . right now?"

No. That's not what I'm saying.

Be Her Now is primarily about *behavior*, not purchases.

I want you to *behave* like the million dollar badass you dream of becoming, not necessarily *spend* like her. (At least, not yet. We'll get there.)

The goal is for you to engage in behaviors that make you *feel like a million bucks*. Do things that make you feel emotionally rich (powerful, inspired, energized) so that you can become financially rich.

You can do things that cost nothing, or almost nothing. You don't have to spend irresponsibly (or rack up credit card debt) to generate the wealthy feeling that you want.

NOTICE THE WORDS YOU SAY TO YOURSELF— TINY WORD CHANGES MAKE A BIG DIFFERENCE

In her memoir, *Own It All,* entrepreneur Andrea Isabelle Lucas, tells the story of how she went from rock bottom (domestic abuse so severe, it almost ended her life—she had to flee her home, bleeding from a head wound, trudge through the snow, and beg a next-door neighbor to drive her to the hospital) to where she is today (million dollar badass, running a thriving yoga and barre fitness studio in New England with five locations and growing).

It took a lot of resilience and creativity for Andrea to go from abuse survivor (and absolutely flat broke) to thriving entrepreneur. A lot of mindset changes, too.

One of Andrea's favorite mindset exercises is to flip the word *"but"* to *"and."* This is so simple, yet powerful.

This little verbal switch feels like flipping a light switch inside your brain. *Boom.* Illumination. You see possibilities you hadn't considered before.

For instance:

> *"I want a tropical beach vacation in the Caribbean,* **but** *I have no money."*

Okay, this is depressing. The word "but" feels like a big stop sign. Dream: dead. Womp womp.

> *"I want a tropical beach vacation in the Caribbean,* **and** *I have no money."*

Okay, now this is interesting. Notice how the word "and" feels like an open door, an invitation to dream and consider different options. Dream: alive.

How could you create a low-cost or no-cost vacation for yourself? Could you convince your employer to send you to the Caribbean for a professional training retreat? Could you get someone to book you for a speaking gig there, all travel expenses paid? Or, how could you generate the money you need? Could you get a side hustle poppin' and generate the $3,000 you need to make it happen? So many options! Hellooo, jerk chicken and muddled mint rum cocktails on a white sand beach! This is doable.

> *"I want to send my kids to summer camp, **but** I have tons of credit card debt."*
>
> VERSUS
>
> *"I want to send my kids to summer camp, **and** I have tons of credit card debt."*

(Cool. How could you make the camp dream happen, in spite of your temporary financial situation? There's got to be a way.)

> *"I want to feel confident, sexy, and gorgeous, **but** I weigh 200 pounds."*
>
> VERSUS
>
> *"I want to feel confident, sexy, and gorgeous, **and** I weigh 200 pounds."*

(Consider: Isn't it possible to feel amazing and not be a size 6? Of course it is! These two things are both possible at the same time, not mutually exclusive.)

> *"I want to become a millionaire, **but** I don't know how to do it."*
>
> VERSUS
>
> *"I want to become a millionaire, **and** I don't know how to do it."*

(Ah! But you can learn.)

Try flipping "but" to "and," and notice what happens to your brain. Small word changes unlock doors in your mind that were previously closed.

TWENTY-FIVE WAYS TO BE HER NOW

Here are twenty-five ways you can begin to be the woman you want to become right now.

1. When you're working, put your phone on Do Not Disturb mode, Airplane mode, Silent, or Off. Create a distraction-free zone so you can focus like a boss. (Your stress levels will drop, and you'll feel ten times smarter.)
2. Get dressed for work, even if you work from home. Even if you're going casual, choose something that makes you feel elevated. Nice top. Hoop earrings. Lip gloss poppin'. You know. Actually care about your appearance.
3. Hydrate.
4. Declutter your home and workspace. Less clutter immediately makes things feel more luxurious. (Have you ever stepped into a five-star hotel lobby that was crammed with unnecessary stuff? Nope. For a reason.)
5. Have an orgasm, with a partner or by yourself. You'll wear that sexy, relaxed glow all day long.
6. Invest in one bottle of perfume that you really love. Spritz yourself daily. Ooh, smells like money up in here.
7. Keep your phone out of your bedroom. Upgrade to a nice (ideally, non-digital) alarm clock.
8. Create spa vibes with a scented candle, incense, or an aromatherapy diffuser.
9. Create a wellness plan and commit to it. Daily walks. Daily workouts (gentle movement totally counts). Fresh air. Nature.
10. Find somewhere in your hometown with a Million Dollar View that you can access for free (a bridge, a cliff, a lake,

a skyline) and stand there. Gaze at the horizon. Soak it in.

11. Do something every morning that makes you feel "pulled together" and "bossed up," whatever that means for you. Mascara. A cute silk scarf. Meditation. Whatevs.

12. Treat yourself to a small luxury that feels amazing, like a notebook to write down your money-making ideas.

13. Make room in your home (and in your life) for your goals. Clear out that garage, attic, spare bedroom, or kitchen corner to create a workspace. It might be small (for now) but make it feel as spacious as possible. Room for you to grow.

14. Hire a personal assistant or virtual assistant. $20 an hour. Five hours a week. Start delegating things that distract you or drain you. (See chapter 9, "Million Dollar Team," for more on why you should absolutely do this, and specific things you can outsource ASAP.)

15. Put cucumber and lemon in your water on a normal Tuesday. Because you can.

16. Create a Million Dollar Moment for yourself, at least once a day, to remind yourself that you can have (and you deserve) nice things. This moment can be reading a book (just for pleasure), watching the sunset, or taking a lil' extra time to style your hair and feel your best.

17. Get your car professionally washed, so it's gleaming inside and out. Or ask your spouse or teenager to do it.

18. Put lotion on your elbows, knees, feet. Get that glow. Like my friend Robert says, "Leave the house looking like somebody loves you."

19. Listen to audiobooks and podcasts that inspire you, because Million Dollar Badasses are continually looking for ways to stay lifted.

20. Slow down when you eat. Savor your food. Let your shoulders sink down and enjoy the moment. Eat like you're a millionaire, not like you're rushing to catch the next train.

21. Declutter your calendar. All those unnecessary commitments that drain your energy and power. Byeee.

22. Put thriving, healthy plants in your home and workspace. Get yo'self a money tree.
23. At restaurants, at least once a week, order the menu item that you really want, not the item that's cheapest. The one you want is probably $5 more, but emotionally, it's worth $5,000.
24. Fix that "one thing" that's been annoying you for too long, sapping your energy. The chipped paint. The squeaky door. The fridge that hums and won't shut the hell up. Get it handled. Ahhh. Serenity.
25. Speak to yourself like you love, admire, and respect yourself.

My friend, we've been on quite a journey together. We've talked about why it's important for you to shoot for becoming a millionaire instead of just settling for six figures, which isn't enough to live comfortably in most cities. We talked about the stories you tell yourself that hold you back and how to reframe them into thoughts and stories that serve you. We've talked about the lies we've been told by the media, our government, and society at large about our abilities to earn and manage money.

We've explored how to start making Million Dollar Decisions instead of Broke Ass Decisions. We've looked at your Weak Ass Boundaries and turned them into Million Dollar Boundaries that you enforce. We've assembled your Million Dollar Squad to support you as you build your empire. And we've weaved it altogether into a beautiful, specific Million Dollar Vision for your life.

Now that we've got your Million Dollar Behavior on lock, you are ready for your Million Dollar Roadmap. In part two of this book, we will work through the steps and the changes you need to make in order to make a million dollars. Don't be scurred. You got this. And I'm here to guide you. Let's go get this shmoney!

CHAPTER SUMMARY

- Give yourself permission to dream and create a vision for your life. Be extravagant with your dreams and don't assume it is out of reach. And, do the math! Figure out exactly how much your dream life costs. Is it $10,000 per month, $35,000 per month, or what? Find the monthly number.
- Big, hairy, audacious and mindful goals are more likely to be achieved than boring, mediocre, attainable goals.
- To achieve success, we need to feel successful. Women must take steps to Be Her Now. Treat yourself the way the most successful version of yourself would treat you. Tap into your desires to start creating your future.
- Being Her Now is not about spending money. You don't need to accumulate debt to start behaving like a woman who makes millions.
- Watch the way you talk about your goals and dreams. Shift your language to lean toward possibility rather than defeat.

Action steps:

1. Use the Million Dollar Vision worksheet from earlier in this chapter to lay out your desires. Figure out what you want your life to look like and then use the worksheet to calculate the actual monthly cost. Once you figure out the monthly cost, begin brainstorming ways to increase your income to that amount.
2. Be Her Now. Choose three ways you can start to behave like the woman who earns the amount of monthly income you want to earn.
3. Shift your language. Use "and" instead of "but" when thinking about the obstacles in the way of having what you want. Use creative thinking to find solutions to those obstacles.

PART II

MILLION DOLLAR ROADMAP

CHAPTER 7

MILLION DOLLAR VALUE

"You better realize your worth and stop settling for bare minimum half-ass sh*t."

—CARDI B

walked down the hallowed, marble hallway, my heels clacking loudly with every step. I paused at the massive carved wood doors that looked like they reached all the way up to heaven. I didn't know what would happen once I was on the other side of these doors.

I was in a federal court; the Southern District of New York, to be exact, the Honorable Colleen McMahon presiding. I was shooketh.

This was not my first time in federal court. I had interned at the Eastern District of New York during law school. But I was not here as an attorney. I was here as a party to a case.

I took a deep breath, pushed my shoulders back, lifted my head high, grabbed the massive brass door handle, and walked in.

HOW DID WE GET HERE?

It all started in February 2013. I was living in Rapid City, South Dakota, at the time. We moved there for my husband to attend a short-term training program and were stuck there for a while, because I was pregnant with my son and on bedrest. It was a high-risk pregnancy, and there was a good chance my son would be born early, possibly too early. As a result, I was reclined in bed 24/7. The only time I got to leave the house was for my weekly doctor's visits. I did have several scares when I started having contractions and had to go to the hospital to stop them.

It was an emotionally trying time.

To cope, I would spend my days working from bed with my laptop and my evenings snuggled up with my one-year-old daughter watching children's videos, and sometimes the TV show, *Bones*, on my laptop. I kept myself busy to keep from worrying about all the things that could go wrong with this pregnancy. I was also still the primary breadwinner for my family and needed to be since my husband was now a full-time caregiver for me and my daughter.

During this time, I got a new client in my law practice. Her name was Amber, and she was exactly the kind of client I wanted. She had a growing business and needed to set up a solid legal foundation. Contracts, business formation, trademarks, and copyrights—she needed the works. This was music to my lawyer-and-expectant-mother-who-needs-the-money ears. We hit it off on our initial call, and within twenty-four hours we were off to the races.

By March, we were friends as well as colleagues. It was during this time I decided to create my first digital product, a legal guide for online-based entrepreneurs with contract templates and do-it-yourself instructions for things like incorporation and copyright registration. I thought it was a great idea and clearly met a need in the marketplace. I was looking to create a secondary source of income for my family that would support us when I went on maternity leave. I shared my ideas for this project with Amber, as she had experience creating and selling digital products.

Amber immediately suggested that we become business partners and create this product together. I would be in charge of the legal content of the product, and she would help with the branding and marketing. She also had an audience of about 11,000 potential customers to whom we could market the product. We would split the proceeds down the middle 50-50, and we would split the startup expenses evenly as well. I thought this offer sounded great, but I did have some reservations.

I decided to reach out to a trusted girlfriend and business consultant who had been helping me systematize my business to ask her what she thought of the deal. Her reply was something like "hell to the no!" She warned me that this joint product was mostly my intellectual property and that I should own it outright. She suggested that I work out an affiliate relationship with Amber instead, where Amber could get a small percentage of each sale for promoting my product to her customer base. (Note: Listen to your smart, knowledgeable girlfriends who have your back!)

I did not take this advice.

Instead, I walked into this partnership with starry eyes, and it cost me greatly.

Throughout the creation process for our digital product, Amber frequently was very busy working on other less profitable projects, like a retreat in Costa Rica where she saw little return on her investment and a book proposal that wound up getting rejected by the agent who requested it. Meanwhile, I did the majority of the heavy lifting when it came to creating our digital product while on bedrest. My son was born (thankfully at exactly thirty-five weeks and six days—just one day shy of full-term), and after three weeks of maternity leave, I was back to work on this project.

We finally launched the project in July 2013. We had more than two hundred customers purchase the digital product during the initial launch, and we made $80,000. That was the most money I had ever made at one time. I was really grateful for all the customers who believed in us, but we were shooting for a six-figure launch. We were hoping to make a minimum of $100,000, which is what Amber had suggested was the likely result when she pitched the partnership. I couldn't help but wonder if we could have done better if Amber had focused more of her time and energy on this project.

Nevertheless, I had launched my first digital product and customers were delighted. This project was a success, and I wanted to move forward and keep generating sales.

A few weeks after the launch, I reached out to Amber to discuss getting affiliates and hosting webinars as we had planned. But she was busy with other projects, as usual. Her plan was to leave the product listed on her site, and she thought this would generate a little bit of additional revenue. But what I wanted was to generate as much money as possible from this product. I had a growing family to support and was not interested in a trickle of cashflow. I wanted a flood.

I decided to put together promotions on my own, even though Amber was supposed to be the marketing genius of our outfit. The promotion I put together generated an additional $30,000. When I sent Amber that $15,000 check for her half of the proceeds, I was bitter. I was doing 80 percent of the work to create, market, and deliver this program, and paying her 50 percent of the proceeds. Our original written agreement required 50-50 payments and 50-50 effort. Our specific duties were all laid out in our agreement, and Amber wasn't doing even 20 percent of those duties most months.

I reached out to Amber to talk about this and tell her how I was feeling. I thought she would tell me how she was feeling as well and then we could rework our duties and financial split for this product so that it felt more equitable on both sides.

Instead I received a response from Amber's newly hired attorney.

That led to six months of negotiations. Eventually, we came to an agreement. The agreement was that I would buy her share in the product for a flat five-figure fee in addition to her having the right to earn a 100 percent affiliate fee on any sales she directly generated for a period of two years and a 75 percent affiliate fee for sales she generated for the third year. It was not an agreement either of us was thrilled about but it was fair. I was excited to finally move on with this product and have the ability to make the kind of money that I knew was possible.

Right after we signed the contract, I did a marketing promotion and the result blew me away. I made $80,000 from that launch all by myself. I could finally see that I didn't need Amber or her customer list to promote and sell my digital product, I had the skill and ability to do it on my own.

But Amber was none too pleased that I had had such a successful launch without her, even though she participated in the launch as an affiliate and made $11,000 from sales she generated. Within two months of dissolving our partnership, Amber violated the contract by creating a duplicate website and continuing to sell the product, which amounted to intellectual property theft. I had no choice but to sue her.

In September 2014, just one year and four months after our partnership began, I sued Amber in federal court. Over a three-year period, there were hearings, depositions, claims, and counterclaims. There was a public smear campaign where Amber wrote lies about me in various articles shared with our customer base and filed a complaint threatening my law license. I received hate mail from my own customers and had potential clients back out of working with me because they googled my name and saw Amber's articles.

There were many sleepless nights, impossible decisions, and anxiety-ridden days. By the end of it, my team had spent countless hours of work gathering documents to support our case. The lawsuit cost me $150,000 in legal fees, and they were only that low because I did part of the legal work myself.

In April 2017, we finally settled the lawsuit and I got 100 percent ownership of my product. Amber got nothing but $400,000 in legal fees and the satisfaction of making my life difficult for a period of years.

The day I signed the settlement agreement, I thought long and hard about what my girlfriend had said to me four years earlier when I was considering entering a partnership with Amber. She warned me that I should own the product myself, and I didn't take heed because I had imposter syndrome. I didn't think I could create and sell a product successfully on my own. And that imposter syndrome cost me greatly. It cost me money, friendships, clients, stress, and the great distraction of a three-year legal battle.

Had I listened to my friend, I would have negotiated an affiliate arrangement with Amber where I paid her 50 percent of any sales she generated and kept 100 percent of the proceeds for the many sales I generated. I might have hired her to help me with some of the copywriting (which would have cost me $10,000 maximum) but I would have retained 100 percent ownership of this product. I would have been actively selling and promoting my product for that three-year period and had no lawsuit costing me clients and distracting me from building my empire. Maybe Amber and I would still be friends and colleagues.

In summary, because I didn't believe that I was capable of writing, developing, and selling a product on my own, it cost me—$150,000 in legal fees, at least $500,000 in lost revenue, a thousand hours of pain and sorrow and time away from my kids, a friend, and then some.

This is the painfully high price of imposter syndrome. As a woman, you are (probably) paying this price daily.

Imposter syndrome is one of the greatest challenges to women's wealth. To earn millions, you first have to stop believing what the world says you are capable of as a Black woman, lesbian woman, disabled woman, fat woman, trans woman, loud woman, bossy woman, or filthy-mouthed woman. Whatever kind of woman you are, the media is sending you messages every day to convince you that you are not good enough. Don't you believe it.

WHAT "IMPOSTER SYNDROME" IS, WHY YOU PROBABLY HAVE IT (EVEN IF YOU THINK YOU DON'T), AND HOW IT'S BLOCKING YOU FROM WEALTH

You've probably heard the term "imposter syndrome" before. What does this phrase actually mean, and where does it come from?

The term was coined by two clinical psychologists—Dr. Pauline Clance and Dr. Suzanne Imes—back in 1978.[1]

Back then—when "Last Dance" by Donna Summer was one of the hottest songs on the charts, and Diana Ross was serving legendary looks in her afro while appearing in The Wiz—Clance and Imes conducted a study on high-achieving women. They found that an astonishing number of these women felt inadequate, inferior, and perceived themselves as a "phony" or "fraud," despite truckloads of evidence indicating the exact opposite.

Clance and Imes labeled this situation "imposter syndrome." Although not a mental illness, per se, it's often accompanied by anxiety, stress, depression, and low self-esteem.

IMPOSTER SYNDROME SHOWS UP IN
MANY DIFFERENT WAYS

It can look like:

- Winning a prestigious award, but secretly believing it was just a fluke, you probably didn't really deserve it, and something like this will definitely never happen again.
- Consistently delivering high-quality work to your boss, receiving praise, or even a merit-based bonus, but quietly believing that you "don't really know what you're doing, and one day, they'll find out."
- Earning a bachelor's, a master's, and a doctorate, plus a slew of additional certifications (certified life coach, certified project manager, certified dolphin trainer) just for good measure, and still feeling like you're "not qualified enough" to go after your dream job, or charge top dollar for your services.
- Receiving an amazing opportunity but chalking it up to "lucky timing" or "just knowing the right people." (As if having the "right people" in your corner and cultivating strong relationships has nothing to do with how awesome you are, *hmmm*? But I digress.)
- Dreaming about doing something really cool (giving a TEDx Talk, writing a book, starting a podcast, hosting a special event) but then procrastinating for years (or never starting at all) because deep down, you worry, "Who'd want to listen to me?" "Others have already done this, and they've done it better than I ever could." "Why even bother?"
- Having an avalanche of evidence (statistics, case studies, testimonials, endorsements) to confirm that you are excellent at fitness training, marketing, designing sleek, contemporary, avant-garde goldfish tanks, or whatever you do, and yet continually doubting that you're "good enough."
- Working for free, or undercharging for your services, because you're terrified that you "suck" at whatever service you're providing. So you figure, if you only charge $15 instead of $1,500,

then "nobody can get mad at you" when they realize that you suck. (This is the most batshit crazy nonsense, but so many of us women do this. It's wild.)

- Or, like me, dreaming about creating something amazing but not believing you're capable of leading the project yourself, and then getting yourself into inadequate partnerships that end up costing you money, time, and sanity.

Do you recognize yourself in any of those descriptions? I'll bet you do!

Valerie Young, author of *The Secret Thoughts of Successful Women*, notes that women of color experience imposter syndrome even more frequently than white women—for obvious reasons. When you already suspect that you're inadequate, and then society continually reinforces your suspicion, then you believe it. *Doubly.*

And here's the thing that's *really* sad: Imposter syndrome doesn't just make you feel shitty about yourself, it also keeps you broke.

LACK OF CONFIDENCE
IS COSTING YOU MILLIONS

How does imposter syndrome keep you broke? Like this:

One study shows that, due to imposter syndrome, 55 percent of self-employed women automatically discount their prices before the client even asks for a lower price.[2]

The cost: If you charge around $100 an hour, work thirty hours a week, and take a few weeks of vacation per year, you'd earn around $150,000 per year. Okay, let's say you discount your services "just a little bit," like around 15 percent. Not too much, but it adds up. That's $22,500 per year you're waving away because you don't think you're good enough to earn more. That's private school tuition. That's a new car. That's a down payment on a house. That's 173 aromatherapy massages. Gone.

Another study shows that many women consistently underestimate their performance on tests.[3] For instance, you take an exam and (before seeing your actual score) you assume you got 60 percent of the answers correct. But in actuality you got 80 percent correct. Your knee-jerk reaction is to assume you did poorly when this is not the case. It is interesting (and not surprising) that men tend to do the opposite—they tend to overestimate their scores and assume they did better than they actually did. (Like that old saying: "Lord, grant me the confidence of a mediocre white man.")

The cost: If you persistently underestimate your intelligence and performance, this means you're less likely to launch your own business, apply for a big grant, or go after that C-level position with a six-figure salary and an assigned parking spot with your name on it. You're leaving millions on the table. Or, like me, you are taking on unnecessary partnerships and not maintaining ownership of your own intellectual property, both of which will cost you financially.

To further drive this point home (and depress you a little more), get this: One study—surveying employees at a major tech company—found that female employees would apply for a promotion only when they believed they met 100 percent of the requirements listed on the job description.[4] On the other hand, male employees would frequently apply even when they met only 60 percent of the requirements.

In other words, highly qualified women would read the job description and think, I'm not good enough. There's no way they'll choose me. There's no point in even applying. I won't waste my time—or theirs. (Sound familiar, ladies?) Whereas significantly less qualified men would read that exact same job description and think, Oh, I'd be perfect for this! Here's my application! Job, please!

For my sisters on the other side of the pond, this one's for you. A United Kingdom survey reports that 60 percent of women who have considered starting a business ultimately decided *not to do it* because they lacked confidence in their abilities and did not feel like "the type of person who could start a business."[5] And that is why, even today, only one-fifth of UK businesses are owned and run by women. *The Telegraph* calls imposter syndrome "women's silent career killer" and I would add, "women's silent money killer," too.

HOW TO PURGE IMPOSTER SYNDROME FROM YOUR LIFE

How can you cure yourself of this terrible, money-stealing plague?

To purge imposter syndrome from your brain, your journey might require mindset coaching from a skilled professional, a transformational church sermon, or perhaps watching the music video for "Spirit" by Beyoncé a hundred times in a row, because this video will heal you. Trust.

I'd recommend all those things, plus these steps:

Acknowledge that you're not alone, and your brain is not "broken."

You might feel broken right now, but you ain't broken. And you're in good company. Virtually every woman on planet Earth either suffers, or has suffered, from imposter syndrome. Even me. Even Michelle Obama (just read her autobiography—she talks about this). Even Maya Angelou—despite winning numerous literary awards—always thought her "next book" would be a failure, and even said so in interviews.[6] You can feel these insecurities and refuse to let them stop you.

Get into the habit of tracking your victories as they happen. Keep a record.

Keep track of your wins, big and small, instead of letting them zip by and go unnoticed.

I have a colleague who offers various writing-related services, including helping people write a book proposal, find a literary agent, and get a publishing deal. She keeps track of her clients and meticulously follows up afterward to find out how they're doing.

Because she tracks things carefully, she knows that—after hiring her—more than 90 percent of her clients go on to successfully secure a book deal. (And the ones who don't, it's usually because they got lazy or got scared and never actually pitched their proposal to any agents.)

Ninety percent is a very high rate of success. Having this piece of information helps her to fight imposter syndrome and keep insecurities at bay. She knows, without a shadow of a doubt: "I'm good at what I do. I have proof. When people pay me, they get results." Because math.

The more you track your victories and record them, the stronger you feel. Use evidence to combat insecurities.

Sometimes, even with a mountain of evidence staring you in the face, you *still* feel inferior. If that's your situation, then . . .

Get therapy.

Therapy means different things to different people. You might need traditional talk therapy. You might prefer group therapy or EMDR. Or maybe you want something that's not strictly "therapy" but feels therapeutic to you—like joining a club filled with women who are determined to make more money (I happen to run one, google me), a space where you feel seen, heard, understood, and get lifted by your sisters.

And if none of that works, then . . .

Become an athlete.

I am not kidding. Did you know that 94 percent of women who hold C-level positions are former athletes?[7] I did not. Until today. And it makes total sense.

When you do something that's extremely challenging and out of your comfort zone (like win a regional soccer tournament or run a marathon when you absolutely did not think you could do it) this experience changes you on a cellular level. You start to wonder, *Well, if I could do that extremely challenging thing, then what else could I do?*

So, go train for a 5K walk-run race, learn how to surf, sign up for archery lessons, or, I dunno, give birth to a child (one of the most badass feats of athleticism on Earth). Walk across the hot coals and let this be a lesson to you: Despite the pernicious insecurities you sometimes hear in your mind, *you can do anything.*

HOW WOULD YOUR LIFE CHANGE IF YOU ACTUALLY BELIEVED IN YOURSELF?

How would you behave if you didn't have a gruesome case of imposter syndrome? How would you behave if you owned your worthiness and understood the immense value you bring to the table? You would behave very differently. Your bank account would look different, too. So, what makes you valuable?

What do you currently offer—or what could you start offering—that is extremely valuable?

What's a skill you've got that's so desirable, so helpful, so life-changing that people would practically sprint across the room to open their wallets and hire you?

What's the ability you've got that's gonna make you millions?

An ability that triggers people to say, "Take all my money!"

This is your Million Dollar Value.

And if you don't know what it is, then it's high time to find out.

WHAT CAN YOU DO THAT IS EXTREMELY VALUABLE?

There is *something* you can do that is extremely valuable. The million dollar question: *What is it?* You might already know what it is. Or you might have no idea.

Many women are blindly unaware of their own value. Many think, *But I don't really bring anything valuable to the table! Me? I'm nobody special!* You are wrong about this. You are appraising yourself incorrectly.

Let's say you're a hairstylist. You specialize in working with Black women. A new client comes in. She has struggled with her hair all her life. She's tried a hundred different styles and systems and nothing has worked out. Her hair is dry and chemically fried. She doesn't know what to do next. All this hair drama is degrading her quality of life.

Enter: *You.*

You teach this client how to become a natural hair goddess. After hiring you, she finally understands how to take care of her hair. She now has her go-to signature styles, and her hair is shiny and healthy. She falls in love with her hair again and feels confident like never before. She carries herself differently. She goes after her dream job. She nails the interview. She asks her crush on a date. Love. Marriage. Baby carriage. And on and on.

You didn't just give this client a hair-styling tutorial. You changed this woman's life *forever!* How much is that worth? A lot more than $50, that's for sure.

This is how I want you to start thinking about yourself, your skills, your expertise—the value you bring to the table.

If you are really good at what you do (and I bet you are), then you are not just offering a "haircut" or a "dance lesson" or "social media marketing services." You are *changing someone's life,* and that is worth a lot.

So, what can you offer that is extremely valuable?

If you don't know, here are some ways to figure this out:

1. Recognize your natural talents.

Your natural talents are extremely valuable.

There's probably something that comes so naturally to you, it doesn't even feel like work or anything special. It might be gardening, cooking, writing, decluttering and organizing, styling bomb outfits, creating custom face cream or confidently strutting across a stage and speaking in front of a crowd.

For you, it's as natural as breathing. For others, it's a headache, boring, confusing, terrifying, or just not a type of expertise that they possess.

As a child, I always got in trouble for talking too much. Every report card would say, "Rachel is an excellent student, and she would have gotten even higher marks if she could learn to talk less." The number one thing my mother said to me every day was "*Shush!*" I had a lot to say, y'all, and I always said it loudly and with verve. Guess who gets paid very well to talk and share all the ideas and thoughts in her head now? Dats right! Your girl is making millions using my natural ability to never shut up!

And I'm sure you know Tiffany Haddish, the A-list movie actress and author of the bestselling memoir, *The Last Black Unicorn.* Tiffany is a natural comedian. Even back in the day when she worked as a baggage attendant for a major airline, she was cracking jokes over the loudspeaker and keeping weary passengers wildly entertained. Comedy pours out of her like heat from the sun. She couldn't stop it, even if she tried. It's her natural gift, and it made her a millionaire several times over. What is yours?

Action step: Write down three things you can do naturally and easily. Even if you think, *Well, nobody would ever pay me to do XYZ,* ignore that voice in your head. You'd be surprised. People will pay you (and pay you very well) to do all kinds of things, because what comes naturally to you does not come naturally to everyone.

Extra credit: Write down the last three compliments you received from friends, colleagues, clients, anyone. Do you routinely get praised for how incredibly neat you are? *Ding!* Natural talent alert! You might be the future CEO of a million dollar home organizing empire, the next Marie Kondo. Do friends thank you for being so supportive and encouraging, their biggest cheerleader? Bang the money gong! You might have exactly what it takes to run a seven-figure fitness studio or life coaching practice.

Your natural gifts can make you millions.

2. Audit your career and make a list of accomplishments.

Another way to identify what makes you extremely valuable is to audit your career. You can look at your past, like a historian, and examine the facts to figure out what makes you extremely valuable.

You've probably done tons of valuable things for your employer or clients. Sometimes you just don't remember all the things you've done, and you need to sit your ass down, pour a glass of iced tea, and think it over. Refresh your memory.

Action step: Make a list of extremely valuable, helpful things you've done for your employer and/or clients in the past, including any freebie work you've done.

Challenge yourself to write down fifty specific ways you've made your company better, made your boss's life easier, or made your clients oh-so delighted.

You saved your last employer tons of money? Write that down! You improved a janky system and vastly increased productivity in your department? Put that down, too. Lawsuits avoided. Sales achieved. Results your clients got, thanks to you. Put it all down on the list.

Read your list back to yourself. Look at all the value you've contributed to the world. Breathe that in. Own it.

Take a closer look at your list. Do you notice any trends? Any repetitive themes? For instance, are you consistently uplifting morale or fixing broken systems or finding just the right words to make a message sizzle off the screen? There's something you do (and you probably already do it regularly) that is immensely valuable. And you could be leveraging this skill to make a whole lot more money.

3. Understand your zone of incompetence, zone of competence, zone of excellence, and zone of genius.

What can you offer the world that is extremely valuable? One of the swiftest ways to figure this out is to understand your zone of incompetence, zone of competence, zone of excellence, and zone of genius. You need to be working in your zone of genius in order to deliver maximum value and make millions. These four zones come from a book called *The Big Leap* by Gay Hendricks. It is one of my favorite books that I have read and reread throughout my career. It's also the book that I regularly gift to my clients and friends. In it, Hendricks lays out four different zones of work.

The zone of incompetence: In this zone, you are engaging in tasks and work that you inherently do not understand or are not skilled at. It's typically pretty obvious to you and others that you are not good at this work. It's also inefficient for you to continue to do this kind of work because your lack of understanding or skill means that it takes much more effort and time to complete this work whereas someone else could do it quickly and efficiently.

An example of this would be if you said to me, "Rachel, I need you to design and build a website." Well, I have zero website programming skills. Could I learn how to do this? Probably, but it would take me a hundred hours or more. Would I do an excellent job? Almost definitely not. (Just take a look at some of my early landing pages that I built myself, or, preferably, don't.) Would the website look busted and basic? Oh, yes. This is my zone of incompetence, so the end result is going to be a hot ass mess.

The zone of competence: In this zone, you are doing work that you can do efficiently but it is likely something that many people can do efficiently. Therefore it is not the kind of work that pays well or provides deep satisfaction.

An example of this might be operating a cash register at a grocery store. It is important work, it's how retail businesses get paid. Maybe you can do this work efficiently and do a good job, but it doesn't exactly light your heart on fire, and you're not fully utilizing your gifts. You're just coasting along. Another example is a family lawyer offering $500 uncontested divorces. There is nothing special about the way this lawyer handles your uncontested divorce as compared to other lawyers. Without any special branding, customer experience, or beneficial skill, customers will choose the lawyer who charges the least amount.

The zone of excellence: This is where things get tricky. In this zone, you are doing work at which you are very skilled. Often, it is work that you have trained for, as well as something that you have practiced and established over time. This is also work for which the world praises you and pays you well. For these reasons, zone of excellence work is often hard to give up.

For example, if you went through college, medical school, and a residency to become a licensed physician, you are likely making good money, and people are impressed when you tell them that you are a doctor. You have cultivated the skills to practice medicine over a great deal of time. However, if this is not zone of genius work for you, you will long to do the work that you are truly meant to do but you will struggle to give up being a physician because you worked so hard to achieve it. Many people stay in their zone of excellence because they're afraid to leave, or don't think it's possible to do anything else. Like golden handcuffs. Your situation is pretty darn good, so why reach for more? Except your heart keeps whispering that "this isn't quite it."

The zone of genius: In this zone, you are doing work for which you have a natural ability. These are your innate skills rather than learned skills. When you are doing this kind of work, you get into a flow state and do not struggle to create. You can produce distinguished and unique results that are unlike what anyone else is doing. When you are operating in your zone of genius, there is little to no competition for your work.

An example of this is an engineer who loves to build things. She might spend hours in her garage tinkering with gadgets and gizmos, taking things apart and rebuilding them in a way that functions much better than before. She invents new products that solve the world's problems all the time. It is easy for her, and she truly enjoys honing her engineering skills, challenging herself with new projects and redesigning incredible products every day. She can charge top dollar for the products she creates, and many companies want to work with her and benefit from her skill.

Zone of genius work is what will produce millions for you. It's important to take "the big leap" from your zone of excellence or competence into your zone of genius in order to experience the kind of success you can't currently imagine.

Working in your zone of genius is all about taking your natural gifts and maximizing them. For example, if you are a great public speaker, take a course on public speaking and become an even better public speaker. This is where you can earn "compound interest" with your work. This is not what most people do. Most people try to get better at things they are really bad at. I say forget what you're bad at and double down on what you're great at. This is where the big money and career satisfaction is.

Action step: Discover your zone of genius by following the call. If you listen closely, there are projects, dreams, and big ideas that have called to you for years. If you look back at your history, you'll find clues in your childhood where you were drawn to similar work that is calling you now. That nagging desire might not reveal exactly what your zone of genius is at first, but if you take the very first tiny step it will begin to reveal itself.

4. Take an assessment (or three).

Still not sure what makes your work valuable—or what you could offer to the world that will make you millions? There are a number of talent and skill assessments you can take to learn more about where your natural talents lie. One of my favorite assessments that I have my clients and employees take is CliftonStrengths (formerly StrengthsFinder).

A few years ago, I was at a mastermind event and met up with several women entrepreneurs in the suite of an attendee. There was a CliftonStrengths coach among us, and it turned out that most of us had done the assessment at some point. We all began pulling out our phones and finding our top five strengths so she could give us her thoughts about our work based on those top five.

When she got to me, she told me that I have no execution strengths. She said that based on my top five, I am a big ideas person and a good strategist. She said I belong on stages and in front of large groups of people sharing my genius and inspiring others. She told me that I should stop doing everything in my business that does not have me on a stage in front of people who could benefit from my work.

At first I was offended. No execution strengths? I had worked my ass off building a business for the last seven years, clearly I can work a to-do list. But after just a few moments of thinking about it, I realized that I had always struggled with delivery. For example, my newsletters were always written on Saturday night when they had to be sent out by 6:00 a.m. the following morning. And I hated having to send follow-up resources to clients after a coaching call. As a lawyer, I drafted contracts at midnight the day before they were due to clients. Sitting my butt in a chair to do focused, solitary work was a real challenge for me. But getting on the phone with clients or on a stage in front of a group of people I could help? I lived for that and would jump at the opportunity.

As these realizations settled in, I felt completely liberated. Hallelujah! I am not good at execution! Praise be! Rather than thinking I was a terrible person with a poor work ethic, I realized that I just wasn't good at the follow up and that I could hire other people to do that work. And that is exactly what I did. From that moment forward, I began hiring a team who could do all the things that I was not good at. And the real magic is that I hired people for whom execution was their zone of genius. So they got to do work they loved and so did I. This was a massive breakthrough moment—and it was the first year that I earned $1 million.

Action step: Take a few talent and skill assessments to get a better understanding of how you work best. CliftonStrengths is a great one. I also recommend Kolbe and DiSC. Each test has a slightly different way of assessing your skills and talents and, taken together, the results can provide clues and insight into your genius work.

OBJECTION!

To recap: the big question is, *What can you offer that is extremely valuable?* We just walked through four different ways to start figuring this out.

I can already hear your objections brewing! Here are some things you might be thinking right now:

But, Rachel, I'm not an amazingly accomplished Boss Bitch. I don't have any skills. I don't have expertise. I don't have a college degree, or an impressive list of accolades. I flip burgers at McDonald's and, honestly, I usually show up late and do a half-assed job. I don't bring much value to the table. Other people are super valuable, but I am not.

Okay, Burger Boo, here's my response to that:

- You might think you suck at your current job. And you might be completely wrong. It's possible (statistically speaking, not just possible, but *highly likely*) that, as a woman, you are experiencing imposter syndrome. Your boss and colleagues might love you and feel you're doing an amazing job—but you just don't believe them. You might be harshly critical of yourself when others feel like you're dope. Consider that you might be viewing yourself in an excessively negative light.

- You might think you suck at your current job. And you know what? You might be right! It's possible you've chosen the wrong career path, one that is not allowing your natural gifts to shine. It happens. This situation is fixable. Get on a new path.

"But, Rachel, I am so lazy. I have a terrible work ethic. I hate waking up early. I am not a go-getter like you seem to be."

I doubt this very much. You are probably not lazy. You are probably extremely *tired*. "Lazy" and "tired" are two very different things.

Most women are exhausted all the time. The American Academy of Sleep Medicine and the Sleep Research Society reports that one in three Americans are chronically sleep deprived. When you roll into work in a fatigued state, your brain power is diminished. Scientists say that trying to work while sleep deprived is like trying to work while drunk. You're bound to make mistakes, miss things, and feel sluggish, stupid, and unmotivated.

We're not just exhausted. We're depressed, too. One recent study shows that 37 percent of moms with toddlers at home exhibit symptoms of depression, including anxiety, apathy, hopelessness, and difficulty concentrating. No wonder you're struggling to shine like a diamond at work.

You have the potential to be extraordinary at *something,* and you absolutely have the capacity to develop systems and offers that generate millions. But if you're so exhausted you can barely keep your eyes open, then obviously, you're not going to rise to your highest potential.

But just consider how much value you already bring to the table, even in a chronically depleted state. You probably did a thousand things today. You successfully kept small humans alive, clothed, and fed. You banged out some time-sensitive emails. You handled a crisis at home, then put out five more fires at work. You even managed to bathe, floss, and you remembered to wish Grandma Clarisse a happy birthday. And that's all before 10:00 a.m. Incredible. Now imagine how much more value (higher-level value, Million Dollar Value) you could contribute if you were well-rested with eight hours of sleep, hydrated, nourished, and fresh from a therapy session. #Miracles

One last word on this topic—what's wrong with being "lazy," anyway?

Lazy might just be shorthand for "someone who craves efficiency and wants to get the biggest results in the least amount of time." In that case, I am very lazy, too! My friend Denise Duffield-Thomas is another proudly lazy woman who makes seven figures per year. She even wrote a book called *Chillpreneur* about how being lazy and taking the easiest, chillest route can lead to success. Google it.

What the outside world may call "lazy" might actually be your zone of genius. In fact, that's exactly what I realized about myself.

MY SO-CALLED BAD WORK ETHIC

When I was a young woman, I felt bad because I thought I had the worst work ethic. I worked for a catering company in which my boss's desk was directly behind mine. It was so close that when I would push my chair out to get up, the back of my chair would hit the front of his desk. My boss was very literally breathing down my neck all day every day.

My job was to organize files, answer phones, send emails, and manage the schedule. I hated all those things. I remember getting physically ill on the train every day on my morning commute. It was a total nightmare. I eventually got fired, and I skipped down the street that day on my way home. I was broke but at least I was free!

I had a series of other administrative jobs: in a real estate office, at a staffing agency, at an investment bank and at a nonprofit. With each job, after the first few weeks, I began dreading going to work. I had trouble concentrating and was always down to the wire with meeting deadlines. When there was a big, exciting project, I would rise to the occasion and do an amazing job. Once the big project was over, I would go back to low output.

My bosses always seemed to be perplexed by me. They liked me a lot and knew that I was smart but couldn't seem to get the level of productivity out of me that they believed possible.

I decided that I must have a poor work ethic and wished I could be more like some of my family members who seemed to be highly valued at work. I figured that I must not have the "hard work" gene and felt terrible about myself.

Eventually I realized it wasn't a poor ethic that was affecting my performance. It was boredom. I was bored to death with the work and tried to get it done in the least amount of time possible so I could spend the rest of my work time talking with coworkers, reading, or applying to graduate school. Administrative work is 100 percent not my zone of genius, and that is why I struggled so much.

In law school, I didn't study as much as I felt I should have but when there were mock trials, mock negotiations, or mock mediations, I would always heavily prepare, stand out, and garner much praise. Why? Because I got to be in front of an audience strategically arguing a case for my "pretend client," and I absolutely loved it. After I graduated from law school and began building my own practice, I really understood just how hard I was willing to work. I never had a poor work ethic, I was just doing the wrong work.

Perhaps that is the case for you. You think you don't have a strong work ethic or special skills because you are in the wrong job. But I promise you that, given the right work in the right working environment, you will soar.

OKAY, NOW WHAT?

By now, maybe you've identified ten different ways you could offer value to the marketplace. You're multitalented! There are numerous things you could do. So, now what?

Just pick something.

Commit.

Choose one thing to focus on for a while.

You love baking cookies? Go all in with cookies. Fine-tune your recipes. Develop a system that leads to cookies so good, they're like crack. Build a fan base, hot demand, and a waitlist for your cookies. Then turn this system into a seven-figure cookie empire.

Or, you've noticed that very few women go after careers in aviation? You want to see more female pilots in the world? Great. Commit 100 percent to solving this problem. Use your valuable skills to develop services, educational programs, youth summer camps, or whatever you want to offer to address this societal problem and fix it.

This is what successful entrepreneurs do. You identify a specific problem in the world. You develop an excellent solution. Then you bring that solution to the marketplace and sell it. *Cha-ching!* The more you focus on one problem, the better you get at solving it and the faster you'll make that coin.

"But I am multi-passionate!" I can hear you saying. "I contain multitudes! My soul is a tapestry woven with infinite threads of possibility! I can't possibly commit to doing just one thing!"

To that, I would argue, go ahead and be multi-passionate—on your personal time.

On your days off and weekends, do it all. Go salsa dancing. Ride ponies. Learn French.

Read romance novels. Practice calligraphy. Bake scones. You don't need to monetize every single one of your passions. You can have a multi-passionate life. But you need to have a uni-passionate career if you want to make serious bank.

Commit to one thing. For now. Roll with it for a while. Give it a chance to blossom into a wealth-building empire. This is not the only way to earn millions but it is the fastest way to earn your first million.

CHAPTER SUMMARY

- You are more accomplished than you think. You probably have a nasty case of imposter syndrome, and this is costing you greatly.
- You are not lazy. You are probably really freaking tired. There's a difference.

- You need to spend some time thinking about the question, "What could I offer to the world that is extremely valuable?" This is the million dollar question.
- The answer might be staring you right in the face. It might be something you already do in your current career (and you just need to start charging a whole lot more). It could be something you do just for fun in your spare time (that you could start charging for). It could be something that comes naturally to you, so naturally you never even recognized that this is a valuable gift.
- Once you identify what makes you valuable, believe it, own it, and charge accordingly, your life will change forever.
- And, you should probably double your rates. Right now.

Action Steps:
- Think through the kinds of things you have been doing naturally since you were a child. These might even be the things that always got you in trouble.
- Do a career audit and take stock of your past accomplishments. There are likely clues that will lead you to recognize the way you add value to the world.
- Take a few talent assessments to better understand your natural talents and skills. I recommend CliftonStrengths, DiSC, and Kolbe.
- Once you have a better understanding of your natural skills and talents, write down a list of all the things that you are excited to do to make money. Then choose one and only one to focus on. Give yourself a chance to make that one thing a big success.

CHAPTER 8

MILLION DOLLAR PRICING

"When they go low, we go high."

—MICHELLE OBAMA

O n May 23, 2011, at 2:14 p.m., a friend and fellow lawyer sent me a DM on Twitter that changed my life.

She said: *love the services—but your prices are waaaay too low. esp for trademark. WAAAAAY TOO LOW! ;-)*

I did not agree with her and, to be honest, kinda thought she should mind her own business. My reply was: *Thanks for the feedback, Lurie. You know I know lawyers who charge even less for some of those services? Okay, something to think about. Thx!*

Unbothered, Lurie said: *Of course. U can always be underpriced. If u compete on price, u lose. Too much work for too little pay. Trust me on this one!!! ;-)*

After this message, I changed the subject of our conversation, because I was uncomfortable and annoyed. What did she know?

Turns out? A whole bloodclot lot.

The friend I am referring to is Lurie Daniel Favors. She is an amazing lawyer and social justice activist. At the time, she was running a solo law practice focused on bankruptcy and also running a nonprofit organization that provided education and empowerment for Black communities. Lurie is pretty badass, was a more experienced entrepreneur than me at the time, and had studied the effects that racism and white patriarchy have on Black people. She knew that I was discounting my value and wanted to help me.

I should have asked her a smart follow-up question like, "How much would you charge for trademark registration services, Lurie?" Or I could have shared the true reason my prices were so low (imposter syndrome). Instead I got defensive, because I felt a bit embarrassed.

While I was annoyed at receiving unsolicited advice, her message stuck with me. I couldn't stop thinking about my one lawyer friend, a white male, who charged $15,000 for trademark services. *But no one would spend that amount of money for me to be their lawyer*, I thought.

Or would they? said the part of my brain that wasn't riddled with fear.

I thought I had really smart, logical reasons for my prices. I am still a new lawyer. This is a new law practice. I don't have an administrative assistant yet. I don't want clients taking too long to decide whether to work with me. I don't have an office. *Blah blah blah*. There were all my weak excuses to cover for the fact that I was too afraid to claim that my work was worth more.

It made me think back to my very first client. She was purchasing a hair salon. I handled the negotiation with the opposing side and drafted the contract for the sale of the business. It took hours of research, contract drafting, phone calls and emails with her and the attorney representing the seller. When I completed all the work and realized that I just helped someone acquire a business that would be the cornerstone of her empire, I realized I had been an idiot for charging a mere $500 for all that work. Insert face-palm.

Finally, after thinking it over for a few days, I decided that I would go for it and take Lurie's advice. I took the prices off of the services described on my website. I made a commitment to myself that the very next client who came to me, I would quote a price that was double my current prices. And sure enough, the moment I made that decision, a potential client emailed asking to schedule a consult with me. My test case had arrived.

On the call a few days later, I did all the usual things I do during a consult. I listened to the client's situation. I asked what his desired outcome was and what his concerns were. I got details about his business and specific timeline, and so on. Once I had gathered all the information from the client, it was time to share details about my practice and how I work. I shared all those details pretty easily and then came the moment of truth. The client and I had talked about everything and were in alignment. The only thing we hadn't discussed was the price.

He finally asked me "So, how much is this going to cost me?" and I took a deep breath, poised myself and said "$1,500 per mark." The moment I said this price, I was horrified. My face contorted (thank God we were on the phone and not in person), and I waited for what felt like six hours (but was really five seconds) for his reply. It was a very pregnant pause, and I was ready to give birth right there on the floor (I was pregnant with my daughter at the time).

Although I was screaming on the inside, I forced myself to say nothing. I knew if I opened my mouth I would start justifying my price or discounting my services. Finally he replied. And his epic reply was "Okay, I'll take two." I was jumping up and down but trying to act like I accepted this amount of money for my services every single day.

Once the call was completed, I ran around my apartment rejoicing. I called my husband and told him I just got a new client and made $3,000. I hadn't ever been paid that much money from a single client before—$3,000 was how much I used to make in a whole month (before taxes) in my previous job as a law clerk.

From that moment on, $1,500 was my new price for trademarks. And I raised my prices on all my other services as well. Lurie was right, and I was grateful that she was willing to tell me what I didn't want to hear.

In case you think raising your prices is only for women working as entrepreneurs or freelancers, think again. As a salaried employee, you can raise your prices, too.

YOU CAN SIGNIFICANTLY INCREASE YOUR INCOME, EVEN IF YOU'VE GOT A NINE-TO-FIVE JOB

A few years ago, I decided I was ready to hire a program director for my company, Hello Seven. Up until then, I had been the de facto program director in addition to handling all my other duties as CEO of my company. That meant I was the one planning the program schedule, creating all the training materials, managing the small team of part-time coaches, planning our live events, and delivering almost every aspect of the programs. It was a full-time job within itself, and I needed to find some help.

I had my eye on a particular person for the role. I had seen her in action and knew she was an excellent candidate. She had all the credentials and experience that I wanted the program director to have. She was very familiar with my work, as she was a former client, and I knew we were aligned on values. I reached out to see if she would be interested in talking about an opportunity with the company, and she was excited.

We went through the entire hiring process, and I was excited about her taking on the role of program director. We met in person at my home and talked through all the various aspects of the role. We were both in complete agreement except when it came to the salary.

I had initially offered a salary of $75,000 per year plus what I thought were great benefits like being able to work from home, three weeks of paid time off, and health insurance. This candidate wasn't going for it. She said she loved everything about the company, the mission, and the role and was so excited to work with us, however, the salary didn't work for her. I hadn't planned on negotiating the salary offer, but I really felt she was the right person for the role so I buckled up for the salary negotiation.

When I asked her how much she was looking for, she said $150,000. She wanted me to pay double what I offered! *Dammit*, I thought. There's no way I could pay that, even if I wanted to. I told her the max I could offer was $80,000, and I explained all my reasons. And she explained all the reasons she felt she was worth $150,000.

Some of those reasons included that she would be bringing in her own intellectual property to benefit the company and further developing Hello Seven IP. She talked about her proven track record for transformational coaching and her ability to train other coaches to do the same. She talked about her insider knowledge as a former client of the very programs she would be directing and improving. I couldn't argue any of those points, and I couldn't think of anyone else who would be better suited to this role. Everyone else I had considered had nowhere near her level of qualifications.

I excused myself for a moment and went upstairs to talk to my husband, Hello Seven's CFO, about it. Could I possibly raise the offer to $100,000? We talked through what that would look like and why it would be worth it. Finally, I came back downstairs and announced that I could offer her $100,000 and that was the highest I could go. Her reply was no. She couldn't commit to the role for $100,000. *Sigh.* I am an experienced attorney and skilled negotiator, but she was wiping my ass with the floor.

Several more rounds of respectful negotiation took place. She was playing hardball and for good reason—she knew the value she was bringing to the table, and so did I. After some time, we finally came to an agreement on a six-figure salary and an additional week of vacation.

Up until that point, I had never paid a salary of $100,000 or more (my company was still relatively small—the only person who made over $100,000 was me). I had also never "lost" a salary negotiation. Remember, I studied negotiation in college, and negotiation was a core part of my job as an attorney for the seven years that I practiced law.

However, my new program director presented me with facts and figures about how she would benefit my company and clients, the amount of work she would take off my plate, and the intellectual property she would add to the company's vault. As a result, I wound up paying her far more than I had initially planned.

My program director doubled her price during salary negotiation and wound up with a salary significantly higher than the initial offer.

Entrepreneurs can double their prices, like I did in my law practice all those years ago, and employees can double their salaries, like my program director did in our negotiation. The key in both situations is to recognize your skills and experience, learn how to communicate the value you provide and ask for what you want. Regardless of your current career situation, you can start earning significantly more than you currently do.

I guarantee that you have colleagues doing similar work as you who are earning a lot more simply because they were willing to ask when you were not. The fact is that most women accept whatever salary they are offered, without saying a peep. Sixty percent of women never negotiate for higher pay, never ever, not even once in their entire career.[1] If you are serious about building wealth, you must stop leaving money on the table.

CHARGE ACCORDING TO THE VALUE YOU PROVIDE

Historically, companies have set the prices for their products and services based on what it cost to produce. Businesses would look at their manufacturing costs or the costs for employees to complete the work, they would add a little bit of profit on top and that is how they would determine their price. Nowadays, entrepreneurs and employees look to what their local competitors are charging or what the labor department says is a common salary for that role in that city to determine what they should be earning for their work. Both of these methods can cause you to leave money on the table. Using value-based pricing is a more effective method of pricing that allows you to earn the true value of your work.

Value-based pricing is a method of pricing that focuses on the value received by the person enjoying the fruits of your labor, whether that be your boss or your customer. With value-based pricing, you are quantifying the results of your labor rather than your labor itself.

For example, let's say you're a copywriter and you write marketing materials for companies. If you're a fairly experienced copywriter, it is very common to charge an hourly rate of around $100.

Now, I know a woman who works as a freelance copywriter. A few years back, a company reached out to her to inquire about hiring her. They wanted her to write ten email newsletters. Each newsletter would be blasted out to the company's mailing list to promote a high-end program, and each would hopefully drum up lots of enrollments.

"How much would you charge to write ten newsletters?" the company asked.

Homegirl thinks: *I can write email newsletters in my sleep. So easy. This whole project will probably take me ten hours to complete, max.* She gives them a quote: "$1,000 please." The company jubilantly agrees!

So, this copywriter writes ten incredibly good newsletters. These aren't just your typical, boring marketing emails. Each one is like a work of art. She brings her years of expertise, creativity, and deep knowledge of the industry into the project and does a smashingly great job. She delivers the project. The company sends out these newsletters. Their subscribers go apeshit with excitement, and these newsletters immediately trigger an avalanche of sales to the tune of $300,000.

The CEO personally reaches out to homegirl, saying: "Wow, great job with those newsletters. You helped us triple our sales compared to the same program launch last year."

And that's the moment when homegirl realizes, *Damn. I think I seriously undercharged.*

To recap: This company paid her $1,000 to provide writing services that directly helped them earn $300,000. Which means, the work she did was worth a whole lot more than $1,000.

She could have easily charged $3,000, $5,000, or even $10,000 for the exact same project, and even at $10,000, it still would've been an excellent investment for the client.

To rub salt in the wound, that very same week, this copywriter was chatting with a fellow writer (who offers similar services and has around the same experience level) and learned this other writer has a $10,000 minimum—starting point—for any project. Period. For $1,000, she won't even get out of bed. This further underscored the grim truth: My colleague had been wildly undercharging for years, leaving (literally) hundreds of thousands of potential earnings on the table. Why? Because she didn't know any better. She didn't know she could ask for more. And because she was only considering the amount of time she put in ("How many hours will this take me to do?") rather than considering the value she's providing ("How will my client's/boss's life improve once I do this work for them?").

I bet you're making the exact same mistake.

Now let's get specific about *hourly-based pricing* versus *value-based pricing*, and break down the difference between these two approaches.

To harken back to the story I just told, say you're a copywriter (or graphic designer, brand strategist, attorney, dog behavioral expert, or whatever you do) and you're doing hourly-based pricing. You charge $100 an hour. A client wants to hire you for a particular project, and you estimate a project will take you ten hours. So you charge $1,000.

A few years roll by. You're even more experienced now. You're sharper and more efficient than ever. A project that used to take you ten hours to complete now takes you just five hours. You've become a zippy lightning bolt! But you're still charging $100 an hour. This means, now you earn $500 for doing a project that, a few years ago, would have generated $1,000. Do you see why this is crazy-town?!

When you charge by the hour, as you become more efficient at your craft, you are literally punished for efficiency. The swifter you work, the less you earn.

With value-based pricing, your efficiency and expertise makes you richer, not poorer. A copywriter doing value-based pricing thinks about the transformation she's delivering, not the time she's spending. She trusts that the client doesn't particularly care if it takes her ten hours to complete the project or five hours or twenty hours or seventeen minutes. The hours don't really matter that much. The client just cares about the value you provide; the results you help the client achieve. And if you help achieve $300,000 worth of results? Then your services are definitely worth $30,000. They're making a very reasonable investment in hiring you, so they can get a massive return on investment.

This is true whether you're an entrepreneur or an employee. Price according to the *value* you bring to the table, not according to the *time* it takes you to saw, nail, and construct the table.

VALUE-BASED PRICING WORKS FOR EMPLOYEES, TOO

When my program director negotiated her salary, she didn't share a bunch of statistics with me about what program directors at other companies make or what the Department of Labor says program directors make. None of that data would have helped her, since all my competitors that I have talked to pay their program directors less than half of what I pay mine. And according to the Department of Labor, program directors make an average salary of $63,000.

Instead, my program director focused on the value of her labor to my company. She showed me the amount of work she was directly taking off of my plate (saving me a minimum of twenty-plus hours per week, time I could use to make more money for the company). She showed me the value of her coaching to our clients and the results we could achieve for our clients with her labor. She also presented the value of the intellectual property she would produce that would make the company good money.

As the owner of my company, when I looked at the value of what she was providing, I could clearly see that paying her the salary she wanted would translate into an increase in revenue for my business. That year, we went on to make $2 million in revenue (that is $1 million more than we earned the year before). Was my new program director the only reason we made that money? No, but she definitely played a significant role in increasing the company's overall revenue. Needless to say, I am happy with the investment I made in her salary.

Are you ready to stop leaving money on the table? Good. Keep reading.

HOW TO RAISE YOUR PRICE

I am thrilled that you are ready to raise your price. The process is really simple: Take your current price (whether it's your hourly rate, your current flat fees, the cost of your product or your salary), multiply it by two, and there you have your new price.

That's right, Boo. It's time to double your rate.

Yes, I'm serious.

The next time someone emails you to inquire about your services, let them know the new price and see what happens. If you are an employee, do the math on how your role is delivering on the desired outcomes of your organization and then negotiate for higher pay or set up a side hustle using your natural talents to earn double what you are currently making. Another option is to start looking for a role where you can get paid significantly more.

I have worked with thousands of women entrepreneurs over the last ten years, and almost all of them were severely undercharging. As women, our imposter syndrome is so severe that it causes us to work for pennies in comparison to the amount of money for which men are willing to work. This is part of the reason women hold a majority of low-wage jobs, whereas men hold a disproportionate number of high-wage jobs. Because we have been historically and systemically undervalued as a collective, and we have internalized the belief that our work is less valuable. In order to correct this economic travesty, we must significantly raise our prices to even begin to come close to charging what our work is actually worth.

Sis, you may be afraid that when you double your prices, your clients will reject you. In my years of watching clients raise their prices, I've seen the opposite. When you value your work more, your best clients will cheer you on. When you charge more, you'll attract people who are delightful to serve.

For example, my client Jane Jones is an editor and coach for academic writers. She decided to take my advice and double her prices for her one-on-one services. After she raised her rates, she found that her clients were way more invested in the work they were doing together. Suddenly clients stopped rescheduling or canceling meetings and were much more willing to take action on her advice.

Overall, her clients respected her and respected the work a lot more when Jane raised her prices. In Jane's words, her clients are "generally delightful" now that she has raised her rates.

Another client, Megan Hale, a therapist and financial coach who teaches women entrepreneurs how to manage their business income and earn more, was surprised by the response to her raised rates. Rather than hate mail or canceled contracts, Megan found that her clients actually cheered her on when she raised her monthly retainer from $350 to $1,550. She received emails from clients who said how happy they were to see her valuing her work even if they could no longer afford her services. Her higher price points bought her more time and resources to market her services, and she has caught the eye of clients who were previously skeptical about working with her because her prices were lower than they expected.

And a life coach client of mine found that her retreats actually filled up faster when she tripled the price. She thought no one would sign up for her previously popular retreats when her rates went up. She was really nervous about announcing her new prices. Instead, the opposite happened. Customers recognized the value and signed up even faster than they had in the past.

WHEN YOU DOUBLE YOUR PRICES, EVERYONE WINS

I assert: When you double your prices (as an entrepreneur) or double your salary (as an employee), everyone wins.

You win. Your clients (or boss/colleagues) win. Your family wins. Your community wins. Society wins. And here's why.

When you're earning double:
- You can afford to hire help around the house: cleaning, grocery delivery, pet care, a personal assistant to run errands, a pool boy to feed you chilled grapes and fan you with coconut fronds (*haha*), or all the above. This means more peace, more joy, and more free time for you. Free time you can spend reading stories to your kids or enjoying a sexy date night with your partner. Your family wins.

- You can afford to hire a paid intern, assistant, and other team members to support you at work. *Boom.* You've become a job creator. You're providing income to another household and changing someone's life. Your employee wins. (And so does your employee's family.)
- You can afford to invest in your mental and physical health at an even higher level. Peloton bike. Yoga membership. Therapy. High-quality organic food for yourself and your family. You have more energy and vitality to do wonderful things in the world. Everybody wins.
- You can treat your clients to the VIP experience, send them snazzy gifts in the mail, and bring your absolute best self to every meeting and project. Instead of showing up to that Zoom room bedraggled, burned out, and exhausted, you show up refreshed and brimming with genius ideas. Your client wins. They're getting the best version of you when they pay more.
- You can become a badass philanthropist and write massive checks. You can do other exciting things with your money, too, like invest in a local small business to help it grow, buy a house for your mom, upgrade to a new car with all the latest safety features, or start a college tuition fund that's so phat, even your grandkids can get an excellent education and graduate debt-free. Damn. Your whole community wins.
- You become a role model and inspiration for fellow women and girls. A teenage girl finds out you're earning $1 million per year and thinks, *Damn. For real? Maybe that's possible for me, too.* Another life transformed because of your wealth. You are helping to change outdated perceptions and reestablish what women's work is worth in our society. Women win. Girls win. Because of you.

Bottom line: When women earn more, all society benefits immensely. The research proves it. I've seen it and felt it. I'm sure you have, too. Instead of just admiring women who earn millions and change the world, become one.

TAKE OUT THE MIND TRASH

Whenever I start talking about raising your rates, doubling your pricing, or negotiating to double your salary as an employee, women freak out. Tons of objections rise to the surface like scum floating on the surface of a pond. As you know, I call these *Broke Ass Thoughts*, also known as *mind trash*.

Well, did you just hear that truck pull up outside? *Beep beep?* Oh, yes. It's garbage day! It's time to take out the mind trash, and I'm your sanitation worker.

Here are some objections you might be thinking, and my response.

"But I can't raise my pricing to $XXX. Because nobody in my industry charges that much! That's just not how it's done."

Oh, nobody in your industry charges that much? Good. That means you're going to stand out.

Do you want to be the bargain bin service provider, or the crème de la crème? I don't know about you, but I want to be Tiffany's, not Bingo Bob's Big Discount Gem Emporium. Charge top dollar and offer high-end services (and high-end results) to match.

"I don't want to charge more, because I don't want to be inaccessible to the people who need me most."

Buckle up, because I have a lot to say on this one.

First, not everyone's going to be able to afford you, and that's okay. In fact, it's more than okay, it's desired. Instead, charge what you're worth. Make tons of money. And then, if you want to serve humanity through charitable giving, great! Get after it! This is a far more effective way to have a positive impact than offering your services for less than what they are worth.

Now that you've become a millionaire, you can start a foundation and donate huge sums—instead of just $20 here and there. If you're genuinely concerned with "helping the people who need you most," then the best way to do this is to become wealthy. When you're signing the check, you have a say in where the money goes, so if you want to make meaningful change in people's lives, money helps a lot.

One of my besties started a college scholarship fund for young women entrepreneurs. She also donated thousands to provide free childcare to single working moms during the COVID-19 pandemic, helping essential-worker moms go to work and earn a living while schools were shut down, knowing their kids were in good hands. My friend is able to do amazing things and help people who really need help, because she has built wealth. It's tough to help on that level when you're broke.

Instead of trying to be cheap and accessible to all, focus on being wealthy and influential to many. You will make a greater impact this way.

Last, if you insist on offering your genius to humanity for free? Cool. Start a podcast. Do a YouTube show. Write a blog. There are plenty of ways to serve a large audience—even the people who can't afford to pay you right this moment. But do it smart. Spend an hour recording your weekly podcast so that thousands can listen and get inspired (smart!) instead of spending twenty hours giving away your services to people for bargain basement pricing, because you're too nervous to ask for more (dumb).

"But how can I do value-based pricing when I'm not really sure what kind of value I am providing—or when the value I provide is difficult to measure? Previously you gave the example of a copywriter. If you're a copywriter, and you write a marketing newsletter, and this newsletter helps a client to make $300,000 in sales, then there's a direct connection between 'the work you do' and 'a huge result.' Cool cool cool. But what if that's not the case for me? I'm not a writer. I do something else. In my line of work, it's difficult to measure the 'value' my client (or boss) is getting because it's not measured in dollars. It's not obvious like that. I'm confused."

Helping a client (or boss) make more money is great, but that's not the only form of value you can provide in this world.

Do you help your clients (or boss) save tons of precious time? Do you make their life tremendously easier and prevent all kinds of annoyances and headaches? That's highly valuable. That's worth a lot.

Do you help your clients keep their marriages intact and avoid divorce court? Priceless. Do you help your clients finally stop emotional overeating and break the ugly pattern of bingeing and starving, which transforms their whole life? That's major.

Do you help your clients stop drinking alcohol excessively? Start a daily yoga practice that brings peace into their lives? Heal from childhood trauma? Or finally have the uncluttered, beautiful, Insta-worthy home of their dreams? All these outcomes are highly valuable.

Consider, "If someone hires me, and we work together, what is the highest possible outcome? What is the best that could happen?" Price according to the highest possible outcome (a thriving marriage, a peaceful relationship with food, a joyful yoga practice, and a gorgeous home), not the lowest possible outcome.

Look at your track record. Gather the receipts. Ask yourself, "Based on what I've observed from my last ten clients/employers/projects/and so on, what is the highest possible outcome? What is the big, exciting result that is not just possible, but highly probable? Highly likely to happen?" Whatever it is, that's what should determine your pricing.

> *"I don't want to charge more, because I'm nervous about clients being angry, feeling like they didn't get their money's worth."*

In the last year, how many times has a client angrily demanded a refund? One time? Zero? I'm guessing not many. This will not change when you increase your fees.

In the unlikely event that a client is dissatisfied with what you've provided, there are ways to handle this gracefully. You can give them a partial or full refund if the situation truly calls for it. You can invite them to book more time with you, at no charge, giving you a chance to make things right. You can meet with them to figure out where things went wrong, and fix it. A client feeling "dissatisfied" is not the end of the world. It happens. And it happens at every price point. It can be addressed. It won't kill you.

I've had a few situations in the past where a client wasn't happy, so I took some time to figure out why. I listened to their grievances. I fixed the situation. Then the client was so thrilled that she became one of my biggest supporters and referred even more clients to me! You can transform disappointment into a win-win victory.

"But nobody will pay that much."

Oh, but they will.

There are people who pay $1,000 to hire professional actors to cry dramatically at funerals. Fact.

There are people who pay $400 an hour to communicate and "learn many things" (according to one site) about their pets via a psychic pet medium.

There are people who pay $4,000 for beautiful human hair for hair weaves and wigs.

NASA will pay you $5,000 per month to participate in a "bed rest study," where you lie down and do nothing, to help gather data about the effects of zero gravity space travel on the human body.

I once paid a lovely woman $275 to take a forty-five-minute plane flight and retrieve a laptop that I'd accidentally left at another airport. She got paid a nice lil' chunk to sit on a plane and watch a Netflix show. And I was delighted to pay! Because she saved me an entire afternoon of schlepping and hassle and stress. Totally worth it.

Whatever products or services you offer, trust and believe, there are people out there who are willing and able to pay, and who will do so joyfully. There is a market for e v e r y t h i n g.

"But people already think I'm too expensive."

Oh, well, too bad for them! Perhaps your pricing will inspire them to hustle and gather the funds they need to hire you.

Hiring you can become an exciting, aspirational goal to work toward. They'll pin a photo of you to their vision board, and think, "One day, I'm gonna hire her! *Yay!*"

Instead of worrying about offending other people with your pricing, start worrying about your own broke-ass pockets. Worry about the fact that you don't have adequate healthcare or funds to retire. Worry about the stress you are under trying to make ends meet. Worry about the legacy you want to leave behind. In other words, worry about things you can actually control, and let go of other people's opinions.

"But what if I raise my prices and then something bad happens? Like villagers come after me with flaming pitchforks! Or I get hate mail! Or all my clients fire me!"

How about you just try it and see what happens?

None of the horrifying things you fear will actually happen. Most likely, everything will be fine. More than fine. Better than ever.

It's time to get paid more, because this is a very good thing for you, your family, and the entire world. When you flourish into wealthy badassery, all humanity benefits.

YOU WANT TO CHANGE THE WORLD? THEN YOU NEED A WHOLE LOTTA CHANGE

Beyoncé is perhaps the best living example of a self-made millionaire who uses her extreme wealth to do extremely great things.

She has donated millions to charitable organizations and has literally bailed out entire cities after natural disasters. When the US government fumbles and doesn't act fast enough, Queen Bey steps in to make things right.

After Hurricane Katrina, Bey launched The Survivor Foundation to provide housing for hurricane victims in Houston, Bey's beloved hometown.[2] Hundreds of distraught, traumatized families and children had a safe roof over their head instead of living in the streets. All thanks to Beyoncé.

A few years later, she came across a rehabilitation center for recovering drug addicts called Phoenix House. She was so moved by the center's mission, she decided to send them a cool $4 million to support the cause. This enabled Phoenix House to launch a cosmetology school so that residents could learn new career skills and reenter the workforce after getting sober. Beyoncé wanted to provide residents with "something that would teach them skills that would give them hope even after Phoenix House." [3]

Can you imagine sitting down and casually writing a check for $4 million? Can you imagine changing (or even saving) thousands of lives because of the money you can provide? Can you imagine providing that level of support and possibility to countless human beings? Beyoncé isn't just imagining. She's actually doing it. How? Because she's rich as fuck.

I could fill an entire book with a list of Beyoncé's philanthropic work—the various foundations she has started, the millions she's given to innumerable causes, the checks she has mailed to the families of victims of police brutality to help with legal fees or college tuition. She is able to provide resources to people who've been neglected, overlooked, and abused, and she can do it on a massive scale. *Because she has massive amounts of money.*

Look, I'm not saying you can't change the world if you're broke. Sure you can. You can change the world with a smile! You can change the world with a song! You can change the world with a sign and a protest (I've watched my friends do it). And that's beautiful. But you can also change the world on an entirely different scale—restore a devastated city, build an entire school, cure a disease, give thousands a chance at a better life—if you've got lots of money to fund the good work you want to do.

Will Smith says, "Money and success don't change people; they merely amplify what is already there." Beyoncé has always been a goddess of generosity. Being wealthy simply enables Bey to be even more generous. It amplifies the goodness that's already within her. And money will do the same thing for you.

Your wealthiest self is your most authentic self—the highest expression of all you can be Why? Because when you no longer are worrying about earning a living, you can use your skills and abilities to focus on what matters most to you.

Chrissy Teigen and husband, John Legend, hired food trucks to provide free meals to hundreds of Black Lives Matter protestors.[4] And donated $100,000 to fight sex trafficking. Taylor Swift donated fourteen thousand children's books to the Nashville Public Library.

Sara Blakely, founder of Spanx (net worth: $1.1 billion) created the Sara Blakely Foundation, dedicated to helping women "globally and locally through education and entrepreneurship." She has already given millions away and has pledged to donate at least half of her wealth to philanthropic causes.

These are the kinds of miracles you can create for humanity when you've got serious money. Once you are actually making good money—no longer burned out, underpaid, and overworked—you can do even more good for the world.

MAKING MONEY AND MAKING THE WORLD A BETTER PLACE ARE NOT MUTUALLY EXCLUSIVE

You don't have to choose. You can have it all. When I started law school, my goal was to work for a nonprofit or for the government. I wanted to advocate for people who were marginalized and didn't have the resources to stand up to powerful forces. Then I started looking at how much student-loan debt I was facing upon graduation. My older sister and other family members sat me down and insisted that I let go of my nonprofit plan. Right before graduation, the financial aid office at my law school sat me down and showed me my total amount of student-loan debt. I was filled with shame about borrowing so much money.

Between the peer pressure from family members and the six figures in student-loan debt I was facing, I decided to give up on my dream of helping people for the sake of making money. So I proceeded to fly all around the country interviewing for jobs I didn't want. I wound up being offered an associate attorney position at a firm that represented Big Oil companies. That wasn't exactly what I had in mind when I thought of helping people. In the end, I turned down that position and wound up building my own business.

Now I make millions of dollars each year and help thousands of women increase their earning potential. As a business owner, I can support activism with my dollars in a way that I never could have if I wasn't making millions. And I am able to bring attention to issues that matter to me because I have a large audience. I invest in #BlackLivesMatter, Mother's Day bailouts, disaster relief, human rights organizations, and friends and family members' dreams every single year.

And I am not the only one. My client, Amanda Brinkman, is the founder of the Shrill Society. She created the viral Nasty Woman T-shirt with the red heart. Many celebrities wore the T-shirt in support of Hillary Clinton's presidential candidacy after Donald Trump called her a "nasty woman" during a presidential debate. Amanda's company is a multimillion-dollar business that has its own warehouse and continues to earn millions every year.

Perhaps more important, Amanda's company has donated more than $100,000 to Planned Parenthood, and also donates significant sums to several other human rights organizations like the ACLU, She Should Run, Houston Food Bank, and more. In addition to supporting human rights organizations, Amanda's company only sells products created by women with materials sourced ethically and sustainably. Amanda is making millions and making a difference.

Another example is my friend, Rachel Cargle. She is an activist who teaches white women how to be truly intersectional feminists. She makes $10,000 or more for every lecture that she gives around the country. She has received a great deal of positive media attention. She's making hundreds of thousands of dollars every year and making the world a better place at the same time. I personally am so glad she is doing the work that she is doing.

Rachel has also created a nonprofit with some of her earnings called The Loveland Foundation. Through this foundation, she raised more than $1 million to cover the cost of therapy for hundreds of Black women and girls.

This is what women do when they make bank:
they make the world a better place.

Research shows that "women's economic participation and their ownership of financial assets speeds up development, helps overcome poverty, reduces inequalities and improves children's nutrition, health, and school attendance."[5] And "working women invest 90 percent of their income back into their families and communities, compared with only 35 percent for men."[6] That's why when NGOs (nongovernmental organizations whose purpose typically addresses a social or political issue) want to rebuild communities ravaged by war or natural disasters, one of the first things they do is invest in women in the community in the form of microloans and other economic aid. Give women economic assets, and they will change the world.

A few years ago, my mom lost her job. She was really struggling to find another job and felt like she was facing age discrimination as she was over sixty. She lives in New York City, and we all know how expensive housing there can be. I was able to immediately start paying my mom's rent the moment she lost her job. I eliminated the stress she was under so she could focus on finding a job she wanted. It felt really good to support my mom and take this financial worry off her plate.

Money isn't everything, but it can solve a whole lot of problems—your own, your family's, and the world's.

However, I want to be clear. I don't want you to become wealthy just so you can give every single penny away and wind up financially and emotionally bankrupt. Because I know some of y'all reading this are probably thinking something along those lines. *Stop.*

It is one thing to be a powerful philanthropist. That's dope. It is another thing to give excessively—to give away so much of your time, energy, and money that you wind up depleted. That's a Broke Ass Decision.

YOU ARE ALREADY GIVING
(MORE THAN) ENOUGH

Research shows that women give more than men across the board—at home, at work, and even when it comes to philanthropy.

The American Time Use Study (released annually by the US Labor Department) shows that working women "put in longer hours on the job, spent more time caring for their children, and did more work around the house" than in previous years. "They also spent less time relaxing or socializing—and less time sleeping."[7] Those quotes come from the *Wall Street Journal.*

We're giving more than ever and spreading ourselves thinner than ever in every realm of life.

At home, in most American households (definitely not mine! LOL), women do significantly more household/domestic chores than men: cooking, cleaning, shopping, keeping the home from crumbling into smithereens. How much more? Some reports indicate two hours more daily.[8] This happens even in households where the woman is the breadwinner.

In terms of charitable giving, it's the same story. We give more than our male counterparts. One study finds that 54 percent of women have given to charity in the past year compared to just 40 percent of men.[9]

Women don't just donate to charity more often than men. We also donate a truckload more money.

Women aged fifty-six to seventy-six years (the baby boomer era) give 89 percent more to charity than men their same age. What the hell are these boomer men doing with their funds, dare I ask? Buying another fishing rod, Steve?

Women are also more likely to support charitable causes aimed at helping fellow women and girls.[10] We lift our sisters higher with our words, actions, and dollars, too.

I want you to become fabulously wealthy so that you can do great things with your money. Donating to charity can, and should, be one of those great things that you do.

At the same time, I don't want you to remain trapped in a prison of excessive generosity.

I want you to understand that you are already giving enough.

You're already giving enough to your household, your boss, your spouse, your kids, your community, your church, and society. You're already giving more than Steve, Greg, and Mark combined. You're already giving more than your fair share, and doing it with less.

Right now, with your current income level, I can almost 100 percent guarantee that you are already giving enough. More than enough. You don't need to become a nonstop giving machine of time and money in order to be a good woman. You already are.

Are tears splashing down upon this book right now, as you recognize how much you've already given, and how little you've acknowledged your own generosity? Good. Keep those tears flowing, because we're going even deeper.

I want you to make a list of twenty-five ways that you are already giving back.

In a typical month, what kinds of support (financial, emotional, and otherwise) do you give to your significant other and to your kids, parents, aunties and extended family, neighbors, friends, colleagues, clients, your religious or spiritual group, young people you mentor, professional connections, your domestic team, your kids' school, charities, boards, volunteer commitments, and complete strangers on the street?

Make a list.

The money you donate to good causes. The coffee dates with people who want to pick your brain and get advice. The late-night phone call with a friend who's grieving a breakup. The extra $5 you stuff into your favorite barista's tip jar. Those two hours you spend working on Sunday so that your boss can look like a genius during that Monday morning presentation. You already give, and give, and give, in so many ways, and to so many people. You are doing enough. Say it with me, "I am doing enough!"

If you want to give even more, okay. That's your prerogative. But acknowledge, right now, that you already give more than enough. Let enough be enough.

If you feel called to serve humanity in an even bigger way, I urge you to focus on becoming a millionaire, because then you can give a lot more without depleting yourself. Those people at the homeless shelter that you want to help, the ones who are there because they were unable to pay rent and were thus evicted, would probably rather you create a job for them than serve them dinner.

Money you can always replenish. Time you cannot.

CHAPTER SUMMARY

- Due to imposter syndrome and systemic racism and misogyny, you are likely way undercharging for your labor. You can and should raise your prices significantly, whether you are an entrepreneur or an employee.
- Use value-based pricing, rather than hourly or comparison pricing, to determine the true value of your work.
- Double your prices to get your wages to a reasonable value. Do not let limiting beliefs (aka Broke Ass Thoughts) prevent you from doubling your prices.
- Studies show that when women earn more, the world improves. Women contribute economically to our greater society at higher rates than men. You can have a much larger impact on the world when you are earning more.
- You are generous enough. Stop giving away your time, effort, and labor and start building real wealth.

CHAPTER 9

MILLION DOLLAR TEAM

"Alone we can do so little; together we can do so much."

—HELEN KELLER[1]

Now that you've got your prices right, it's time to live that A-list life.

No more schlepping, stressing, and dealing with messes. You are ready to value your time on a whole 'nuvha level and live your life like a celeb.

In December 2019, America's favorite (or least favorite, depends on whom you ask) tweetalicious celebrity, Chrissy Teigen, decided to bless the people by dishing on how she and hubby, John Legend, live that good home life.[2] Chrissy shared that they have a house manager who works at their home daily to handle day-to-day business, manage household staff, plan personal events for the family, and really manage all the inconveniences that come up in daily life. Thanks to this support, Chrissy can spend time working on her Cravings website, modeling, and hosting career as well as time with her wee ones.

Chrissy also shared that they have an accountant who receives their mail, pays bills, and monitors income and spending. She and John have four nannies who rotate to assist with caring for their kids. When they travel, they use a private terminal and bring their various staff members, including their hair and makeup stylists.

For celebrities and other high-net-worth individuals, it is not uncommon to have a household staff that makes life more convenient. There are staffing agencies, many of them located in Los Angeles, specifically designed to staff the households of A-listers. A colleague of mine used to be a house manager for several A-list celebrities and shared some of the details of how they run their homes.

Typically at the top of the hierarchy is an estate manager (if there are multiple homes) or a house manager (if there is one home) who is in charge of everything. They are not unlike the general manager of a luxury hotel, and their pay can be anywhere from $100,000 to $300,000 annually. Additional typical staff members include private chefs ($70,000 to $200,000), housekeepers ($65,000 to $100,000; one for every 4,000 square feet), nannies ($65,000 to $185,000), butlers ($85,000 to $125,000), drivers ($80,000 to $100,000) and personal assistants ($65,000 to $150,000). A household staff of this size can easily cost $500,000 per year or more. Each celebrity household is a miniature economy.

Each member of the household is a crucial piece of the puzzle that allows wealthy individuals to generate significant income. Having a trusted team of people who have your back when you are off filming a movie, recording an album, or negotiating a deal means that high-net-worth individuals have time to focus on their careers and not be distracted by the various daily tasks that take up time and energy.

It makes sense to have a domestic staff when your net worth is $75 million (the reported net worth of Chrissy Teigen and John Legend, as of this writing), but what about the rest of us schmoes? Well, as I'm about to elucidate, even if you don't have Teigen-Legend-level wealth (yet!) you can—and should—have a household staff supporting you. Let's talk about why and, most important, how to make it happen ASAP.

FEELING JEALOUS?

Remember in chapter 6 we talked about how jealousy points you to the things you want for yourself. And those desires are valid and possible to attain. So often we count ourselves out, saying we could never have the thing we want when that's only true because we've decided we can't have it. Decide that you can have it.

Explore exactly what is it that you would like some support with? What would make a world of difference in your everyday life? What would make you feel more held so that you can go out there and make bank? What things would you really like to get off your plate?

Once you have identified what those feelings of jealousy are pointing you toward, brainstorm ten ways you could satisfy those desires. (And I have lots of ideas for you below.)

Everything you want is within reach if you are willing to work for it.

WHAT'S FOR DINNER?

My husband and I used to argue a lot.

The main source of our arguments? Dinner.

After a day full of teaching classes, calls with clients, meetings with my team and writing and recording new content, I was beat by 5:00 p.m. and ready for my jammies. All I wanted to do was curl up on the couch surrounded by my babies and watch an episode of *Too Cute* (a show about newborn kittens and puppies. It's basically free therapy—we're obsessed). But unfortunately these kids had to eat.

My husband would basically turn into a pumpkin at 6:00 p.m. and be mentally checked out. And for good reason. He works part-time in our business as the chief financial officer. He makes sure all the bills are paid, the books are processed, and the taxes are managed. He also handles payroll and human resources for our team. When he wasn't working, he would handle the domestic tasks around the house. Making breakfast for the family, taking the kids to school, dropping our dog, Stone, off at the groomers, running errands, ordering household supplies, grocery shopping, and so on.

So, every night we would look at each other, completely spent, and wonder "Who the hell is gonna feed these kids?!" Some nights, he would grill some chicken and take care of it. Some nights, I'd have a plan for leftover ziti and get it in the oven early. Most nights we would either a) order takeout (pizza, Chinese, Thai, or burgers on rotation) or b) fight about who was making dinner. On the nights I "lost," I wound up passive aggressively slamming every drawer, pot, and utensil as I angrily prepped a meal—not my proudest moments.

My husband and I had done a good job up until that point of outsourcing household help. We used a laundry drop-off service; had a personal assistant to run errands, plan birthday parties, and handle returns and shipments; we had a cleaning service come in every other Friday; and we used regular babysitters so we could have date nights. We thought we were nailing it, but after our youngest was born we officially reached capacity.

I started calculating our food budget and realized we were spending an insane amount of money on takeout every week. I wanted my children to eat more vegetables, and I wanted to stop arguing with my husband, so I got the crazy idea of hiring a chef. A few of my entrepreneur friends had done it. I knew it was expensive and pretty much out of my budget, but I had to get food stress off our plates. I figured I would find a way to make a little more money so I could cover the cost of the chef.

I put an ad on Craigslist and waited for applicants to come pouring in. I only got four applicants. One of them was an experienced chef from Brazil. She was a former restaurateur who had just closed her business due to the immense stress of running a fine dining restaurant. She was looking for something much more relaxed. We hit it off right away and after doing a test run, we hired her.

When I say our chef changed my life, I am not exaggerating. Suddenly delicious healthy meals were happening every night. She made lunches and snacks and cake for birthdays as well. She handled Thanksgiving and prepared an incredible meal for a dinner party I hosted for friends. She also handled meal prep for my company retreats. She's at our house Monday through Friday and is now a member of our family. She loves to cook, and we love to eat her food. It's a win-win.

My business team noticed a marked difference after we hired our chef. I was less stressed and waltzed around with an inner calm. I was able to focus and wasn't exhausted all the time (even though I still had a toddler in my house). As a result, I made more money, which I used to expand the employee benefits my company offers, create more jobs, serve more clients, afford the things that my family needs and wants (like a nice vacation), and give more back to my community. And, best of all, my husband and I stopped arguing.

Hiring a chef may seem indulgent or like something only celebrities do, but the fact is building a team around you is not only an essential step to building wealth, it is an essential element of happiness in the modern world.

And once you find out how much it costs to hire a chef, a gardener, a driver, or whatever would make your life easier, you're often surprised to discover that it's not as astronomically expensive as you might have thought. Celeb-level help is within reach. And once you get a taste, you realize, "This is absolutely worth every penny."

FINANCIALLY RICH BUT EMOTIONALLY BROKE? NO THANKS.

Many people who increase their incomes are working eighty-hour weeks and constantly stressed and strapped for time. They don't tend to have healthy lifestyles or good relationships with their loved ones. This leads to an increase in things like divorce, stress-related health problems, and mental health concerns. The constant grind to make money doesn't increase happiness, it diminishes it.

I saw early on as a new lawyer how constantly overworked most lawyers were. This is why lawyers have very high rates of substance abuse, depression, and, sadly, suicide. I refused to go down that path. I had young children almost immediately after graduating from law school, so I had to figure out a way to make money that didn't require me to work insane hours and severely limit my quality time with my husband and children.

The solution, for me, has never been to make as much money as I can, no matter what it takes. Rather, I have always been interested in finding creative ways to increase my income without increasing my work hours.

CAN MONEY BUY HAPPINESS?
TURNS OUT, IT CAN

A recent study led by researchers from Harvard concluded that if you want to be happier, spend your money on buying time.[3] The study looked at 6,300 households from four countries—the United States, Canada, Denmark, and the Netherlands—and found that time famine is a real drag on well-being.

In recent decades, incomes have risen in many countries from Germany to Korea to the United States. With that increase in income has come greater time scarcity and time stress, which lead to reduced happiness, increased anxiety, rising rates of obesity, and insomnia. Some evidence suggests that wealthier people spend more time engaging in stressful activities, such as commuting to work. Other research shows that leading people to feel that their time is economically valuable induces them to feel that they do not have enough of it. Wealthier people may also have more professional opportunities, which can result in time scarcity if not managed appropriately. Regardless of the reason, the solution to time scarcity is buying back your time by hiring help.

Working adults in the countries studied reported greater happiness after spending money on a time-saving purchase rather than on a material purchase. The households studied spanned lower- to upper-middle class and found that people benefited from buying time regardless of where they fell on the income spectrum.

In conclusion, you know the classic question, "Can money buy happiness?" Well, the Harvard research proves, if you're using your money to buy domestic help and clear chores off your plate (aka "buying back your time") then, yes! Money does buy happiness.

So, if hiring help is the key to happiness, why aren't more of us doing it?

I work with many high-earning women who make anywhere from $200,000 to more than $1 million per year. They are incredibly smart and savvy, and yet they lose their minds when I suggest they stop doing their own laundry and running their own errands. They can't wrap their minds around the idea of asking someone else to do things that they can do for themselves.

It's not just my clients who are uncomfortable with outsourcing. When researchers surveyed eight hundred Dutch millionaires who had no issues with being able to afford outsourcing, only a slight majority of them said they spent money on timesaving tasks.[4] And when they asked ninety-eight working adults in Canada how they would spend an extra $40, only 2 percent said they would steer money toward time-saving services.[5]

The idea of a Protestant work ethic that emphasizes hard work, discipline, and frugality may be at play. From my working-class parents, I learned that work was always hard and making money was hard. With that kind of thinking drilled into my head, I used to think that I should spend my time making money and never even considered the idea of spending my money to make time. That is, until I became a time-starved working mom.

Women are more miserable than ever, and being time-starved is the culprit.

Women's life satisfaction has gone down in recent decades and I believe it is due to the "second shift" discussed in chapter 4. Our society does a good job of making women feel obligated to not only work a full-time job but to also complete all or most domestic work themselves when they get home.

Even Beyoncé struggles with work-life balance stress as she shared in *Elle* magazine. She states: "Many of us grew up seeing our parents act as if they were superheroes. Most women have been conditioned to ignore symptoms and just 'tough it out' and focus on taking care of everyone else before themselves. I am no longer one of those people."[6] Me neither, Bey.

Committing to hiring help and letting go of the obligation to do everything yourself will liberate you, make you happier, and, incidentally, increase your income.

MY TEAM OF HOUSEHOLD HELP

I'm not on Chrissy Teigen or Beyoncé's level (yet) but it does take a village to make my business and home life run. Here's who's on my team:

Nanny: I have four children (one bonus child who is now an adult and three children under ten years old). My husband was a stay-at-home dad for six years until he started working in the business. When my youngest child arrived a few years ago, we decided to hire a full-time nanny, which cost us $50,000 in annual salary plus payroll taxes and benefits like health insurance and two weeks of paid time off. Over a year-and-a-half period, we went through four different nannies, each of whom was with us for several months. They just weren't a good fit, didn't want to do the things I asked them to, were unreliable, or, in one case, wound up moving out of state to follow a boyfriend. It was a frustrating process.

Eventually, we got lucky, and my mother-in-law, whom I adore, moved in with us and became the children's full-time caretaker. Thank God! At some point in the future, if Grandma is no longer willing to care for the kids (she's got a busy social life, you know), then we will search for a nanny again using a placement agency to expedite the interview process.

Cleaning: We have a team of cleaners led by an amazing man named Victor. Victor and his wife run a small cleaning company, and their team comes to our house every two weeks to do a deep clean. Victor will also do extra cleaning for us before holidays and when we have events. We have a pretty big house, and we pay Victor $300 every two weeks for cleaning.

Chef/House Manager: I've already told you all about our incredible chef. She used to come to our house twice per week to handle cooking for the week. She did all the grocery shopping, meal planning, and bulk cooking. She organized all the meals and side dishes in the refrigerator in containers so it was easy for us to pull out a vegetable and main dish each night to feed the kids. On the days that she was here, she made us a beautiful plated lunch. We sat down as a family and have a restaurant-quality lunch together every Monday and Thursday.

Eventually, our chef offered to take on more work for us. So we added two additional days. So now, in addition to cooking, she also runs errands, does grocery shopping, handles laundry, straightens up the house, helps plan events, and organizes handymen and other people who come to our home. She is a godsend. We pay our chef/house manager $4,000 per month for four workdays per week plus the cost of payroll taxes, health insurance, and paid time off. If $4,000 a month seems wildly extravagant, consider that prior to hiring our chef, we were routinely spending $3,000 a month on takeout, delivery, and going to restaurants to feed our family of seven: Mom, Dad, four kids, and Grandma. So $4,000 is not much more—and we get higher quality meals—way more nutritious food. Plus all of the support around managing our household. Worth it.

Personal Assistant: My part-time personal assistant handles things both business and personal. She will do things like organize my office, respond to emails, handle scheduling, book travel, deal with packages and returns, help plan birthday parties and gifts for my kids, do holiday gift shopping, and really any other errands or tasks that need to be done. She will also babysit and otherwise help out with the kids when needed. She is young, organized, and reliable. I pay my personal assistant $20 per hour.

That is who is on my home team, but I also have a team of people who work in my business. They include a program director, operations director, finance director, resident coach, developer, salesperson, program assistant, operations assistant, marketing assistant, technology assistant, customer service rep, designer, copywriter, bookkeeper, accountant, and publicist. About half of these folks are full-time employees, and the other half are part-time contractors.

For each member of my team, we pay a competitive salary, provide health insurance and a retirement plan for those who work twenty-five hours per week or more, provide paid time off, and profit sharing. We are kind and respectful to all our team members. They are each an extension of our family, and we treat them as such.

Without this crew of twenty, I would not be able to operate my life and business this smoothly, and I could not generate the amount of revenue that we do. I am able to make multimillions, pay all these peeps well, and still personally earn more than $1 million annually. I am proud to be a job creator and the leader of a micro-economy. Knowing that both my family and this team of twenty depend on me keeps me motivated to be the best CEO I can be and push myself to the next level.

YOUR FIRST HIRE

Ready to start building your entourage? If not, get ready, my friend. You cannot build this empire alone. You need lots of support and a wide array of talent. As I always tell my team, we are stronger together.

But there's one little problem: You're not a millionaire yet.

Good news: That's not a problem at all! You absolutely do not have to be a millionaire to start outsourcing tasks and hiring support. You do not have to start with hiring twelve full-time staff members. You can begin with one part-time person, and I promise it will change your life.

When I begin working with a new client, one of the first things I have the client do is hire a personal assistant for just five hours per week. At $20 per hour, a part-time personal assistant will cost $100 per week or $400 per month. In exchange for that $400, the client can buy back twenty hours of time.

What could you do with twenty hours of free time every month? Take on more clients, have time for self-care, spend more quality time with your loved ones, write an op-ed and get it published, rest, sleep, have sex, or have fun. A lot of magic can happen in twenty hours.

One of my clients, Shandra, took my advice and hired a personal assistant for the first time. Shandra is a photographer, and she tends to work a lot in the evenings and weekends when weddings and other events take place. She put an ad on Craigslist for her dream personal assistant and received several great applicants and wound up hiring two personal assistants (extra credit for Shandra!).

She had one of the personal assistants handle physical tasks like taking her car to be serviced, dropping off packages, picking up equipment, mailing out cards, and straightening up her work space. The other assistant wasn't able to travel but was great at working on the computer. The second assistant would schedule appointments, respond to emails, book travel, and order household supplies.

With the forty hours per month that Shandra saved, she launched a new business coaching amateur photographers who wanted to become full-time professional photographers. She launched a You-Tube channel, created weekly videos, hosted webinars, built a Facebook Group full of eager potential clients and did multiple sales calls a week with potential clients. She also created a course for photographers and spent several hours per week running the course for her new clients.

Shandra was able to do all this while still running her own photography business, because she had the support of two personal assistants. After just two months, Shandra was making an additional $20,000 per month in income and landed herself on an episode of *Ellen*. Not bad for an investment of $800 per month.

HOW TO HIRE YOUR FIRST PERSONAL ASSISTANT

Step one: Write down the personality traits, skills, and talents of your dream personal assistant. This list will serve you well when you are deciding between your top candidates.

Step two: Draft a job description for the role.

Step three: Post the job description on Craigslist, community forums, and job boards.

Step four: Review résumés and choose the top three or four candidates to interview.

Step five: Have your top two candidates do a "test day" where you pay them to handle a few tasks for you before you commit to hiring one. This allows you to determine who is a good fit.

Step six: Make the offer to your top candidate and provide an official offer letter.

Step seven: Celebrate! You got yourself a personal assistant!

Here's a sample job description for a personal assistant that I have used in the past. Use this as a guide to craft your own job description for your dream assistant. Post it on Craigslist or another community forum and make your first hire.

PERSONAL ASSISTANT NEEDED
[THREE DAYS PER WEEK]

Busy business owner and mom of 4 looking for a great local personal assistant.

I would love to find a detail-oriented and experienced personal assistant who loves organization, enjoys hanging out with kids as well as generally helping out with whatever is needed.

Duties include:

- Scheduling personal appointments for myself and the children (doctors appts, lawyer appts, school volunteering, playdates, etc.)
- Booking travel arrangements (flights, hotel, car service, etc.)
- Managing my inbox including drafting and sending emails
- Keep my spaces organized, including office, closet, files, and so on

- Managing returns and other errands such as shopping, picking up dry cleaning, post office, and so on
- Sort mail, deliveries, and so on
- Order, wrap, and ship gifts
- Coordinate scheduling, travel, events, and so on with my nanny as well as my business team
- Packing and unpacking before/after travel
- Light cleaning when needed
- Occasional help with the kids when needed—driving them to appointments, picking them up from school, helping out with birthday parties, holding the baby while I do my makeup (LOL, but not kidding), and so on
- Occasionally travel with me on business trips

My kids are an eighteen-year-old girl, six-year-old girl, five-year-old boy, and four-month-old boy. My business is a successful and busy consulting practice with a team of ten. An ideal schedule would be 2:00–6:00 p.m., Monday, Wednesday, and Friday.

If you're always punctual, reliable, a nonsmoker, and a self-starter (plus can craft a great email), I'd love to talk to you.

Please reply to this ad (either in writing or with a quick video on your phone) with:

- your name
- what city you live in
- your phone number
- what days and times during the week you are available
- why you'd be great for this position
- what you do on the other days of the week (other jobs? parenting? school?)

Please use the word "bacon" in the subject line (to ensure you've read this post in its entirety).

Thank you!

ONCE YOU HIRE A PERSONAL ASSISTANT, THEN WHAT?

What kinds of tasks can you delegate to this new, fabulous member of your team?

Maybe you've already got a list of a hundred things you want to assign to your new PA. You are chomping at the proverbial bit and cannot wait!

Or maybe—like many of my clients—this is brand-new territory for you. You're drawing a mental blank. You're not sure where to begin. *"Uh,* I dunno. What should I delegate?"

So, what kinds of tasks can you assign to your PA?

The short answer is:

- Anything you dread. Unpleasant, boring, tedious tasks that you just don't want to do. I'm sure you can think of a few.
- Anything that drains your energy and makes you feel like a depleted, wilting sunflower, thereby diminishing your ability to earn money.
- Anything that steals your time, time you could be using to generate income or enjoy your damn life! A good question: "Is XYZ the highest and best use of my time right now? No? M'kay, then I'm going to delegate XYZ to my PA."
- Anything you suck at doing. Remember previously when I mentioned your zone of incompetence? That. You might be incompetent at reading technical manuals or assembling Ikea furniture or baking cakes. It takes you ten times longer than it should, and the end result is a disastrous 9-1-1 emergency call. Delegate that stuff, for sure.
- Anything that would make your life a little more beautiful, delightful, and joyful. It is okay to assign tasks to your PA purely because it brings more joy into your life.

Let's talk specifics. Here are twenty-five things you can delegate to your personal assistant immediately:

1. Drive around town to run errands that you don't want to do, like standing in line at the post office to mail packages, or taking your broken vacuum to the repair shop.

2. Take your vehicle to the car wash and bring it back to your home, sparkling clean and smelling like a pine forest. No more toddler-Cheerios scattered across the floor.

3. Email your family members, friends, and colleagues to find out everyone's birthday, and enter all the dates into your calendar so you never forget anyone's birthday again.

4. Shop for birthday, holiday, and anniversary gifts, wrap them cutely with a bow, and mail them out two weeks ahead so they arrive on time, and you look like the greatest, most thoughtful human to ever grace the earth.

5. Straighten up your home—make the bed, fluff the pillows, reset the coffee maker so it's ready for tomorrow morning and all you have to do is stumble out of bed, press the red button, and magic! Coffee starts brewing! A miracle of Biblical proportions.

6. Google, read reviews, and compare prices to find the best roof repair company, best lawn-mowing service, or best whatever-service-you-need, and then present you with the best option, so all you need to do is nod and say, "Approved!"

7. Do grocery shopping and basic food preparation—wash veggies, peel fruit, slice into chunks, get things prepped so you've got ready-to-snack items in the fridge.

8. Read all those emails from your kid's school about school holidays, pajama day, parent-teacher conferences, and so on, and plug important dates into your calendar.

9. Make sure the house is always stocked with essentials (toilet paper, shampoo) and with things that bring you joy ("I got more of those shortbread cookies you like, and your favorite tea, and refilled the lavender bubble bath dispenser in the bathroom") so that you feel like a queen.

10. Tackle all those things you've been meaning to do but never get around to doing, like building an earthquake emergency preparedness kit, or compiling an up-to-date list of your friends' snail-mail addresses.

11. Take your dog for a walk (or an extra/bonus walk) daily to tucker her out, so she's a calm, chillaxed pup instead of a furry hellion.

12. Drive you to an important meeting while you sit in the backseat, listen to calm, classical music on your headphones, and review your notes one last time, so you can arrive chill as a cucumber and slay that presentation.

13. Go into your bloated inbox with 8,974 unread messages, click to unsubscribe from a zillion newsletters you don't need, delete irrelevant messages, and then reply politely (on your behalf) to the scant handful that are actually important.

14. Plan the ultimate family vacation (location, accommodations, flights) and book everything, based on the preferences and budget you provide.

15. Scan invoices, receipts, contracts, and other important documents you want to keep, so that you can get rid of all those piles of paper and keep things organized and sleek, digital style.

16. Set up all your recurring bills on auto-pay so you never worry about it again.

17. Be "the person to speak to" when the pest control guy arrives at your home. Your PA can give him a tour of the home, answer questions, hand him a check, and so on, so that you can work peacefully, undisturbed, blissfully unaware that disease-ridden rodents are being captured and whisked away from the premises. *Ahh*!

18. Do a walk-through of your home, office, or business to make a list of things that could be improved. Peeling paint. Dirty windows. Pile of unsorted papers. Printer ink cartridge running low. And then handle every single thing. Upgrades all around.

19. Plan and execute a fabulous party. Menu. Decorations. Playlist. Clean up, too. So you can relax and enjoy quality time with your fam or besties, instead of scurrying around cleaning up empty beer bottles that guests have left scattered around.

20. Be a "second brain" for you. Sit down with your PA, talk through a project or plan, then ask, "What do you think—am I missing anything?" A second pair of eyes can help fill in the gaps you're not seeing.

21. Create a beautiful chore chart for your kids, with gold stars to celebrate tasks they've completed, and, let's be honest, this

chart will be 100 percent prettier than the janky-ass one you would begrudgingly create.

22. Deal with breakdowns, meltdowns, tech issues, and other annoyances. Internet not working? Power mysteriously went out? Your son's bicycle has a flat tire? PA can get on the phone, do whatever needs to be done to get it sorted out.

23. Find opportunities for you. You'd love to write an advice column for the local paper? You want to speak onstage at a conference? Win an award? Get a grant? Your PA can do the legwork and compile a list of opportunities for you: "Here are ten grants you could apply for, and the deadlines for each."

24. Hunt and find things for you. Like that one episode of WNYC's *Radiolab*, where they talk about how different cultures have words with no English equivalent, and the researcher says something brilliant at the very end, and you kinda remember the quote, but not totally, and you want to find the exact quote so you can include it in an article you're writing? Your PA can listen, find out, type the quote, and email it to you.

25. Literally anything on your to-do list that causes you to sink heavily into your chair, and go, "*Ugh*, but I don't wanna."

If you delegate these twenty-five things to your PA, the result is:

- You free up thousands of hours of your time every year.
- You clear thousands of pesky distractions out of your brain.
- You feel happier, healthier, more peaceful, way less distressed.
- You can focus on high-level pursuits, like finding dream clients, getting articles published, trademarking your ideas, launching new revenue-generating offers, and building serious wealth.

You can spend 1,000-plus hours per year dealing with household chores like laundry, or you can delegate like a mofo, buy back your time, and then use your time to exponentially increase your income and quality of life.

The choice is yours.

This really shouldn't even be a tough choice. It's a no-brainer.

You need an assistant. Five hours a week. For starters. Get a taste of what it feels like to have help, and how much it can change your life. You will never look back. And your bank account will never look the same.

DELEGATION FOR
FUTURE MILLIONAIRES

Do you want to be a martyr or do you want to be a millionaire? That is the question.

Learning to delegate is an essential step toward becoming a millionaire. Stop killing yourself for the cause and realize that the cause is better served when you utilize the talent around you. You are building your own micro-economy. You cannot do it alone, but I bet you will try.

As of 2018, 76 percent of small-business owners in the United States employ only the founder.[7] They are solopreneurs. That means the survival of these companies depends entirely on the owner. They are doing the marketing, the selling, the delivering, the financial planning, and the business modeling. They are thoroughly exhausted. Hell, I'm exhausted just from typing that sentence. If solopreneurs burn out, have a personal emergency, or even just get distracted with things like life, their company's revenue will suffer.

And suffer it does.

Those approximately 25 million companies that are run by a solopreneur with no employees generate only 4 percent of total small business income in the United States. Yes, my friend. Four. Percent. The other 96 percent of US small-business revenue comes from the 24 percent of small-business owners who have employees. And it's not just revenue numbers for solopreneurs that are depressing. The survival rate of these companies is incredibly low as well.

This is why 20 percent of new businesses fail during the first two years of being open, 45 percent during the first five years, and 65 percent during the first ten years.[8] I believe this great rate of failure has a lot to do with not having a team and, therefore, not delegating.

If you aren't delegating, you aren't leading. And you must be a leader in order to build wealth. You have to go from *doing* to *leading*.

The sooner you step into leadership, the sooner you will foster others to become leaders as well.

If delegating is something you are just starting out with, here is a hierarchy that I recommend. First, outsource household tasks. These are the domestic items that take time like cleaning, laundry, transporting kids, running errands, cooking, and so on. Your capacity to build your company will grow immensely when you reclaim mental real estate from household tasks. This is work that is incredibly important to your quality of life and well-being but is not so specialized that you have to be the one to do it.

You will feel uncomfortable when you first start relying on household help. Know that discomfort leads to growth. You are growing as a leader when you have to talk to your personal assistant about your favorite kind of milk or how you like your laundry hung instead of put in drawers. These uncomfortable conversations where you provide clear direction to those you employ are stretching your leadership muscles and getting you ready for the next level of delegation. Note: you are not an asshole for asking for what you want. You are an asshole if you ask for what you want in an asshole way.

Once you have your household running smoothly and are feeling supported, the next step is to outsource administrative tasks. Delegating things like scheduling, email, paperwork, bill paying and invoice sending, file organization, and travel arrangements go a long way in freeing up your time. When you get the necessary administrative tasks related to your work off your plate, you will have much more time to do the work that makes you money. The average professional spends 30 percent of their time on administrative tasks.[9] What could you do with 30 percent more time? Probably make 30 percent more money. Doesn't that sound delightful?

Incidentally, this is exactly why I not only hire administrative help for myself but for my team as well. When I have a really great employee who is busy (great employees are always busy—they get lots of assignments because they can be relied upon to do good work), I hire them an assistant. This increases their productivity and the bottom line for my business. My great employee feels supported and happier in her role, and we can provide a job to an assistant. Everybody wins.

If you work at a company and don't have an assistant, ask for one. You can use the evidence that you are losing 30 percent of your productivity to administrative work and the evidence that a great assistant will provide a win-win scenario for everyone involved as your argument. You will be happier in your role and therefore probably stick around longer, and your new assistant will have a job that previously didn't exist, and your employer will make more money. Win-win-win.

Okay, so let's say you've got some household help poppin', and you have an administrative assistant to help you with your work. What's next?

This is where the delegation meets the dollars, because the next thing you delegate is your income-generating tasks. If you are an interior designer with household help and an administrative assistant, the next role you need to hire for is another interior designer to begin taking the income-generating duties off your plate. This is how you expand your capacity to serve more clients and make more money without being an exhausted, burned-out solopreneur. Two interior designers can serve more clients than one interior designer.

Eventually, you might grow to having four interior designers and two administrative assistants. Now you are leading a firm with ever-increasing capacity to serve more and earn more. You are also creating jobs and expanding your micro-economy into an empire. It's a beautiful thing.

Once you are delegating on this level, you may be wondering: *What the hell do I do if I have hired all these other people to do my job?*

Great question! What you are going to do is lead. You will lead your company, you will manage your team, you will make deals and you will dream up more ways to make money and make an impact. Eventually, you might hire someone else to manage your team and lead the company. At some point, you may be an owner of the business, but not necessarily work in it every day. Then you are free to go build another business, launch a nonprofit or foundation, become an activist, or just stay home and spend quality time with your loved ones. The choice is yours.

Of course, you also have the option to continue to work in your company until you retire, if you wish. You get to do whatever you want. And therein lies the entire point of delegating: Freedom.

The sooner you start, the sooner your liberation will arrive.

OBJECTION! FREEDOM SCARES ME. CAN'T I JUST STAY BUSY, BROKE, AND TIRED?

When it comes to hiring help, many women (I would even say *most* women) have a million objections.

"No, I can't. No, that's crazy. No, I can't afford it. No way, what will people say?"

Your million objections are blocking you from earning millions. So let's address each one and burn 'em up.

"Hiring a personal assistant [or some other help, like a nanny, housecleaner, dog walker, house manager, private magician, and so on] sounds great! But I can't afford it."

Are you sure about that?

Have you actually researched to find out how much your dream situation would cost?

It might be within reach.

And, like I've emphasized, you can start small. Hire a personal assistant, five hours a week, for $20 an hour. That's $400 a month. A relatively small financial investment that will free up twenty hours of your precious time (at least!) and priceless amounts of energy. This alone will change your life.

You are telling me that you cannot rustle up $400? Bish, please. I know you can. You know you can. You've accomplished far greater feats in the past. If I told you, "You need to magically come up with $400 today so you can have brunch with Beyoncé and Lizzo," you would be like, "Be right back, gimme just one sec," and you'd be brandishing that cash within minutes! You can do this.

And if a personal assistant is truly out of reach right now, what about outsourcing some of your errands to TaskRabbit? And using a grocery delivery app like Instacart to save the time of grocery shopping? Or a meal prep service like HelloFresh? What about asking your niece to walk your dog every week for a small weekly allowance? There are lots of ways for you to get into the outsourcing game until you can afford more permanent help.

"I don't want people to hate me or think I'm a snob."

Do you hate Oprah because she has a personal chef who makes heart-shaped grilled cheese sandwiches for her and Stedman on Valentine's Day? Do you hate Michelle Obama because she has a pro stylist who chooses those oh-so-perfect dresses to create iconic style moments? I am guessing, you don't.

Maybe you feel jealous, in a good way. Maybe you feel inspired and motivated. By hiring help, you can become that same inspirational role model for other women in your life.

And if others "hate" you because you hire an assistant, that is an issue they need to work out with their therapist or pastor or both. It has 0 percent to do with you, and 100 percent to do with their own emotional issues. Bless them and wish them well on their journey of self-discovery.

Drop the shame and step into the life you want. #normalizedelegating.

"Delegating is too hard. It is easier if I just do things myself."

Sister, you must be a Greek goddess, because this right here is an outright myth! A fable! If you think it's "easier to do everything yourself," you are lying to yourself.

Delegating is a skill you can learn. It might not come naturally at first, but you can master this skill and become a delegating-ninja. Eventually it becomes so easy, it's like a game. You wake up wondering, *"Ooh*, what else could I delegate today?" Like Pringles potato chips, once you pop the top, you can't stop!

And delegating is an essential skill that all leaders must master.

Whether you are leading a social justice movement, a parent-teacher association, a growing company, or a household, you must learn to delegate the tasks that must be done. Why? Because you are a human being with finite energy that deserves free time, well-being, and rest. You also deserve hobbies, time with your loved ones, and fun. You cannot and should not try to do it all and be it all. This is a recipe for failing in your mission and misery. I doubt you want either. Be a leader and learn to delegate like a boss.

"I don't want someone in my home or rifling through my underwear/ personal items/financial documents/and so on."

Security is important, and that's why you can vet candidates, do background checks, check references, and hire someone who is completely trustworthy. You can even install cameras (as long as you disclose it to those who work for you) and whatnot if that helps you feel more secure.

But ultimately, if you want to become a millionaire, you simply need to accept that you're not going to climb this mountain alone. You need help.

If you are stubbornly committed to "being the one and only person on earth who is allowed to wash my own panties," then you will also continue being broke. Have fun with that laundry.

"I'm totally down with the idea of hiring help, but my spouse won't get it."

You can sit down with your spouse and have an exciting conversation about why you want to hire help, exactly how much it will cost, the benefits of doing this, and why this is a win-win situation for the entire household.

If you don't know how to have this conversation, see the sample script you can follow in this chapter.

If your spouse is a reasonable person who (a) wants you to be happy, well-rested, and in the mood for sex a lot more often, and (b) wants you to make millions, then they will quickly get on board.

SCRIPT FOR DISCUSSING DIVISION OF HOUSEHOLD LABOR WITH YOUR PARTNER, SPOUSE, ROOMMATES, OR WHOEVER YOU LIVE WITH

This would probably be best as a face-to-face conversation with your partner—assuming you live together and share household expenses—rather than an email or a video meeting.

EXAMPLE

Hey! I was hoping we could sit down and have a conversation about the house. I have some exciting ideas I wanted to share with you.

Let's talk tomorrow morning, after we've slept and we've got fresh brains. Cool?

[The next morning, after you've both enjoyed a good night's sleep, had your coffee, and feel revived and ready for the day . . .]

Okay, so I did a really interesting time tracking exercise this last week.

I was curious to find out, how much time do I typically spend every week doing household chores—laundry, vacuuming, mopping, making the beds, grocery shopping, cooking, cleaning up kitchen, putting away dishes, and other tasks like that.

I downloaded an app called Toggl and I tracked my time for one week.

Wanna guess the number?

[Partner guesses]

It was 15 hours in one week, which adds up to 780 hours per year.

Obviously change 15 to whatever it actually was for you.

[Partner gasps in shock, and says, "Nooo! That's awful! You are my Queen and this is outrageous!"]

I know, right? 780 hours is so much time!

This got me thinking, "If I had an extra 780 hours of free time every year, what could I do with that time?" I mean, for starters, I would love to . . .

- Work on my career [start my side hustle / grow my business / earn more money]
- Invest way more time into my health [meditation / gym time / daily walks]
- Spend quality time with YOU [and the kids!]
- And so many other things.

An extra 780 hours per year would significantly change my energy levels, my health, my ability to work and earn more money—it would change my life. Really, *both* of our lives.

[Partner agrees—Yes, it definitely would]

So, here's what I'm thinking.

I would like to hire someone to help around the house.

I propose that we start small—for instance, get a personal assistant who can help with laundry, meal prep, and running errands. We could start by hiring someone 5 hours a week, at $20 an hour. So, that's $100 per week, $400 per month.

[Partner might say—"Great, when do we start?" Or, "But how can we pay for that?"]

I have a plan to pay for this!

[Explain your plan—you'll sell a consulting package, you'll find 2 more clients, you'll negotiate for a raise at work, you'll sell some furniture, whatever you intend to do.]

Hiring someone costs money, that's true. But I feel confident that this investment will pay for itself, many times over.

This will free up so much time and energy, and enable me to [strengthen my business / hugely increase my income]. Plus, more quality time for us to [snuggle together / have amazing sex / go on hikes / do anything besides fold laundry, hooray!]

Are you cool with this plan?

[Let your partner express any hesitations they might have, and address each one]

At this point, you can agree to a plan and wrap up the conversation. Done. Hooray!

Or, if you feel like you need to keep discussing things a bit more, here are some great questions to discuss with your partner.

- Around the house, what are some things you really enjoy doing? (Cool, keep doing that stuff!)
- Around the house, what are some things you *don't* enjoy doing? (Okay, let's delegate these tasks to someone else!)
- What kind(s) of helper(s) do we want? (Housecleaner, nanny, personal assistant, virtual assistant, gardener/lawn care, pet care, what else?)
- How many hours per week?
- How much will that cost? (Look at websites like taskrabbit.com and upwork.com to find pricing)
- How are we going to get those funds? What's the plan?
- When can we start?

I don't want to exploit low-income workers.

Then don't.

Pay your team members a good living wage. I pay everyone on my team a minimum of $20 an hour (which is more than double the current national minimum wage) and several benefits as well. Give bonuses for exceptionally good work. Give paid time off. Give annual raises. Offer a flexible schedule. Treat them well, and be the dopest boss who ever lived.

Plus, like the old saying goes, "a rising tide lifts all boats." You can be that rising tide, lifting your team even higher.

Maybe your nanny eventually wants to run a nanny agency and become the childcare tycoon of Tampa. Maybe your dog walker dreams of attending veterinary school and running her own clinic one day. Find out your helper's long-term dream, encourage that dream, and help your helper take steps in that direction.

You can pay your team well, listen to their big goals, and help unlock doors for them. This is the opposite of exploitation. This is mentorship.

"I can't bear to hire someone, because I don't want to have to fire someone. The thought of doing that just stresses me out."

Firing someone doesn't have to be like one of those movie scenes where briefcases get hurled across the room, shouts ring out, and then the door slams as your former employee marches out ("You can't fire me, because I quit!") to write a scathing undercover journalism piece about what a demon boss you are. No.

It can be a civilized, compassionate conversation between two adults, and it can end with a win-win moment where you both feel confident that this is the right move.

"But I'm not making good money yet. How can I possibly justify hiring an assistant when I am making less than $100,000 per year, and I have tons of debt and all that stuff? It seems irresponsible."

Most women think, *I need to start making big money, and then I will hire an assistant.*

It's actually the reverse.

You need to hire an assistant, and then you will start making big money. The end.

CHAPTER SUMMARY

- Earning more can have a lot of positive effects on your life, but it can have negative effects on your time. If you want to be happier, spend your money on buying your time back.
- Your first hire should be a personal assistant who can help you handle a variety of tasks. Even if you can only afford five hours a week of help from a PA, you will find that it has a profound impact on your ability to generate income.
- Most women feel they can't afford or don't deserve to hire help. Blame the Protestant work ethic we have all been taught. Hiring other people enables you to serve others by creating jobs and being a great boss. Building a Million Dollar Team isn't exploitive unless you choose to exploit those who work for you. Instead, building a team is empowering.
- Learning to delegate is an essential step toward becoming a millionaire. Learn to have uncomfortable conversations with those you employ. Learn how to manage other people. Mastering delegation is the key to having not only financial freedom but time freedom as well.

CHAPTER 10

MILLION DOLLAR SYSTEMS

"Stop treating every dollar like it's your last."

—MY HUSBAND

always believed I was bad with money.

And I had lots of evidence to prove it was true.

I did my first year of higher education at Hunter College in New York City. It just happened to be down the street from Bloomingdale's flagship store. I quickly got a Bloomingdale's credit card and would spend my breaks in between classes shopping the sales racks and charging new coats, shoes, and dresses.

I loved walking through this bougie department store, pretending that I wasn't broke. I even "looked the part," because my sister had done an internship at Chanel and acquired a beautiful Chanel handbag that she would let me borrow. I'd walk through the beautiful designer sections with Chanel bag in hand and pretend that I was the kind of person who had an apartment on Park Avenue and could easily afford to buy $700 shoes. Of course, the fact that I only browsed the very small sales sections might have given my ruse away.

When I think back on it now, what I was buying with my credit card was an escape from the challenges of being broke. The clothes

I bought were an attempt at upward mobility. If I could look the part, maybe I could become the part.

It wasn't long before I acquired additional credit cards and was in way over my head. Interest racked up but my income did not. Eventually, I started paying late and then missing payments. Before I knew it, I had a 480 credit score and the shame to go with it.

In addition to my unpaid credit card debt and poor credit score, I regularly overdrafted my bank account. I was so used to overdrafting my bank account that, over time, I figured out exactly what sob stories worked well on the bank's customer service reps. I had the script memorized. Every time my bank account would overdraft, I called with my sad story (the real sad part: often my outlandish stories were completely true) and get them to reverse the fees.

As you can imagine, this song and dance was exhausting, embarrassing, and wasting mental space that I could have been using to figure out how to make more money. I was ambitious and focused on getting the education I needed to advance my career, but I didn't know how to make money in the meantime.

After a year at Hunter College, I transferred to State University of New York at Stony Brook. I was insanely jealous of my friends whose parents paid for college and bought them a truckload of dorm room furniture and decor. Most of my college experience was on credit. I negotiated for grants and found a way to showcase just how broke my family was as a way to squeeze a few more pennies out of my tightfisted college financial aid office. In other words, I was a natural-born hustler by necessity.

I remember when my greatest financial goal was to eat at a restaurant without fretting about the bill. I wondered what it must feel like to go out to eat and not have to mentally calculate the cost of what I was ordering, including tax and tip. There were so many times when I would be out to eat with a group of friends, and they would order pitchers of fancy beverages and appetizers "for the table."

I would literally be sweating through my shirt wondering if my rent check was going to bounce after I paid for this meal. The bill would arrive and one of my friends, who was obviously way more flush with cash than I could even dream of being, would announce

MILLION DOLLAR SYSTEMS 199

that we should just split it four ways evenly. Drats! My exact calculations would go out the window.

I'd put down my debit card, and my stomach would churn while I waited for the waiter to bring back our cards. I would be silently praying to God that my card would go through, and I wouldn't be embarrassed in front of all these people with a decline. Every time it went through, I would thank God and then go home and call Con Edison to see if I could talk them into not running my card for the electric bill that month.

Even when I became a "successful" entrepreneur, I was still living hand to mouth, because I had so much old debt to pay off. I'd have just enough money to cover the cost of attending a conference, but I never factored in the "let's get lunch" together that inevitably happened. Someone would choose a fancy place, and I'd be dying inside. The bill would come and everyone would drop their platinum Amex cards, and I'd sheepishly drop my credit union debit card in the pile. While folks were talking, I would surreptitiously check my balance on my phone to be sure my card would go through.

I actually might have PTSD from all those "decline" moments. A decline of my credit card felt like a decline of me. A decline of my constant struggle to get to a better place financially but always failing to succeed. A decline of my pride, my ambition, and my hopes and dreams to one day stop living in the struggle.

What those broke ass years taught me is the story that money is scarce, and spending money to enjoy life will lead to poverty and humiliation. Even after I became a millionaire, I could find myself dropping back into scarcity thinking when I felt challenged by a financial situation.

I couldn't treat myself to nice things unless they were directly connected to advancing my career. Luxury retreat? Only if I commit to networking my ass off and parlaying this opportunity into additional income. Nice clothes? Only if they are for a branding photo shoot or speaking gig that can raise my visibility and get me in front of more potential clients. I didn't even allow myself to buy a nice home until we had so many kids that I had no room for workspace, and I thought, *Well, if I have a nice home then I will feel good, and feeling good will lead me to make more money.* And then, of course, I had a lengthy discussion with a group of entrepreneurs more successful than me to confirm that this was true before I would take the leap to buy my house.

It wasn't until I started dating my husband that my financial mindset began to shift.

SCARCITY BEGETS SCARCITY

My husband had grown up even poorer than I had, but somehow he managed to have an abundance mindset. He would tell me, "Stop treating every dollar we have as if it's our last." He had no problem spending money solely for our joy and entertainment. He showed me that every single cent spent does not have to have a financial ROI to be worth it. My husband's thinking was "There is more where that came from." He trusts himself and trusts me enough to know that we are smart, resourceful, and capable, and that if shit ever really did hit the fan, we would figure it out.

> At the end of the day, that's what being "good with money" is about: trusting yourself with money.

When scarcity thinking takes hold, you don't trust yourself, and this lack of trust actually leads to terrible financial decisions. Scarcity might cause you to sign up for a credit card with a high interest rate when you buy a new mattress, instead of using your savings to pay the full amount with zero interest. Suddenly, your $1,200 new mattress turns into a $3,600 mattress that takes you two years to pay off. That's $2,400 worth of interest and two years of mental space wasted.

Or because of scarcity thinking, you are afraid to set up automatic retirements savings that go into your retirement account every month. You are afraid of not having enough if you start automatically saving, so you don't set up the financial systems that can create more abundance in your life. This is how scarcity begets more scarcity.

When you believe in your ability to make money and your ability to figure out any financial problem that may come your way, the constant financial anxiety starts to dissipate and you start making better financial decisions.

One of the simplest ways to learn to believe in your ability to figure out financial problems is to create financial systems that combat scarcity. Once you have systems in place that are designed for abundance, you will be making abundant financial decisions "automagically" every month. This means you're not relying on how you feel on a given day to make your money go *vroooom*.

Another reason you want to set up Million Dollar Systems is because at some point you have to grow up to glow up. Setting up systems for success is the definition of adulting. Systems are essential to our well-being, especially as women who are often overworked and underpaid by society. Increase your mental capacity by making smart financial decisions in advance, create a system where those decisions are executed automatically and then let them ride you into a bountiful future.

Okay, one more reason Million Dollar Systems are a must. You are valuable. The work you do is valuable. You are likely creating intellectual property that has immense potential. Your legacy is incredibly important, so you must protect it. Predators abound in our white-male-driven capitalist society. I can't tell you how many femmes have seen their work stolen and turned into millions by large corporations that don't compensate the creatives they steal from.

And last, wealth is important. Wealth is not the same as income. Income is something that you create entirely on your own and often use to take care of yourself and the people who depend on you. Wealth is something that should be created over generations. Wealth is made of assets that increase in value. These assets not only take care of you in your lifetime but also take care of your children and your children's children.

If you are Black, due to the legacy of slavery and the unfulfilled promise of reparations, chances are you have not and will not inherit wealth. In 2016, the net worth of a typical white family was $171,000. This is ten times more than the typical Black household's net worth of $17,000.[1] And since then, the numbers have gotten worse, not better. That is an appalling wealth chasm, which makes it even more of a priority for those of us who are Black to build systems to create wealth for ourselves, our communities, and the next generation. This is one of the most powerful ways that we can change the world.

It's not only Black people who experience a massive wealth chasm. The median white family has twenty-two times more wealth than the median Latinx family.[2] And poverty affects women of color worst of all. The national poverty rate for white women is 9.7 percent while 21.4 percent of Black women, 18.7 percent of Latinx women, and 22.8 percent of Native American women experience poverty.[3]

Sis, this is devastating, but we can fix this. Let's start by fixing our own personal financial systems, so we can get to a place where we can spread the wealth.

It's up to us to learn how to make smart financial decisions that capitalize on our income, intellectual property, and other assets so they can take care of us and also take care of other people who need us. We are the saviors we are waiting for. And it starts with bookkeeping.

WHAT GETS MEASURED GETS MANAGED

When it comes to challenging things, like managing money, many of us want to put our head in the sand or appoint someone else to do it for us. But I know you picked up this book because you believe it's possible for you to become a millionaire. And managing the money you have now, however large or small a sum it may be, is the training ground for reaching millionaire status. Avoiding your money situation will only lead to less money and less power to create a better world. I promise you: You can do hard things.

Tackling hard things begins with one small step and your willingness to look into the shame and guilt. You need to start tracking exactly what's happening with your money once it reaches your possession. In other words, establish a good accounting system. Trust me, you don't want to wait on this. This is one of those lessons I chose to learn the hard way.

I started my business on September 1, 2010. That was the day after I left my job as a law clerk and the day I got my first official client. I created an excel spreadsheet to begin tracking my business expenses and income. On day one of committing to build wealth, I couldn't have imagined actually having enough clients and money coming in that it would be hard to track with pen and paper or a simple spreadsheet. But after a few months in business, it happened.

I completed my first official year in business with about $60,000 in income, and my finances were a hot mess. I had to hire a bookkeeper to go back and dig through a year's worth of financial transactions. You know what's more expensive than purchasing accounting software or hiring a bookkeeper to do your books? Hiring a bookkeeper to do forensic accounting because you didn't track things properly in your crappy little spreadsheet. That cost me a pretty penny and tons of time digging through drawers and file folders and closets for all the receipt information that was needed so I could do my books and pay my taxes.

I didn't set up the proper systems for my business in the beginning, because I didn't believe in my potential. Don't do what I did. Make an energetic claim for the wealth you're building by setting up proper systems to manage your soon-to-be empire.

Plan for the financial life you want, not the one you have.

Plan to be big. In fact, plan to be *huge*. When you believe that you are headed for big things, you'll see the value in taking care of the financial and legal needs of your future piles of cash.

You gotta grow up to glow up, Sis. It's hard to build wealth when your financial life is messy and it all feels overwhelming and defeating. Instead, commit to taking charge of your finances.

Mind your business, and take that first uncomfortable step now.

Eighty-five percent of Americans feel anxious about money. Fifty-six percent feel awkward discussing finances with someone else. Twenty to seventy percent (depending on which study you look at) would rather endure a painful dentist visit than meet with a financial professional to discuss their money.

And one in five Americans would rather spend an hour in jail than sit down and figure out a five-year financial plan.

But the tragic thing is, if you're unwilling to look at your money, talk about your money, make a plan for your money, and create systems for your money, then you are keeping yourself in a financial prison. And you're serving a life sentence. By choice.

Whether you are thirteen years old or eighty-seven years old, it is never too early or too late to set up proper financial systems to protect yourself, your family, and your income. You can do this. I repeat: *It is never too late.*

You can take a few small steps this week, and a few more next week. Over time, you can clean up your financial world and feel beautifully organized. From hot mess to *oh yes!* Tiny steps add up to big things.

I know it sounds cliché, but it's true: When it comes to cleaning up your finances, the hardest part is just getting started. You have to take that first step to get things moving in the right direction.

For you, the "first step" might be logging in to actually look at your checking account balance—to see the number and face it instead of avoiding it.

Or the first step might be emailing a professional tax preparer to inquire about hiring them. Or figuring out how much debt you owe. (When I decided I wanted to get out of debt, I created a spreadsheet of every debt I owed and slowly paid each one off, one by one, until they were all gone, but it started with just putting together that spreadsheet and facing my reality.)

That first step might trigger all kinds of uncomfortable emotions: shame, guilt, a wave of anxiety. Trembling hands. Sweaty palms. A sick feeling in your stomach. You would rather do literally anything but this.

That first step might *suck.*

But it's like ripping off a Band-Aid. Once you finally do it, you'll realize, "That wasn't as awful as I feared. It's done. Cool. Now I can move on!"

SHATTER THE SHAME WALL

So, what's stopping you from taking that first step? Most likely: *your own thoughts!*

If you feel intense shame about your financial situation (as millions of people do), this shame becomes a massive, solid, impenetrable brick wall blocking you from taking action and getting the help you need.

You must find a way to shatter the shame wall, or you'll feel stuck forever.

Here are some grim, bleak, shame-riddled thoughts you might be thinking right now:

- "My credit score is practically minus-200. Abysmal."
- "I have $5 in my checking account. I'm a clown! A joke!"
- "I have no savings. I have student loan debt, credit card debt, and probably other debt I am not even aware of because I've pushed it out of my mind or stopped opening bills months ago!"
- "I haven't paid taxes in two years, and the IRS is probably gonna start sending me terrifying letters soon. *Ugh.*"
- "I am a Disaster with a capital D, which rhymes with P, which stands for Poor, which rhymes with Floor, which is what I want to disappear beneath."
- "My situation is such a mess. Even if I work my ass off, I will never climb out of this hole. I'm beyond help."

If you're thinking thoughts like those, you need to slam on the brakes and stop. Those kinds of thoughts are unproductive and only keep you depressed, hopeless, and trapped.

Toss out the mind trash, and start talking to yourself differently.

Here are some much better thoughts. These are truthful, empowering thoughts that get you in motion rather than keeping you stuck:

- "My credit score isn't great, that's the truth! But I can improve. If I keep taking action, things will shift in the right direction."

- "I don't have much in my checking account—yet! But I am determined to expand my income. This year, I will earn more than ever before."
- "I have no savings—yet! That's about to change. Watch me, world."
- "I have debt—okay, so what? Millions of people have debt. The US government has debt. Practically everyone has debt! I can work toward paying it off. Debt doesn't make me a 'bad' person."
- "I haven't paid taxes/bills/loans/and so on in a while. I am behind. That's real. But guess what? I am not the first human being to fall behind on payments, nor will I be the last. It happens. It's okay. I am creating a plan to get caught up, and it feels good to take action."
- "I'm not where I want to be, yet. But I have a clear vision of where I want to go. Every day, I can make Million Dollar Decisions that carry my life in the right direction. Things are improving. The best is yet to come."

Talk to yourself differently and get support from your Million Dollar Squad, and your wall of shame will crumble into dust.

SYSTEMS CAN BE JOYFUL

Did you ever read *The Life-Changing Magic of Tidying Up* by Marie Kondo?

If you didn't read it, I bet you've heard of it. This book became a global sensation and caused millions of people to catch decluttering fever.

After reading the first chapter or two of Kondo's book, you march into your bedroom, determined to clean up the mess.

You pull everything out of your closet. You toss aside anything that doesn't "spark joy." Old clothes, tattered clothes, things that no longer fit, those awful puke-green-colored pants that you bought for reasons unknown—bye!

You neatly fold your "keep" pile and put things back in an orderly fashion. You feel lighter and happier. A ten thousand pound weight has lifted from your shoulders. You step back and admire your new-

and-improved closet with pride and joy. Ahhh! Serenity!

Maybe your closet still isn't "perfect" but whoa, what an improvement! Things are shaping up and lookin' good!

That's the exact same energy you can bring to your finances.

Just like cleaning up your closet, cleaning up your finances and creating new systems can feel exciting! Energizing! Even joyful! It doesn't have to be a miserable experience.

You can decide, "I will bring a spirit of joy into this. Joy, not shame."

Your shame serves no one. It doesn't help you work faster. It doesn't help you earn more. It just makes you feel like putrid garbage and keeps you stuck. As you clean up and systemize your finances, don't invite shame to the party. Invite hope. Invite joy.

CREATE YOUR MILLION DOLLAR SYSTEM

It's time to go pro. Here are the top things I would do today if I were getting started with creating Million Dollar Systems upon which I could build my wealth. Let's do this!

1. Track your net worth.

When I graduated from college, Mint was a new software that could help you track all your financial information in one place. It was heavily marketed to college students, and I thought I'd give it a try since it was free. I logged in, connected all my financial accounts (my bank account, credit card accounts, and student loans). Little did I know that once I plugged in all my information, Mint would tell me what my current net worth was. When I saw that it was a negative number due to my student loan debt and low income, I was horrified. I quickly logged out and never logged back in. Thanks, Mint, but nobody asked you to tell me my net was worth nothing.

Well, fast forward about fourteen years: I eagerly log in to my current financial software to check on my net worth every month. I delight in knowing what the total value of my assets is, and it's fun to look at the numbers and see what I have created. It's especially enjoyable because I started with the numbers looking so very different.

As uncomfortable as it may be, knowing what your net worth (your total financial assets minus your total financial liabilities) is and tracking it on a monthly basis is important if you want to build wealth. You may be like me, starting with a large negative number, but I promise you if you follow the advice in this book, you will start seeing that number improve significantly over time. Seeing it one time is informative. Seeing how it changes on a monthly basis, depending on the financial decisions you've recently made, will influence you to make more and more Million Dollar Decisions. It's a way for you to face the music every month and build in automatic encouragement for more MDD.

2. Track your credit score.

As you already know, I spent many years with an abysmal credit score. The media will try to convince you that your value as a human being is directly connected to your FICO score. Fuck that noise! Your credit score has nothing to do with your value and, as we already know, the American financial system is rigged against you as a woman and especially as a woman of color.

That said, I've had terrible credit, and I've had excellent credit. Excellent credit is better because it gives you options. The better your credit, the more access to capital you have to do things like lease office space, buy a home, finance large purchases like a car or equipment for your business and get a business loan or credit card. While my personal preference is to have little to no unsecured debt, the reality is that there may be times where acquiring debt so that you can make an important Million Dollar Decision is really smart. Not all debt is bad. Debt has helped me build the empire and the net worth I have today.

In summary, good credit gives you options. I want you to have all the options in the world. So sign up for Credit Karma or go to freecreditreport.com to get a copy of your latest credit report. You can also get your credit report from your current bank or credit card company. I also recommend signing up for Equifax or Experian's monthly credit tracking account. Each month it will send you a reminder to check your credit, and it will notify you of any significant changes on your credit report. Again, what gets measured gets managed. The more you keep track of your credit and can see what makes your credit score go up or down each month, the more you will be influenced to make financial decisions that lead you toward abundance.

3. Research incorporation and open a business bank account.

If you want to be a millionaire, your greatest chance of doing so quickly is as a business owner. While 39 percent of millionaires built their wealth working for someone else, it usually took that group twenty-five years to acquire their average net worth of $3 million. The vast majority of millionaires are self-employed and on average acquired $7 million in net worth in twelve years.[4]

One of the first steps to building a business, even if it's a side hustle for now, is to do your research on creating a business entity. While this is an important step, it's not something I recommend you do before you have a few paying customers. Once you are regularly accepting money from clients on behalf of your business, do your research, meet with trusted professionals like a small business accountant and a small business lawyer, and decide on the right business entity for your company with their advice. Please do not skip the important step of meeting with trusted professionals (most accountants and lawyers will meet with new potential clients for a short introductory meeting for a relatively low cost) prior to choosing a business entity. Setting up the wrong business entity or setting one up before you need it can become a costly headache.

Once you have a business entity, be sure to get an EIN (Employer Identification Number, in other words, a tax ID for your business) and use your Articles of Incorporation and EIN to open a business bank account. When your business is up and running, you'll make all business purchases out of your business bank account, and when you get paid by customers, you will deposit the money in your business account. You will also pay yourself regularly out of your business bank account (if your business is making money, you should be getting a regular income from it, even it's only $100 per week to start).

There is nothing quite like a brand-new business account just waiting to receive cash to motivate you to get out there and keep selling.

4. Get a bookkeeper and check your finances daily.

Millionaires watch their money like a hawk. I check on my bank accounts daily, sometimes multiple times per day, so I always know what's going on with my funds. I recommend that you do the same. Create a habit of checking on your bank account balances and recent transactions every morning. Set a calendar reminder, if you must. The daily check in is important so you can catch issues before they arise and so you can notice patterns in your spending and earning. The patterns will give you ideas for how to improve the way you manage your money.

I also recommend purchasing bookkeeping software (like Mint or Personal Capital for your personal finances and Xero or Quick-Books for your small business finances). If you already have an established business or side hustle, hiring a bookkeeper is nonnegotiable. Whether you go with software or a human, it is imperative that you get a profit-and-loss statement and balance sheet for your business expenses every single month. Again, these reports will reveal patterns and show you how investments in your business have panned out and when there is an increase or decrease in your earnings and what caused it. Reviewing your financial reports, even if it's just your bank account statement, every month will help you make Million Dollar Decisions in your business and life, and improve your skills as a smart CEO.

5. Go to Money Church™ every week.

In my coaching membership club aptly called We Should All Be Millionaires, we have a session called Money Church every Friday. This is a group coaching session where we discuss money mindset issues and coach our clients on the important decisions that affect their finances. Even if you aren't a member of We Should All Be Millionaires: The Club, you can have your own personal Money Church every week. Money Church is not about worshipping money, it's a weekly, pleasurable date with your money. Carve out a weekly, recurring ninety-minute time slot in your calendar where you will not be distracted to host your personal Money Church session.

During this time, review your books and your latest bookkeeping reports. Write down any patterns you notice and personal *ahas* you have after looking at the numbers. Then spend some time examining your limiting beliefs. What's a money story you have been telling yourself lately? See my "Quick and Dirty Guide to Thought Work" in chapter 1 to examine those thoughts and reframe them into more helpful, positive thoughts. Last, use your remaining time to brainstorm new money-generating ideas and set financial goals. I recommend writing down at least twenty-five ideas you have for making more money every week. Then think of how you will reward yourself once you execute one of these ideas. For example, your goal might be "I'm going to get three new clients for my dog-walking service this month." And the reward might be "Once I get these three clients, I am going to reward myself with those new running sneakers I've been eyeing."

When you take the time to focus on your money every week, three things will happen: 1) You will become more confident about your ability to manage your money, 2) You will challenge and, over time, eliminate your limiting beliefs around your earning potential, and 3) You will get better at making money. Think of Money Church like going to the gym; it's an opportunity to stretch your money-making abilities and get stronger. The more you go to Money Church, the more money you'll make. In other words, what you focus on will expand.

These are the start of your Million Dollar Systems for building wealth. Is this everything you will need to do to manage your money-making capabilities? No. But it's a really solid start and will get you on the right track. Choose one of these items to take action on right now. Get 'er done and get on the path to making millions.

Ready for some bonus material? Some of the other things you'll want to take care of as you build your empire are hiring a lawyer, protecting your intellectual property (if you are creating content, new products, new proprietary methods and brands—those are valuable assets; protect them so they don't get stolen), using contracts with any clients, creating a system for managing customer inquiries, creating a system for booking appointments (this can be done with scheduling software like Calendly) and, most important, creating a system for getting paid (like setting up a merchant account or a PayPal account).

Now that you understand what Million Dollar Systems look like for building wealth, let's talk about the not-so-great financial advice you've been getting.

WHY PERSONAL FINANCE
GURUS DRIVE ME NUTS

If you pick up any personal finance book or listen to the Dave Ramsey Show, the advice is always the same: cut expenses, save save save, and live as frugally as possible on the limited income you have for a reward that will come later in life. I can tell you with certainty that this is not how most millionaires think.

There are some folks who save their way to a million dollars in assets. They do it by living well below their means, saving as much money as possible, carefully and prudently investing the money they've saved and, last, waiting. Saving your way to millions takes approximately thirty-two years.[5] That's thirty-two years of scrimping and cutting every cost until you reach millionaire status.

Ummm, no thanks.

Remember that personal finance gurus are gearing their advice toward employees who are paid a finite amount of money and don't plan on doing anything else to generate income. Therefore, the focus is on telling you what to do with the limited money you've earned from work and how to make it go further and last longer, despite the rising cost of living expenses. This requires an increase in your labor (for example, making every meal and never ordering out) and sacrifice (for example, going decades without vacations). My advice is the opposite.

Instead of only focusing on what to do with the limited income you have, cutting corners and saving every dollar you can, I want you to focus on earning more. Yes, *earning more*. What a revolutionary concept!

Rather than spending lots of hours and energy considering the best possible ways to divide your paycheck, I want you to consider how you can earn more money right now.

I want you to consider the skills that you have, or that you can immediately acquire, that can be used to earn additional income. And I am even going to suggest that you invest money in acquiring those skills or bringing those skills to market. *Gasp!*

With the technology available today, it has never been easier or cheaper to learn new skills via online courses, connect with an audience of potential customers and sell your services or products. I have clients that within twenty-four hours of hiring me have come up with an offer, found a few customers to offer it to and sold the offer. And this has happened a lot. If you are motivated and focused, you can significantly increase your earnings in a relatively short time.

So, I want you to spend time thinking about all the ways you can increase your income, rather than all the ways you can divide your paycheck. It's important to consider how to spend your money and track your expenses so you know what's going on with your money and how well it's working for you. But if you want to become a millionaire, get a lot more focused on your ability to earn more.

Sometimes earning more requires you to go into debt temporarily. Personal finance gurus hate debt and discourage it in all circumstances. However, especially for women, debt is sometimes the only way you can make investments that increase your earning potential.

LET'S TALK ABOUT DEBT

Many financial experts talk about debt like it's an embarrassing, sexually transmitted disease. Something to fear, avoid at all costs, or eradicate as quickly as possible. *Gross! Awful! How could you get yourself into this horrendous situation? Oh, no! You have got to clear away that debt, ASAP, or else you will never be successful, dateable, or lovable! Focus on erasing debt, first, then focus on everything else!*

I do not agree.

Debt is nothing to be ashamed of.

Having debt does not mean you are stupid, reckless, careless, lazy, or "bad with money." It doesn't necessarily mean any of those things. In fact, your debt might signify the exact opposite.

CONSIDER WHY YOU HAVE DEBT

If you have debt right now, any amount of debt, any type of debt, consider—why?

Why do you have debt? Really, *why?*

- Maybe you have debt because you value *education.* You want to learn, grow, and better yourself, no matter the cost. Is desiring education a bad thing? No, it's a beautiful thing.
- Maybe you have debt because you're an *entrepreneurial spirit.* And maybe you took a risk (like hiring a website designer to build a new site for your business), and this risk hasn't paid off financially . . . yet! Is this bad? No. It signifies that you're ambitious, you're courageous, and you're willing to take risks that others are too timid to even consider.
- Maybe you have debt because *you love your friends and family* immensely. You generously treat them to meals, drinks, and beautiful experiences. You want them to have the best things in life.
- Maybe you have debt because *you want your kids to have the best possible life,* too, and every possible chance at success. And you've made personal sacrifices (including racking up debt) to make this happen.
- Maybe you have debt because when your loved ones are struggling financially, *you help them out,* even when it costs you greatly.
- Maybe you have debt because when someone needs to see you (grandma is in the hospital, a girlfriend is grieving a divorce, your college-age child has mono), you buy a plane ticket without a second thought, and *you show up for the people you love.* Always. No matter what it costs.
- And maybe you have debt because, once in a while, the heaviness and agony of the world are too much to bear, and you buy a nice

pair of shoes or a massage, because you just need *something* to alleviate the pain. Who could blame you for that? *You are human.*

You don't have debt because you are "stupid" or "careless." Quite the opposite. You likely have debt because you are intelligent and committed to education. Because you care deeply. Because you are willing to take risks. Because you love fiercely. Because you are generous. Because you take care of your people. And, because you are human. Also, let's not forget that you likely have debt because you are a woman or woman of color dealing with the realities of systemic financial oppression.

This is not a free pass to accumulate debt but rather an acknowledgment that we all don't jump into debt for stupid reasons. It's important not to punish yourself for having debt in order to get free from it. The shame will weigh you down and actually make it harder to eliminate the debt.

When you view your debt in this light, you can see that debt is nothing to be ashamed of. Are you ashamed of trying to better yourself or for taking care of your family? No. So, don't be ashamed of debt.

Your debt represents big lessons you've learned (priceless ones) and all the ways you've invested in yourself. Your debt is a monetary representation of your best qualities, not your worst ones. Challenge yourself to view your debt in this entirely new light.

WRITE A THANK-YOU LETTER TO YOUR DEBT

Write down ten positive things that debt has brought into your life. Say "thank you" to each thing, whether it's an experience or possession or maybe an expensive-but-valuable lesson. The more you can view your debt with gratitude, the lighter it feels, and the faster you can move onward and upward with your life.

TO ERASE DEBT, FOCUS ON EXPANDING, NOT SHRINKING

Women are often told that the best way to erase debt is to trim expenses and tighten their belts even more.

"Stop drinking so many lattes!" "Stop buying all those shoes!" "Do you really need that Fenty highlighter by Rihanna? Restrain yourself, you silly frivolous female!"

This is absolute nonsense. And this is patriarchal drivel.

This so-called financial advice is really just white men barking at women and saying: "Strip good things out of your life. Scrimp and save. Be frugal. Tighten up. Shrink your ambitions. Make do with less. Make your life smaller."

This is offensive and ridiculous, and I am sick of it.

Consider this: If you stop drinking your daily $4 latte, you will save around $1,460 per year. Rather than telling women, "Deprive yourself, stop drinking nice coffee, and then you can save $1,460 annually," we should be telling women, "Believe in yourself, start thinking bigger, and figure out how you can generate an extra $14,600 every month."

Now *that* is a far more exciting and empowering conversation. And it's much more likely to make a real difference to your bottom line.

Which option will make you a millionaire?

Option (a) Shrinking

You can spend five hours this week focusing on how to trim your budget down to the bare bones.

You can cancel your Netflix subscription. You can clip coupons. You can argue with your cell phone company and convince them to lower your monthly bill by a few bucks. You can choose the budget peanut butter instead of the nice organic one.

And maybe you will end up shrinking your expenses by $50 or $100 or some other relatively small amount.

Or Option (b) Expanding

You can spend five hours this week coming up with a plan to generate an extra $15,000 through your new side hustle.

You can email clients to pitch your offer. You can send out invoices and confirm bookings. You can do fabulous work and get paid for your genius. And you can celebrate with a caramel-drizzled latte or whatever your heart desires.

Guess which is a better use of your precious time and energy? Option (a) or (b)? Shrinking or expanding?

And guess which enables you to get out of debt *and* build wealth *and* enjoy a higher quality of life?

This is a rhetorical question, because the answer is obvious. *Expanding!* Duh!

When you focus on expanding rather than shrinking, this is a Million Dollar Decision that changes your financial situation *forever.*

Have your latte. And get those coins.

CHAPTER SUMMARY

- Scarcity thinking begets more scarcity thinking. Stop treating every dollar as if it's your last and challenge your limiting beliefs around money. I promise you: You can make so much more money than you think you can.
- Commit to paying attention to your money. Do not outsource your financial management or decisions. Instead put on your big girl panties and handle it.
- Set up your Million Dollar System for managing your money, which includes tracking things like your net worth, credit score, and daily spending. It also includes researching and creating a business entity and business bank account and going to Money Church every week.
- Stop listening to personal finance gurus who tell you to scrimp and save every dollar you have and that debt is the devil. Instead focus on earning more and recognize that debt is sometimes necessary to increase your earning potential.

CHAPTER 11

A MILLION DOLLARS NOW

"The beginning is always today."

—MARY WOLLSTONECRAFT SHELLEY

The "impossible" is only impossible until you do it.

When I started my business, my only goal was to replace my $41,000 per year government salary and be able to afford health insurance. If I could do that while working from home in my own business, that would be a dream come true.

It felt impossible until I did it. It took me less than twelve months to earn that much in my business.

Once I did that impossible thing, I decided to try other "impossible" things.

Could I make $100,000 in annual revenue in my business? Done!

Could I launch an online course and have it make me money even when I wasn't working? Check!

Could I make enough money to hire a full-time employee? Turns out I could!

And could I find a way to buy the ultimate dream house for my family? Did that, too!

I kept trying the impossible things until I was running a $2 million business with a team of ten employees.

Just when I thought I was out of impossible goals to try, the CO-VID-19 pandemic hit and our revenue wasn't looking good. My salesperson was twiddling her thumbs, because no sales calls with potential clients were getting booked. We had clients emailing us daily informing us that they wouldn't be able to make their payment this month. We were more than halfway through the month, and we had only made 20 percent of what we needed to cover the month's expenses.

It was spring 2020, just a month after the World Health Organization had declared the COVID-19 crisis a pandemic. More than 30 million Americans had filed for unemployment in the previous six weeks, and I was watching small businesses that I used to frequent, like my Pilates studio, close their doors with no idea when they might reopen. I am a pretty optimistic person, but this crisis had me shook.

Would all my clients stop paying, one by one? Would our services become irrelevant to the people we were serving? Would I wind up having to lay off my team? That was my worst nightmare. I have the job security to know that my skills are highly valued, and I could always make a significant income consulting, but the thought of having to lay off my entire team was terrifying. I had a business savings account with enough of a safety net to carry the business for a few months. But no one knew how long this crisis would last. The US economy had come to a grinding halt. I knew I couldn't carry the business on savings long term.

I had two choices. I could hope for the best and ride out the wave. Or I could fight.

By now, I think you know me well enough to know that I am a fighter. So, I chose to fight for my business and my team (while also sheltering in place and homeschooling my children . . . good times!). I would need to pull off another impossible feat. Good thing I had plenty of practice.

My team and I came together to discuss possible ways we could pivot the business to restore our revenue. We realized we had thousands of potential clients who listened to our podcast, read our newsletter, and engaged with us on social media daily. We decided to go straight to the source and ask how we could support them during these challenging times. Their answers led us to create a new offer, a coaching membership community for women entrepreneurs who want to become millionaires. We call it We Should All Be Millionaires: The Club (or just "The Club" for short).

It took us a few weeks to build out The Club. We used intellectual property we already had, a member website we had already built, and the coaching team we had already hired. In other words, we used what we had and combined it in a new and special way to meet the current needs of our clients.

We launched The Club in April 2020, and in the next few weeks, there was a ton of interest. With that one launch, we replaced the lost revenue from all our high-end retainer clients. The Club was a success, and the business was saved. I breathed a massive sigh of relief.

LET'S GO FOR A MILLION!

Well, one impossible goal leads to another.

In June 2020, we had an uptick in demand for The Club. Every day, twenty more women would sign up to work with us. My team and I were in awe. Week after week, we watched our revenue climb. Finally as we moved toward the end of the month, our revenue was more than three times the amount we usually made.

And that's when I got another impossible idea.

"I have a crazy idea," I told my best friend, Robert.

"What's your crazy idea?" he said, accustomed to my shenanigans.

"I think my business could make a million dollars this month. We're more than halfway there. I know there's only two days left in the month, but what if we do it? What if a Black woman who grew up low income could build a company that makes a million dollars in a month? Wouldn't that be wild?"

I proceeded to tell him all the reasons it would be hard and why I was scared to even try. Robert listened intently as I spoke, but said nothing. After a long, pregnant pause, he started talking.

"Listen. I have two questions for you, but you have to be completely honest when I ask you these two questions."

Shooketh, I said, "Okay."

"One: Where is your current monthly revenue at?"

"We've made $647,000 this month so far."

"Okay. Two: Do you want to make a million dollars this month?"

"Hell yes."

"Then no more questions or asking for permission. Go do it."

And so I went for it. With only twenty-four hours left in the month of June, I sent an email to our company mailing list, told them that I was challenging myself to make $1 million before the clock struck midnight, and I asked them to help me reach this goal by joining The Club or spreading the word about The Club. I posted the same on social media as well. What happened next was incredible.

I received a ton of support from clients, friends, and even strangers. It felt like the whole world had rallied around my business to help me reach this epic milestone. I posted videos on social media and sent additional emails. Even influencers and well-known authors helped to spread the message.

And it was down to the wire, but we did it. We made over $300,000 in twenty-four hours and hit our goal.

My company, Hello Seven, made $1 million in a month. File that under "possible."

NOW I WANT TO CHALLENGE YOU

I want you to experience what it feels like to have the ability to make money whenever you want to. I need you to experience the freedom and liberation of knowing that you can make money happen on demand.

> You, today, have all the skills, talents, and intelligence you need to generate an income significantly higher than the one you have right now.

And you don't have to work like a dog for it. You don't have to never see your kids for it. You don't have to deal with a terrible boss for it. Despite what the world has taught you, you can have it all. And I want to invite you to prove it to yourself starting now.

On this journey, we have reframed your Broke Ass Story with your Million Dollar Story. We have examined the Million Dollar Lies that society has sold about what women can earn. You've started making Million Dollar Decisions and started establishing Million Dollar Boundaries. You've assembled your Million Dollar Squad so it can support you as you pursue your Million Dollar Vision.

You've also acknowledged your Million Dollar Value and stopped playing small. You've set your Million Dollar Pricing and started building your Million Dollar Team and your Million Dollar Systems. Now it's time to take everything you learned and turn it into cash money.

The best way to learn how to become a millionaire is for you to challenge yourself to start today.

So here is my challenge. Here's the impossible goal I am setting for you: I want to challenge you to make $10,000 in ten days.

Yes, ma'am, I said it. Ten thousand dollars in just ten days.

I promise you this is possible.

$10,000 IN TEN DAYS

So why attempt to make $10,000 in ten days?

There are a number of reasons you might like to have an extra $10,000 in your bank account.

You can use the proceeds from this challenge to pay off debt that's been stressing you out. You can use the money to hire a personal assistant and get some help around the house so you can free up more of your time. Perhaps you have been wanting to take your kids on a vacation, and this would give you the funds to do it.

Whether you want to donate $10,000 to charity, redecorate your living room, or just have the peace of mind knowing that there are ten thousand extra smackers available to you should you need it, all these reasons are valid.

The reason I am specifically challenging you to earn an extra ten thousand dollars is because ten thousand dollars can do a lot of things for you. This is a life-changing amount of money. Ten thousand dollars can get you moved into a nicer apartment in a better neighborhood. Ten thousand dollars can buy you a new car. Ten thousand dollars can cover six months of preschool for your little one.

It's also a large enough number that it will be a challenge to make happen in ten days.

However, if the idea of making $10,000 in ten days makes you want to hurl. If it causes debilitating fear to rise up within you and makes you lie in the corner in a fetal position, it's okay to go with a different number.

If $10,000 is not the right amount for you, here's how you choose the number that's right for you. I want you to imagine that you need to come up with a sum of money in just ten days for something very important. You would have to put effort in to come up with this amount of money but you are confident that you can do it. What is that number for you? Write it down.

Now, I want you to add 30 percent to that number, and that is the number you want to challenge yourself to earn in ten days. For example: if you feel that $500 is the most you could possibly come up with in ten days, then I want you to multiply $500 by 30 percent, which equals $150. So $500 (what you think you can earn in 10 days) + $150 (the 30 percent tax I'm adding to ensure you don't play small with this challenge) = $650. That is the number you will shoot for over ten days.

Okay, now that you know what your number is, let's talk about why this works.

Back in chapter 6, we talked about setting Big Hairy Audacious Goals (BHAGs) and how setting those larger, more challenging goals makes it more likely that you will achieve them. That's because the goal is electrifying. It causes you to feel hopeful, believe in possibility, and get your creative juices flowing with ideas to make this goal happen.

It is very motivating when you identify a purpose or reward connected to a goal. That's why I want you to decide how you are going to reward yourself once you complete this challenge. What are you going to be able to do or purchase once you achieve this goal? Decide how you will reward yourself for earning this amount of money in ten days.

Whatever you decide to do with the money is awesome, but it will pale in comparison to the real reward of this challenge. The real reward is whom you will become in the process of executing this challenge. You will build a powerful, money-making muscle. This is training for even larger financial goals that you might set for yourself in the future (like earning $1 million). Once you prove to yourself that you can earn large sums of money whenever you want, you will experience an incredible freedom and be ready to smash any other "impossible" goals you have as well.

HOW TO MAKE $10,000 IN TEN DAYS

Okay, so you're in. You're ready to commit to making an extra ten thousand clams in a ten-day period. But now you're wondering: *How, Sway?*

Don't worry, I got you.

There are lots of ways to make money in a short period of time, and I am going to provide you with a handy-dandy list in just a moment. But first, let's go over my principles for generating cash quickly. (Yes, of course, there are principles. What do you think this is?)

So, generally, you are looking to create a method to generate income that:

- *provides a decent amount of capital upfront.* This is not the time to sell your $10 eBook unless you already have an audience of thousands of people who are likely to buy it. A $10 eBook just won't add up to very much money in a short period if only ten people buy it. This is also not the time to create an offer with a lengthy payment plan. For example, if you are selling your consulting services that can be delivered over a two-month period, you want to ask for the full amount of the services upfront. Do not offer a two-month payment plan because the goal is to get $10,000 in the door within ten days.
- *does not commit you to something long-term.* The key to generating cash quickly is not trading said quick cash for future misery. We

don't want no payday loan vibes (in other words, cash in the door now, but insane cost later). You want to create an offer that provides a lot of cash to you upfront without making you miserable for months or years to come. This means you don't want to offer a year's worth of services or a six-month program during your $10,000 challenge, unless it's something you know you will enjoy delivering to your clients over this longer period of time.

- *is not taxing on your time or soul.* The goal of this challenge is to give you the feeling of liberation. So you don't want to earn a bunch of money to deliver a service that makes you die inside a little bit every time you have to do it. For example, let's say you are great at tutoring children and know you can sell some math tutoring packages quickly, but the thought of sitting with those snotty-nosed kids and digging deep for the patience to teach them math makes your soul cry for freedom. Don't do it. It's no fun to accept cash for services or products you have zero desire to deliver or create. Chances are you already have a job you hate. Why not sell something that would be fun for you to deliver?

- *is sexy and exciting to your potential clients.* Excitement matters! Do not underestimate the power of wowing your potential customers. If you can create an offer that gets your potential clients all hot and bothered, they will be thrilled to make a purchase and put some cash in your pocket. In order to figure out what kind of offer would excite your customers, put yourself in their shoes and think of what would get you excited if you were them? Clients get excited about things that are new (you have that going for you if this is something you've never offered before!), things that don't last forever (like a live event or one-time offer that expires soon), bonuses (when free things are thrown in with the offer) and things that solve their problems. For example, say you are a lawyer who offers business formations that may not be all that exciting. But what if you offered a Business Formation in a Day, where your client could have their LLC or S corporation fully formed on a specific day and not have to wait a long time to get this service completed? Now your offer is a lot more exciting.

HERE ARE THE STEPS
TO ACCEPT THIS CHALLENGE

Now that you have the criteria for creating an offer that generates cash quickly, let me hit you with three ideas to get your creativity flowing.

1. Sell a VIP Day.

A VIP Day is when you dedicate an entire workday to helping someone accomplish a specific goal. VIP Days are one of my favorite things to offer for a quick cash infusion, because they are expensive (hiring you for an entire day ain't cheap!), they provide a quick solution for your customer's problem and that creates an excitement factor, and they are over in a single day (so they won't provide cash today while stealing from your future). No matter what you do, you could sell a VIP Day.

For example, if you are great at lawncare you could sell a day where you go over to someone's house and fix up their janky yard and have it looking fabulous by end of day. You could spend a day providing organization to someone's messy closet or basement full of clutter. You could spend a day helping someone create their first website. Or spend a day teaching someone how to do their own makeup (in fact, I would totally buy this!). When I sell a VIP Day, I help companies rebuild their business model to be more scalable. By the end of the day, they have a plan for a better business model.

2. Charge for your advice.

You have probably been guilty of giving your time and expertise away for far too long, so why not start charging for your advice? Paid consultations are an excellent way to raise capital quickly. If people often ask to "pick your brain," let them know they can pick away as soon as they pay this here invoice. And, even if you are already charging for your expertise, make sure you're charging enough and that you don't have any other revenue leaks you're missing related to giving advice.

For instance, are you answering questions for existing clients that aren't within the scope of your current work? While you don't want to nickel and dime your clients, if they're asking for substantial advice or work outside of what they've initially paid you for, you are losing money. Fix that revenue leak by charging for giving advice. Once you've determined how much you're going to charge for your session, spread the word that you're available for paid consultations or strategy sessions.

3. Host an event.

Events definitely meet that excitement factor. People love having something to do and somewhere to go. Your event could be anything. I've seen my clients host amazing dance parties with a fabulous DJ, business conferences, online workshops (let's meet on Zoom!) and weekend retreats. You could host a crafty event where you walk your guests through how to arrange a beautiful flower bouquet. Or your event could be a conference where you help parents learn strategies to reconnect with their children. You could host a one-day virtual workshop where you walk clients through how to create a personal brand. Like VIP Days, events happen and then they are over, so it won't be something that takes up a ton of your time for an entire year (unless you are hosting the equivalent of a wedding . . . maybe don't do that). Charge for tickets to your event over a ten-day period and voila! $10,000 in your bank account.

MORE IDEAS FOR EARNING $10,000 IN TEN DAYS

- Finally launch that program you've been tinkering with for months now.
- Forgive yourself for not using the treadmill/fancy stand mixer/bicycle/inherited antique armoire/designer handbag, and sell it.
- Sell a killer Seven-Day Challenge with an upgrade offer at the end.

- Ask your employer for a raise.
- Create a short-term group offer that brings all your favorite 1:1 clients together so you can try working with them in a group setting.
- Follow up on your unpaid invoices.
- Dust off an old product, freshen it up with an update, and put it on sale.
- Rent out a spare room. Or that cabin your family has that no one uses.
- Buy old furniture. Sand it down, paint it, and sell it on Craigslist for a profit.
- Create an incentivized offer for your monthly retainer clients to pay for the remainder of their contract now.
- Negotiate bonus pay for that extra project you've been managing at work.
- Dog sit, babysit, or house sit for your neighbors.
- Raise your rates effective in thirty days and offer current clients a way to purchase ahead at your current price.
- Sell a workshop/training/seminar to a group you know would benefit from your expertise.
- Reach out to a former client or five with a refresh offer or workshop.
- Host a yard sale.
- Go on a cancellation spree, and free yourself from all the little monthly charges for services you don't use much (definitely keep what sparks joy, though).
- Evaluate everything you give away for free, and use your most popular freebie as the seed for an evergreen mini-course.

Okay, my friend, you are officially ready for the $10,000 in Ten Days Challenge. Here are all the steps to accept this challenge and make ooh-gobs of money in just ten days:

1. **Choose the amount of money you will commit to earning in a ten-day period.** If $10,000 sounds too large or too small,

choose a number that you think you could earn in ten days and then increase that number by 30 percent. There's your goal. Or just go with $10k—that's a life-changing amount of money.

2. **Decide what your reward for reaching your goal will be.** Will you move to a bigger place, fix your old car, buy some new outfits, send junior to a better school, hire a cleaner to clean your home twice per month? Your goal should be something your heart desires, because that will motivate you as you embark on this challenge. You are worthy of having that thing you want.

3. **Choose the thing(s) you will sell.** What services or products will you sell? What alternative methods to save cash will you try? Create a game plan so you are ready when the ten-day challenge begins.

4. **Schedule the ten days you will embark on this challenge.** Look at your schedule and find a ten-day period in the next thirty days when you can commit to taking money-making action. Resist the temptation to put this off. Remember that the goal is to take action and reap the rewards as soon as possible.

5. **Gather your cheering squad.** Tell a few friends, family members, coworkers, past clients, everyone who follows you on Twitter and anyone else who will listen that you are embarking on this ten-day challenge. Ask them to hold you accountable. I implore you: Do not skip this step! This challenge will be, well, challenging. You are going to need a support squad to cheer you on when the going gets rough. And added bonus: When you tell people that you are challenging yourself in this way, they will want to help you! They might purchase your services, spread your sales message, refer clients, and maybe even buy your old vacuum. Let people support you! And use #hello10kin10days on social media and tag me on Instagram (@RachRodgersEsq) so my team and I can support you as well.

$2.3 MILLION IN TEN DAYS

In July 2020, I decided to challenge the members of We Should All Be Millionaires: The Club to the $10k in Ten Days Challenge. After the challenge was over, we did a post-challenge survey to collect results.

Here's the final scorecard:

- 350 women agreed to participate in the $10K in 10 Days Challenge.
- Each participant set their own personal monetary goal for the challenge. Some were shooting for more than $10k, some were shooting for less.
- 75 percent of participants said that they were able to earn additional money they wouldn't have earned if they hadn't done this challenge. That means most of those who participated made extra money! Proof that this challenge works!
- 98 percent said the challenge motivated them to make Million Dollar Decisions (aka: high-quality decisions that bring you prosperity, peace, and joy).
- 90 percent said the challenge made them feel like a CEO, and feel powerful instead of powerless.
- Collectively, these women generated a grand total of $2.3 million over the course of ten days. (Two! Point! Three! Million!). That's an average of $6,571 per participant!
- One woman (who is five months pregnant) asked a family member to watch her toddler during the day so she could focus on the challenge. She made $21,041 by raising her prices and selling as much as she could to her current client base.
- Another woman (a single mom) used this challenge as an opportunity to declutter. She held a big yard sale and made $1,400 in a single day. She also collected from a client who had a past due invoice (just by following up) and landed

several new clients at her newly raised prices. Her grand total was $10,200 in ten days.

- One woman went into beast mode and challenged herself to "get uncomfortable" and "sell every day." She contacted previous clients. She contacted major brands. She emailed her mailing list. She wound up making $25,649 in July 2020. This is wild especially considering that in June 2020, she only earned $250 bucks total. All hail the comeback Queen!

Moral of the story: You think you can't, but you can.
You are more powerful than you can even imagine.
There's always a way to make it happen.

ALL THE THINGS YOU DON'T NEED

Right now you may be thinking, *But Rachel, in order to make more money, I need a fancy website! I need a professionally designed logo! I need two more college degrees! I need a publicist! I need Oprah's endorsement!*

False.

You don't need any of that stuff.

Here's a list of seven things you don't need to start making more money now:

1. A big mailing list (or massive social media following).

If you've got a mailing list filled with thousands of loyal, devoted subscribers who love your work and can't wait to purchase from you, amazing! Good work, boo.

But a mailing list (or any kind of online fanbase) is *not* required.

If you want to make $10,000 in ten days, you can start by making a simple contact list of friends, family, colleagues, teachers, mentors, previous (or current) clients, employers, local business owners, and other people who already know you, or who might like to meet you. Type all their names into a Word document and title it, *"People I will contact soon,"* or something like that. Just make a list.

Then email each person on your list individually to either (A) invite them to hire you or (B) ask them to help you get hired.

When emailing a potential client, you could send a note to say:

"Hey! I'm a big fan of you (or your company), and I wanted to introduce myself. I do XYZ. I'm not sure if you're looking for XYZ right now, but if you are, I'd love to work with you!"

If you're emailing a friend or family member, you could say:

"Hi! I have some exciting news: I've decided to start a side business, and I'm offering XYZ. I have space for a couple new clients right now. If you happen to know anybody who needs XYZ, feel free to give them my email address. Send 'em my way! Thank you!"

That's it. Keep it simple.

I know several seven- and eight-figure companies that got started with a handful of personal emails just like those. Mine did, and yours can, too.

2. A website.

You don't need a snazzy website.

If you've got one, cute! If you don't, write a simple email (see above) with a few sentences describing what you're offering: dog training, wellness coaching, public-speaking seminar, graphic design services, whatever, why it's awesome, and how much it costs. *Boom.* Done.

3. Business cards.

Nope. Unnecessary.

Can you even remember the last time you requested, wanted, or desperately needed a business card? Naw.

Worst-case scenario? Scribble your email address onto a napkin or piece of scratch paper and hand it over. More often than you'd think, lucrative deals get secured just like that.

4. A business name.

I know plenty of successful people who never came up with a "clever" business name. Their business is simply their own name.

For instance, Farnoosh Torabi is one of the top-ranked podcasters on the planet and a badass entrepreneur, and her company is simply called . . . wait for it . . . Farnoosh Inc. Yup. It's just her own name. And she's making seven figures per year.

If you eventually come up with an exciting name for your business (like "The Pampered Poodle Dog Grooming Services"), that's great! But it's not necessary right now.

5. A cool tagline.

A cool, memorable tagline (like Nike's tagline: "Just do it") is a great thing to have. And it's optional.

You don't need one in order to make money. Plenty of successful companies have no specific tagline.

6. Amazing aesthetics, logos, images, branding, and so on.

Friend, let me tell you. I have seen (with my own two shocked eyeballs) numerous websites and other marketing materials that are hideously ugly.

We're talking red, yellow, and electric neon green font, fuzzy images, janky-looking design, truly, the absolute worst. And yet this person is still making bank.

You can bring money in the door, consistently, even if you have branding that looks like a drunk toddler did it, or no branding at all. In fact, I launched my business and worked with five paying clients before I ever had a website.

7. To have it all figured out.

Nope. You don't need to "have it all figured out" in order to start selling your stuff and making your clients delightfully happy.

Nobody has it "all figured out" when they're just getting started. My company generates millions per year and I still don't have everything figured out.

Just take the first step. Send the first email. Schedule that first phone call. Do the thing you feel nervous to do. And you will learn as you go.

As you swing into motion, the answers arrive, and the path becomes clear.

To recap, in order to start making more money, you do *not* need a mailing list, website, business cards, business name, tagline, amazing aesthetics/branding, or "everything all figured out."

Eliminate all the fictitious obstacles between you and the cash and get this shmoney!

NOW, HERE'S WHAT YOU DO NEED

There are a few legitimate things that you do need to make some money. Here is that very short list.

1. A clear offer that takes your client from Point A to B.

You need a clear offer.

When I say "offer," this means a service, package, program, course, seminar, class, retreat, workshop, physical product, digital product and so on. Something you are "offering" to the marketplace. Something to sell.

And *(this part is crucial, please read closely)* you need an offer that delivers a *specific result*—an offer that takes your client from Point A ("I'm so frustrated!") to Point B ("Joy to the world! Things are so much better now!").

Here's an example of what I mean.

Let's say you offer SAT tutoring services.

Point A: The student is getting an abysmally low score.

Point B: After hiring you, the student's score has vastly improved. This child now has a serious shot of getting into college. Joy of joys!

Or, let's say you offer a dog-training program.

Point A: The puppy is devouring $500 designer shoes, peeing on the carpet, and ruining the owner's life. Misery. Woe. Despair.

Point B: The puppy's behavior is so much better. No more shoe-snacks. Potty trained. Heaven on Earth!

If you want people to hire you and fork fistfuls of cash in your direction, you need a clear offer that guides your client from Point A to B.

Spend a little time asking yourself:

"For my client or customer, what is Point A? What is Point B? How can I create an offer that guides them from A to B as quickly / simply / joyfully as possible?"

If you're fuzzy on Point A, or you're confused about Point B, or you can't really explain things clearly, then other people will be confused too, and they *will not hire you.*

You need to be crystal clear about what you're offering.

A conversation with a potential client should go something like this:

"Ah, okay, I see you're at <Point A> and I know that's really frustrating. I offer XYZ and I can get you to <Point B>. How does that sound? Okay, great! Let's get started! And yes, I do take payments via PayPal, Venmo, check, cash, and all major debit and credit cards, why thank you so much."

So again, you need a clear offer. You also need:

2. Some way to tell people about your offer and invite them to say, "Yes!"

Like I mentioned earlier, a simple email can do the trick. Send a personal email to potential clients, letting them know about your delightful offer and inviting them to buy it.

Or you can mail postcards. Or make flyers. Or talk to people face-to-face. Or schedule phone calls. Or post on social media. Or all the above.

Challenge yourself to tell fifty people about your offer in ten days.

If that seems psychotic, do the math. It's only five people per day.

Are you willing to send five quick emails per day, so that you can earn $10,000 or more? I hope so. And it's entirely possible you will reach $10,000 in sales before you've contacted all fifty people.

To recap, you need an offer. You need to announce your offer to the world. You also need:

3. A price.

This may sound obvious, but you need to decide—in advance—how much your offer is gonna cost. Because when an interested client says, "Great! I'm in! How much?" You don't want to reply with, "Um, uh, hmm, I mean, I guess, whatever you want to pay me is fine."

No, ma'am! Choose a price that reflects the value you provide. Review chapter 8 to refresh your memory about value-based pricing.

Most likely, whatever you're offering (SAT prep, dog training, wellness coaching, personal training, legal services, marriage counseling, and so on) is worth *a lot*.

Consider: How much is it "worth" to get into your dream college with a big scholarship? To avoid a lawsuit? To save your marriage? To finally feel comfortable and confident in your own body? I will tell you—it is worth $1,000 *at least*. Bare minimum. Price your offer accordingly.

Whatever price you originally come up with, double it.

And last, but certainly not least, you need:

4. Some way to take payments.

Venmo. PayPal. Stripe. Wave. An empty baseball cap so people can stuff cash payments inside. Whatever! Just figure out some way to take people's money and get those sales.

Nowadays there are many options, and they're all super easy to use. Later on, if you want, you can upgrade to a more "sophisticated" payment system, but for starters, just pick something and run with it.

YOUR *EARN $10,000 IN TEN DAYS* CHECKLIST.

Okay, future millionaire! Let's pull it all together! Action time!
Here's a checklist for you. How many items can you tick off?

- [ ] I came up with an offer and I'm excited about it.
- [ ] I am pretty confident that my offer will take each client from Point A (frustration, stress, stuckness) to Point B (joy, delight, success).
- [ ] I chose a price for my offer.
- [ ] Just kidding! I have now doubled the price, because I realized that my initial number was way too low. Haha, silly me. Fixed now.
- [ ] I have some way to take payments: PayPal, Stripe, and so on.

☐ I wrote a brief, simple description about my offer that explains what it is, why it's awesome, and how much it costs.

☐ I made a contact list of fifty people whom I can contact to (A) invite them to hire me/purchase my offer or (B) ask them to help spread the word.

☐ I've already reached out to five people, because I am not stalling.

☐ Ooh, I just reached out to five more people. Look at me go!

☐ I have an amazing idea for how I will celebrate and treat myself once I reach $10,000.

The sales are coming in! It's happening! You're moving toward $10,000, but you're not quite there yet.

Selling your offer is one way to generate cash and reach $10,000.

But you can generate cash in other ways, too. If you need to whip up another couple grand real quick, you could . . .

- Sell furniture, clothes, concert tickets, and other items you don't want or need.
- All those peeps you loaned money to? Call in those debts. Yes, that includes your cheating ex from five years ago. It's time to pay the piper!
- That one client who's thirty days late paying his invoice? Nudge him and make sure it gets paid.
- Temporarily rent out a spare bedroom (airbnb.com) or temporarily rent out your car (turo.com).
- You might have unclaimed money owed to you due to a class action legal settlement, insurance refunds, an inheritance you didn't know about, tax refund, economic stimulus/emergency relief payments, or some other reason. Occasionally this happens—especially if you've moved to new addresses numerous times or changed your phone number. People may have tried to find you, but couldn't. There are websites that can help you figure out if there's any money floating around out there that is rightfully yours. The US government's official Treasury site (https://www.fiscal.treasury.gov/unclaimed-assets.html) is one place to start. You can also try unclaimed.org (https://unclaimed.org/search-for-your-unclaimed-property-its-free/). It can't hurt to check.

- You sold your offer to an awesome client? Circle back with an upsell. Maybe she wants to upgrade to a VIP package and work with you in a more elevated, luxurious way.

Do whatever it takes to reach $10,000 in ten days.

Get creative. There's plenty of money out there for you. Go claim it.

One way or another, come hell or high water, by land or by sea, by hook or by crook—you can get that money in the door!

You will feel so proud of yourself once you hit that $10,000 milestone. It will forever change your perception of yourself. A major confidence bump. And some nice padding for your bank account.

Conquering this first $10,000 challenge will get you on the path to wealth. Paving the way to your first $100,000. Your first $1 million. And beyond.

GET HONEST ABOUT WHAT MOTIVATES YOU

A colleague decided to do the $10,000 in Ten Days Challenge, once upon a time. But she was having trouble getting motivated. She was feeling low energy, unfocused, sluggish, and was struggling to believe that it was really possible.

She kept reminding herself, "I need this money! I'm going to buy a new mattress, pay off a little debt, and it's a good thing."

But "new mattress" and "less debt" weren't compelling enough to motivate her.

Then, she made a bet.

She chatted with her partner, and they came up with a plan.

She told him: "Okay, here's the deal. If I make $10,000 in ten days, then I am taking us both out for an amazing spa day with massages and everything. And I'm getting us that brand-new mattress we've been wanting. And then *you* are gonna pick up all the dog poop for the next six months. Sound good?"

He said: "I love it. Deal. I'm in! I believe in you, honey!"

For whatever reason, the prospect of not picking up dog poop was the burst of motivation she needed. Every day, she would wake up, head to her desk, start hustling, and practically chant to herself, "No poop, no poop, no poop for meee!"

This massively motivated her. She knocked out $10,000. No problem. In fact, she went above and beyond. Her final total was closer to $12,000. The money-floodgates opened!

Then a few months later, she set an even more ambitious goal: $45,000 in forty-five days. She hit that, too. In fact, she soared over it. She's at $82,000 (and climbing) as I am typing this sentence. Look what dog poop (or rather, lack thereof) can do!

Moral of the story:

Everyone is motivated by different things. You might be motivated by pedicures, fancy dinners, new clothes, freedom, security, peace of mind, house-cleaning services, a new house, social impact, or the joy of never having to touch dog feces again.

Figure out what motivates *you*, and then structure your $10,000 in Ten Days plan so that your personal flavor of motivation juice is flowing through your veins daily. This will awaken the moneymaking dragon that's sleeping inside of you. And once she's awake, look out world. Because you are unstoppable.

CHAPTER SUMMARY

- Impossible is only impossible until you do it. If I can successfully pivot in a pandemic and make $1 million in a month, you can make the impossible happen, too!
- Take the $10,000 in Ten Days challenge so you can prove to yourself that you are capable of making large sums of money in short periods of time, whenever you want.
- In order to make $10,000 in ten days, sell an offer that 1) provides a decent amount of capital upfront, 2) does not commit you to delivering work long-term, 3) is not taxing on your time or soul, and 4) is sexy and exciting to your potential clients.
- Say yes to this challenge by taking the following steps: choose the amount of money you will commit to earning in a ten-day period, decide what your reward for reaching your

goal will be, choose the thing(s) you will sell, schedule the ten days you will embark on this challenge, and gather your cheering squad to hold you accountable.

- You don't need a bunch of fancy bells and whistles to make money. All you need is a clear offer, a way to tell people about the offer, a price, and a way to accept payments.

CONCLUSION

"Wealth is the ability to fully experience life."

—HENRY DAVID THOREAU

What I want for you more than anything else is to be a millionaire.

I want you to fully experience all that life has to offer with your limited time on Earth. I want to see you taking up space, stomping through boardrooms, and dropping off bags of money at the bank.

Why? Because when you, a woman, make bank it's evidence.

Evidence that no matter where you come from, no matter how many financial mistakes you've made, and no matter how many opportunities have been unfairly snatched away from you, your future can be better than your past.

Your next chapter can be one of affluence and joy.

You can win.

The facts: I am a Black woman from a low-income family. I have four kids. I speak up loudly about racism, misogyny, and other systems of oppression that are toxic and damaging. I say things that people don't want to hear. I make people uncomfortable. And I used to be terrible with money (I had a 480 credit score, y'all).

My million dollar victory proves that you can be all these things—Black, female, outspoken, political, a parent with teenagers and toddlers at home, not exactly "naturally gifted" with money—and you can still make bank.

To be clear: I'm not satisfied with simply being wealthy myself. I'm on a mission to help every person who has been systemically marginalized and underestimated become a millionaire. So, let's talk about you.

In order to become a millionaire, you need to start making Million Dollar Decisions.

A Million Dollar Decision is any decision that brings you peace, power, prosperity, or all the above.

Raising your pricing is a Million Dollar Decision.

Having a hard conversation is a Million Dollar Decision.

Hiring someone to handle groceries and laundry (and paying them a living wage to do it) is a Million Dollar Decision.

Standing up for what you believe in. Getting a fantastic haircut. Upgrading your closet so you feel like a #boss. Leaving a soul-sucking relationship. Joining a club filled with badass humans who inspire you to level up. Officially setting up your business as an LLC and going legit. All examples of Million Dollar Decisions.

What is the next Million Dollar Decision that you need to make?

Make it. Then make another. And another.

That is how you will have your first million dollar year. And eventually your first million dollar month. First of many.

If I can, you can, and your daughter can, and her children can, too.

We should all be millionaires.

We should. We can. We will if I have anything to do with it.

APPENDIX:
100 REASONS YOU SHOULD
BECOME A MILLIONAIRE

On your journey to become a millionaire, there will be challenges. There will be days where you ask yourself "Why am I doing this?" I created this list of 100 reasons you should become a millionaire to answer that question on those tough days. The first ten reasons are from me and the rest came from my clients, who are all on the journey to become millionaires as well.

1. Because when you make more money, then you can become a job creator and offer employment to people, and then you send fun gifts to your employees and their kids.
2. Because you can hire someone to handle your laundry, and this will change your whole life.
3. Because you can write a five-figure check to your favorite charity and feel like Oprah.
4. Because having more money frees up huge amounts of space in your brain. Instead of having 90 percent of your brain occupied with noisy money stress—like how you're going to make rent—all that space is freed up to focus on other things— like how you're going to change the world.

5. Because high-quality bed sheets are just better, and that is a fact.

6. Because you can book a boat for your birthday party and basically be Rihanna.

7. Because you can build a phat college fund or trust fund for your kids and give them a competitive edge for the future.

8. Because you can pay off your mortgage and own your home in full, nothing owed, by the time you are fifty, and this creates immense peace of mind for your golden senior years.

9. Because when you have more money, you never, ever, have to take a nightmare client or deal with a soul-sucking boss or stay locked in a crappy, demoralizing job "just because you need the money." You have the freedom to leave or say no.

10. Because you like expensive shoes.

11. To have political power. To have a seat at the proverbial table. —*Pamela Brown*

12. To be the example for the next woman who doesn't think she is worthy of making a million dollars. —*Katie Collins*

13. To be a badass wife who retires her husband. —*Katie Collins*

14. Because one day, a little girl who looks like you will say to herself, "If she could do it, so can I!" —*Melanie Ramiro*

15. Because f**k patriarchy. —*Athenee Mastrangelo*

16. To be able to give back in unprecedented ways! —*Laura Andrea Gonzalez*

17. You should become a millionaire so that you can spend less time thinking about making money, and more time thinking about what you're going to do with all your money. —*Justine Chenel*

18. Because no one should wake up every day feeling like they have to survive. —*Telanna Swan-Jeffers*

19. To truly be free and do what you love. —*Angela Matthews*

20. To pay for my daughter's college education in cash! —*Brenda Lomeli*

21. To change the narrative and raise the expectation of Black and brown girls around the world! —*Michelda Johnson*

22. Because, why not?! —*Uzoma Obidike*

23. We should be millionaires, not because it's our turn, but because we have so much good to do in the world, and we can't fully do it if we're surviving instead of thriving. —*Nicole Salvatore*

24. To fund research that can save lives. —*Sarah Elizabeth*

25. To be my ancestors' wildest dream. —*Melissa Elysian*

26. To prove to yourself that you can. —*Marissa Willits*

27. Create a new lineage of money makers. —*Tracy Neely*

28. You should become a millionaire because no one ever told you that you could become a millionaire. —*Katherine Rose*

29. Because we need to give future generations hope and inspiration. —*Eleanor Healy*

30. Because personal sovereignty and wealth are inextricably intertwined. —*Liz Dennery*

31. Because we need to be self-sufficient! Too many women especially are trapped in relationships because of money. God bless the child who's got her own. —*Kronda Adair*

32. Because you f*cking can. —*Erika Royal*

33. To have the power and influence to build new systems and create a more loving world. —*Lisa Hall*

34. To throw a boatload of money at environmental causes and global warming awareness. —*Jen Nobles*

35. So I can lay in a hammock at the beach and read a novel whenever I damn well please. —*Julie Wolk*

36. Because it's fun! —*Kaeli Sweigard*

37. Because we are worth it, and we have to start living according to our worth. —*Malika Williams*

38. Because I once had a boss (when I was barely making more than minimum wage) sincerely say to me, "I hear you saying you want to be a great employee. But I also hear you saying you want to be a great mom. I think you're going to have to make a choice here." Women need to be millionaires so they can run companies that don't force other women to make these insane "choices." —*Suzi Istvan*

39. I want to be a millionaire because it's my desire and birthright to have an epic life. —*Tavona Givens*

40. I want to become a millionaire not for the million dollars but to become the person who can make a million dollars. —*Afrin Sopariwala*

41. Because Black people can't continue to start from scratch with every generation. —*Ifeoma Ibekwe*

42. Because, as women, we always have to be ready for plan B. —*Grace Van Cleave*

43. So can I pay off my parents' mortgage and help my dad finally retire. —*Patricia Valera*

44. Because our free labor built this country and being a millionaire is just an ounce of the reparations we are owed. —*Erica Jordan-Thomas*

45. So you can be your juicy, delish self any and every time you desire. Be, do, and have all the things that make you tingle!!! —*Wendy Petties*

46. To support strong habits of compassion. —*Judy LaPrade*

47. Because my voice has been silenced for too long and becoming a millionaire will loosen my tongue, unclench my jaw, and allow the power of my words to speak through dollar bills. —*Alice Agnello*

48. Because it's time to stop these oppressive systems, and we need money to do it. —*Naomi Clark*

49. Because my parents sacrificed everything they had so I could have the chance to become everything I dream of. —*Mary Grace Sandoval*

50. Because it's lonely at the top, and Rachel and Beyoncé need some ladies to brunch with. —*Chrissy Mize*

51. You should become a millionaire because a six-figure income doesn't go as far as we need it to in today's world. —*M. Angelique Lucas*

52. Because we are most ourselves when we are generative and generous. —*Julie Ordoñez*

53. When women and marginalized people control the money, we control economies, which control governments, which create laws that end discrimination and marginalization. It is our duty to make millions. —*Sara Kalke*

54. To fund the revolution. —*Amy Walsh*

55. You should become a millionaire, because you have to check that off your list before you become a multimillionaire. —*Delania B*

56. Because who gon' stop you, Boo?! —*Lindsey Vertner*

57. Because looking at your account and seeing all those commas (and all that possibility) unlocks new levels of care and creativity in your little corner of the world. —*Rachel Cargle*

58. To change my family's relationship with money and heal all the women in my lineage. —*Lindsay Padilla*

59. Money helps me be more of who I already am. —*Shamel Leonard*

60. Because it is about damn time. —*Abby Howard*

61. Because I am worthy. —*Carli Jo*

62. To reclaim your childhood and dreams lost to trauma, doubt, and fear. —*Kim Morris*

63. So that any woman becoming a millionaire becomes as normal as all the old white guys that already are. —*Christine Fahy*

64. To heal my ancestors. —*Brandi Jordan*

65. To have more choices to create the world you want to live in. —*Rae McDaniel*

66. Because people less awesome than you have that money, and they're doing bullshit things with it. —*Paige How*

67. You don't need a good reason. —*Melissa McCreery*

68. To redeem the sacrifice of our female ancestors. —*Anne-Lise Jasinski*

69. You should become a millionaire so that you won't have to settle for subpar medical treatment and access to tests that could save your life! —*Diane Thompson*

70. So I can educate girls living in poverty, because education is the key to freedom. —*Nicole Barham*

71. Because it's time to outgrow scarcity narratives that have kept us oppressed and luxuriate in the beauty of life. —*Camila Smith*

72. To have the power to smash the systems that devalue women during pregnancy and childbirth, and create new systems that center, honor, and value a woman's life, body, instinct, and voice as she brings a new life into this world. —*Parijat Deshpande*

73. To prove wrong everyone that ever doubted you. —*Kristen Roberts*

74. To stop generational curses and break the cycle of poverty that affects many women of color. —*Jasmin Haley*

75. To reclaim, at my age of fifty-five, freedom from a lifetime of financial and emotional abuse, live my best and financially free life, retire with security, and simultaneously help other women abandoned by weak-ass controlling men do the same. —*Leanne Banna-Pritchett*

76. So I can give back to the children's hospital that helped my family. —*Carol-Anne Schneider*

77. To write a new story about the role of women in society that isn't wrapped up in their capacity to birth or raise children. —*Nicole Catenazzi*

78. Because they don't teach you this in school. —*Nikki McKnight*

79. You should become a millionaire to not only have a seat at the table, but have the authority to tell others to go ahead and take several seats. —*Amanda Darling Taylor*

80. To have full agency over our time, creativity, and life choices. —*TC Cooper*

81. So we can put our money where our beliefs are. —*Jessica Hitchcock*

82. Because our children learn the most by observing us. —*Julie Lieberman Neale*

83. To smash white supremacy. —*Courtney Shaughnessy*

84. To cocreate a world in which we and all our future generations thrive, in our sovereignty, diversity, and interdependence. —*Stephanie Francesca Kohler*

85. To advocate for others who haven't yet found their own power to become a millionaire. —*Kendra Cote*

86. So you never ever have to ask for permission to buy all the things you want. —*Sheryl Shield*

87. So I can spread joy. —*Mia LaMotte*

88. Because fuck The Man. —*Jennifer Lambert*

89. To not just have a seat at the table—*own* the table, the property it's in, and the very ground it all sits on. —*ML Jaye*

90. Because equity requires power. —*Jade Connelly-Duggan*

91. To rewrite the history of where the world's wealth is distributed so future generations don't see the wealth disparity as it exists today. —*Franka Baly*

92. I don't want me or my children or children's children (and so on) to ever need to ask a white man (or his institutions) for a single thing. Period. —*Shunta Grant*

93. So that your children don't have to look to examples on TV, but they can feel empowered by the influence in their own home. —*Cori Brock Cooper*

94. So you can boldly and unwaveringly walk out God's purpose for your life. —*Alaya Linton*

95. So I can contribute to higher education for Black and Latinx folks and create opportunities for us to thrive in all things. —*Mirna Valerio*

96. So that you can buy things for your home and your children or pay for your family to go on a vacation without checking in with your husband. —*Nsenga Knight*

97. To fund an epic game that appeals to women with a great story line. —*Jenny Chan*

98. To feel safe. —*Sara Vartanian*

99. To fund the arts. —*Tia DeShazor*

100. Money is access. —*DeAnn Ferguson*

ACKNOWLEDGMENTS

Writing and producing a book takes a village. There were so many champions, supporters, and experts involved in getting this book in your hands.

I would like to express my sincere thanks to the following humans:

Dediako, my partner in business, life, and love for more than fifteen years now. Thank you for staying up late with me while I edited, traveling to conferences that you had no interest in to support me, watching the kids while I wrote, and making me delicious lattes every day. You have always been so supportive of my dreams and believed in bigger and better for me before I ever did. You never let me succumb to haters or wallow in imposter syndrome. Your partnership and support have helped make me the badass woman I am today. Thank you, my love.

My babies, thank you for lending your mama to the world on various occasions and being such magical and understanding little humans. You inspire me to build a better world for each of you. I would never have bothered to work this hard without you motivating me daily. I love you so much. Thank you, my loves.

Mom, when I was a kid and said that I wanted to be an astronaut, doctor, or lawyer, you always encouraged me. You told me I could be anything that I wanted when I grew up. And I believed you. That is why I am who I am today. Thank you for always believing in me.

Angela, thank you for always letting me borrow your cute clothes, reminding me that I am smart, lending me money when I needed it, and telling me to get my shit together when I needed that too. And thank you for telling all your friends to buy this book. I wish everyone could have a sister as amazing as you. Thank you, Sissy.

Brittany and the Hello Seven Team, where do I even begin? Without your support and expertise at Hello Seven every day, I would not have had the space or time to think about this book, let alone write it. With your help, encouragement, feedback, and belief in our shared mission, this book was made possible. Thank you, Team.

Alexandra, thank you for inviting me to come to Hawaii for a week to finally get started on writing this book. It was a magical week, and your continued coaching, guidance, expertise, and editing has made this book so much stronger. You are a genius. Thank you, friend.

Robert, thank you for always being available for laughs, tears, and pep talks, and reminding me of *who I is* on a regular basis. You always hold space for my ideas and hold me accountable to my vision. You never let me punk out. I wish everyone had a best friend like you. Thank you, bestie.

Sara, my amazing editor, thank you for choosing this book and working so hard to ensure that it's in the hands of as many women as possible. I appreciate your ideas, edits, and gracious deadline extensions. Thank you, Sara.

Steve and Jamie, you are wonderful agents, and I am thankful to have you to both kick my ass and talk me off the ledge when I need it. I so appreciate the way that you believe in me and my ideas and how you help me bring those ideas to the world on a larger scale than I could have imagined. Also, thank you for ensuring that this Black woman got paid well.

Emma, Farnoosh, and Meghan, your introductions, strategic advice, and feedback helped this book take shape. Thank you for being champions of women building wealth. I appreciate your contributions in the early days of this book's life. Thank you, ladies.

Members of The Club, your stories, struggles, and visions for the future motivated me to write this book. I wrote it so that you would have a handbook for how to become a millionaire and a constant reminder that you are worthy and capable. Thank you for choosing me to be a mentor. Thank you for sharing your wealth journey with me. It is an honor to serve you. Thank you to every Club member and every client I have ever coached.

To all my family, friends, teachers, colleagues, and cocreators, thank you for believing in me, in my ideas, and that we should all be millionaires. I couldn't do it without all of your support.

ENDNOTES

Introduction

1. "Quantifying America's Gender Wage Gap by Race/Ethnicity," National Partnership for Women & Families fact sheet, March, 2020, https://www.nationalpartnership.org/our-work/resources/economic-justice/fair-pay/quantifying-americas-gender-wage-gap.pdf.
2. Laurie Goodman, Jun Zhu, and Bing Bai, "Women Are Better Than Men at Paying Their Mortgages," Urban Institute research report, September 6, 2016, https://www.urban.org/research/publication/women-are-better-men-paying-their-mortgages/view/full_report.
3. Alicia Adamczyk, "This Is the Most Important Money Move That Women Aren't Making," CNBC.com, March 5, 2020, https://www.cnbc.com/2020/03/05/the-important-money-move-that-women-arent-making.html.
4. Brian O'Connell, "American Women Are 80% More Likely Than Men to Be Poverty Stricken in Retirement," The Street, March 4, 2016, https://www.thestreet.com/retirement/american-women-are-80-more-likely-than-men-to-be-poverty-stricken-in-retirement-13482919.
5. Emma Hinchliffe, "Funding for Female Founders Increased in 2019—But Only to 2.7%," *Fortune*, March 2, 2020, https://fortune.com/2020/03/02/female-founders-funding-2019/.
6. "Behind the Numbers: The State of Women-Owned Businesses in 2018," Women's Business Enterprise National Council blog, October 10, 2018, https://www.wbenc.org/blog-posts/2018/10/10/behind-the-numbers-the-state-of-women-owned-businesses-in-2018.
7. Isobel Owen, "Do Women Really Make Better Investors Than Men," *Financial Times*, April 30, 2019, https://www.ft.com/content/f3835072-66a6-11e9-9adc-98bf1d35a056; Stephanie Denning, "Why Have Women Leaders Excelled At

Fighting The Coronavirus Crisis?," *Forbes*, April 26, 2020, https://www.forbes
.com/sites/stephaniedenning/2020/04/26/why-have-women-leaders-excelled
-at-fighting-the-coronavirus-crisis/#5c49b08c543e.

8. Kari Paul and Quentin Fottrell, "The No. 1 Reason You're Still Broke Even If
You Received a Pay Raise Last Year," MarketWatch, January 20, 2019, https://
www.marketwatch.com/story/despite-wage-growth-the-average-american
-suffers-as-cost-of-living-rises-at-a-faster-pace-2019-01-10.

9. Anne Helen Petersen, "I Don't Feel Like Buying Stuff Anymore," BuzzFeed
News, May 18, 2020, https://www.buzzfeednews.com/article/
annehelenpetersen/recession-unemployment-covid-19-economy-consumer
-spending?fbclid=IwAR2KHvC_v8xEQCTct3dxuC3rQn2h9iu4lTaRWeq6snQN-
TOaVN_byg1B8tUI.

10. "The State of Women-Owned Businesses in 2018," Women's Business Enterprise National Council (WBENC), WBENC Blog, https://www.wbenc
.org/blog-posts/2018/10/10/behind-the-numbers-the-state-of-women-owned
-businesses-in-2018.

Chapter 1

1. Christian Larson, *Your Forces and How to Use Them* (Cambridge, UK: Bright
Publishing, 2013), https://www.google.com/books/edition/Your_Forces_and
_How_to_Use_Them/_AlzCwAAQBAJ?hl=en&gbpv=1&bsq=greater%20
than%20any%20obstacle.

2. Heather Long, "Fresh Evidence Women Are Better Investors Than Men," CNN
Business, March 8, 2017, https://money.cnn.com/2017/03/08/investing
/women-better-investors-than-men/index.html.

Chapter 2

1. T. Shawn Taylor, "For Steinem, Women Should Mean Business," *Chicago Tri-
bune*, April 30, 2003, https://www.chicagotribune.com/news/ct-xpm-2003
-04-30-0304300108-story.html.

2. Anne Boden, "Why We Need to #MAKEMONEYEQUAL," Starling Bank,
March 13, 2018, https://www.starlingbank.com/blog/make-money-equal/.

3. Boden, "Why We Need to #MAKEMONEYEQUAL."

4. "UBS Study of Women Investors Reveals the "Divide and Conquer" Approach
to Managing Finances Is a Multi-Generational Problem," UBS Global Wealth
Management press release, March 6, 2019, https://www.ubs.com/global/en
/media/display-page-ndp/en-20190306-study-reveals-multi-generational
-problem.html.

5. Sallie Krawcheck, "Just Buy the F***ing Latte," *Fast Company*, May 6, 2019,
https://www.fastcompany.com/90343899/sallie-krawcheck-saving-money-latte
-advice.

6. Aaron O'Neill, "Black and Slave Population in the United States 1790–1880,"
Statista, Feb. 12, 2020, https://www.statista.com/statistics/1010169/black-and
-slave-population-us-1790-1880/.

7. Reginald Washington, "The Freedman's Savings and Trust Company and
African American Genealogical Research," *Federal Records and African American
History*, Summer 1997, Vol. 29, No. 2, https://www.archives.gov/publications
/prologue/1997/summer/freedmans-savings-and-trust.html.

8. Martha S. Jones, "For Black Women, the 19th Amendment Didn't End Their Fight to Vote," *National Geographic*, August 7, 2020, https://www .nationalgeographic.com/history/2020/08/black-women-continued-fighting -for-vote-after-19th-amendment/.

9. National Park Service, "Between Two Worlds: Black Women and the Fight for Voting Rights," series: Suffrage in America: The 15th and 19th Amendments, https://www.nps.gov/articles/black-women-and-the-fight-for-voting-rights.htm.

10. Al Jazeera, "Who got the right to vote when?" https://interactive.aljazeera .com/aje/2016/us-elections-2016-who-can-vote/index.html.

11. "Quantifying America's Gender Wage Gap by Race/Ethnicity," National Partnership for Women & Families.

12. Brian Kreiswirth and Anna-Marie Tabor, "What You Need to Know About the Equal Credit Opportunity Act and How It Can Help You: Why It Was Passed and What It Is," Consumer Financial Protection Bureau, October 31, 2016, https://www.consumerfinance.gov/about-us/blog/what-you-need-know -about-equal-credit-opportunity-act-and-how-it-can-help-you-why-it-was-passed -and-what-it/.

13. Shelley J. Correll, Stephen Benard, and In Paik. "Getting a Job: Is There a Motherhood Penalty?" *American Journal of Sociology* 112, no. 5 (2007): 1297–1339, https://gap.hks.harvard.edu/getting-job-there-motherhood-penalty.

14. Rebecca Hersher, "Obese Women Make Less Money, Work More Physically Demanding Jobs," NPR, November 8, 2014, https://www.npr.org/2014 /11/08/362552448/obese-women-make-less-money-work-more-physically -demanding-jobs.

15. Virginia Hughes, "Why Do Obese Women Earn Less Than Thin Women (and Obese Men)?" *National Geographic*, November 3, 2014, https://www .nationalgeographic.com/science/phenomena/2014/11/03/why-do-obese -women-earn-less-than-thin-women-and-obese-men/#close.

16. Emma Mishel, "Discrimination against Queer Women in the U.S. Workforce: A Résumé Audit Study." *Socius: Sociological Research for a Dynamic World* 2 (2016): 1–13, https://gap.hks.harvard.edu/discrimination-against-queer-women-us -workforce-resume-audit-study.

17. YW Boston Blog, "Workplace Inclusion of Women Must Integrate Trans Women," October 28, 2019, https://www.ywboston.org/2019/10/workplace -inclusion-of-women-must-integrate-trans-women/.

18. "(1982) Audre Lorde, 'Learning from the 60s," Black Past, August 12, 2012, https://www.blackpast.org/african-american-history/1982-audre-lorde -learning-60s/.

19. "The Powerful Lesson Maya Angelou Taught Oprah," Oprah's Life Class, video aired on October 19, 2011, http://www.oprah.com/oprahs-lifeclass/the -powerful-lesson-maya-angelou-taught-oprah-video.

20. Laura Garnett, "How Can Women Make as Much as Men?" *Inc.*, August 14, 2014, https://www.inc.com/laura-garnett/can-women-be-as-rich-as-men.html.

Chapter 3

1. Stuart Wolpert, "UCLA Neuroscientist's Book Explains Why Social Connection Is as Important as Food and Shelter," UCLA, October 10, 2013, https://news- room.ucla.edu/releases/we-are-hard-wired-to-be-social-248746.

2. C. Nathan DeWall, Timothy Deckman, Richard S. Pond Jr., and Ian Bonser, "Belongingness as a Core Personality Trait: How Social Exclusion Influences Social Functioning and Personality Expression," *Journal of Personality* 79, no. 6 (December, 2011), 1281–1314. doi: 10.1111/j.1467-6494.2010.00695.x. Erratum in: *Journal of Personality* 80, no. 1 (February, 2012), 253. PMID: 22092142.

3. Marianne Cooper, "For Women Leaders, Likability and Success Hardly Go Hand-in-Hand," *Harvard Business Review*, April 30, 2013, https://hbr.org/2013/04/for-women-leaders-likability-a.

4. Patrick Collinson and Sarah Coles, "Eight Reasons You Make Bad Financial Decisions," *The Guardian*, May 30, 2015 (#8, Richard Taffler, professor of finance at Warwick Business School) https://www.theguardian.com/money/2015/may/30/eight-reasons-bad-financial-decisions.

5. "Pay Gap Is Only the Start of Financial Inequality for Women," Cision PR Newswire, May 6, 2019, https://www.prnewswire.com/news-releases/pay-gap-is-only-the-start-of-financial-inequality-for-women-300844184.html.

Chapter 4

1. Sabrina Barr, "Women Still Do Majority of Household Chores, Study Find," *Independent*, July 26, 2019, https://www.independent.co.uk/life-style/women-men-household-chores-domestic-house-gender-norms-a9021586.html.

2. Olga Khazan, "Emasculated Men Refuse to Do Chores—Except Cooking," *The Atlantic*, October 24, 2016, https://www.theatlantic.com/health/archive/2016/10/the-only-chore-men-will-do-is-cook/505067/.

3. Lisa Wade, "The Invisible Workload That Drags Women Down," *Money*, December 29, 2016, https://money.com/women-work-home-gender-gap/.

4. Mia de Graaf, "The Invisible Workload of Modern Mothers: Most Women Still Carry Most Responsibility for the House, Kids, and Family Plans—and It's Damaging Their Mental Health," *Daily Mail*, January 22, 2019, https://www.dailymail.co.uk/health/article-6619433/The-invisible-workload-modern-mothers-damaging-mental-health.html.

5. Stacey Lastoe, "This Is Nuts: It Takes Nearly 30 Minutes to Refocus After You Get Distracted," The Muse, ND, https://www.themuse.com/advice/this-is-nuts-it-takes-nearly-30-minutes-to-refocus-after-you-get-distracted.

6. Fierce Conversations (survey), "Research Finds Majority of Employees Fearful of Sharing Ideas, Opinions & Concerns," https://fierceinc.com/culture-of-nice-survey-2019?_ga=2.223340123.1162052279.1594824867-694912362.1594824867.

7. Timothy A. Judge, Beth A. Livingston, and Charlice Hurst, "Do Nice Guys—and Gals—Really Finish Last? The Joint Effects of Sex and Agreeableness on Income," *Journal of Personality and Social Psychology* 102, no. 2 (2012), 390–407, http://ww.timothy-judge.com/documents/Doniceguysandgalsreallyfinishlast.pdf.

Chapter 5

1. "You Can't Do It Alone," *Harvard Magazine*, May 25, 2011, https://harvardmagazine.com/2011/05/you-cant-do-it-alone.

2. "Guide: What Does a Sherpa at Mount Everest Do?" BBC Newsround, ND, https://www.bbc.co.uk/newsround/27130467.

3. "Guide: What Does a Sherpa at Mount Everest Do?"

4. Aimee Groth, "You're the Average of the Five People You Spend the Most Time With," *Business Insider*, July 24, 2012, https://www.businessinsider.com/jim-rohn-youre-the-average-of-the-five-people-you-spend-the-most-time-with-2012-7.

5. Meta Brown, Elizabeth Setren, and Giorgio Topa, "Do Informal Referrals Lead to Better Matches? Evidence from a Firm's Employee Referral System," IZA Discussion Paper No. 8175, SSRN: https://ssrn.com/abstract=2441471.

6. Diana Rau, "80% Of Jobs Are Not on Job Boards: Here's How to Find Them," *Forbes*, October 2, 2017, https://www.forbes.com/sites/dianatsai/2017/10/02/80-of-jobs-are-not-on-job-boards-heres-how-to-find-them/.

7. Lisa Calhoun, "30 Surprising Facts About Female Founders," *Inc.*, July 6, 2015, https://www.inc.com/lisa-calhoun/30-surprising-facts-about-female-founders.html.

8. Gregory Lewis, "LinkedIn Data Shows Women Are Less Likely to Have Strong Networks—Here's What Companies Should Do," LinkedIn, March 11, 2020, https://business.linkedin.com/talent-solutions/blog/diversity/2020/women-less-likely-to-have-strong-networks.

9. Meg Garlinghouse, "Closing the Network Gap," LinkedIn, September 26, 2019, https://blog.linkedin.com/2019/september/26/closing-the-network-gap.

10. Brian Uzzi, "Research: Men and Women Need Different Kinds of Networks to Succeed," *Harvard Business Review*, February 25, 2019, https://hbr.org/2019/02/research-men-and-women-need-different-kinds-of-networks-to-succeed.

11. Uzzi, "Research: Men and Women Need Different Kinds of Networks to Succeed."

12. Paul Gompers and Silpa Kovvali, "The Other Diversity Dividend," *Harvard Business Review*, July–August 2018, https://hbr.org/2018/07/the-other-diversity-dividend.

13. Elizabeth MacBride, "Diversity In Venture Capital: In the U.S., It May Be Getting Worse," *Forbes*, July 31, 2019, https://www.forbes.com/sites/elizabethmacbride/2019/07/31/diversity-in-venture-capital-in-the-us-it-may-be-getting-worse/#555a7e0b7edb.

14. First Round, "10 Year Project," http://10years.firstround.com/.

15. Katie Abouzahr, Matt Krentz, John Harthorne, and Frances Brooks Taplett, "Why Women-Owned Startups Are a Better Bet," Boston Consulting Group, June 6, 2018, https://www.bcg.com/publications/2018/why-women-owned-startups-are-better-bet.aspx?utm_source=201807Q2TOP&utm_medium=Email&utm_campaign=201807_Q2TOP_TOP10_NONE_GLOBAL&redir=true.

Chapter 6

1. David Desteno, "Three Emotions That Can Help You Succeed at Your Goals," Greater Good Magazine, January 12, 2018, https://greatergood.berkeley.edu/article/item/three_emotions_that_can_help_you_succeed_at_your_goals.

2. Leigh Buchanan, "How to Achieve Big, Hairy, Audacious Goals," *Inc.*, November 1, 2012, https://www.inc.com/leigh-buchanan/big-ideas/jim-collins-big-hairy-audacious-goals.html.

3. Edwin A. Locke and Gary P. Latham, *New Developments in Goal Setting and Task Performance* (New York: Routledge, 2013), https://onlinelibrary.wiley.com/doi/abs/10.1111/peps.12113_5.

4. Art Kleiner, "Ellen Langer on the Value of Mindfulness in Business," strategy+business, February 9, 2015, https://www.strategy-business.com/article/00310?gko=ddca6.

5. "Mindfulness in the Age of Complexity," *Harvard Business Review*, March 2014, https://hbr.org/2014/03/mindfulness-in-the-age-of-complexity.

6. Online Etymology Dictionary, https://www.etymonline.com/word/jealous.

7. Matthew Hutson and Tori Rodriguez, "How Clothes Influence Our Performance," *Scientific American*, January 1, 2016, https://www.scientificamerican.com/article/dress-for-success-how-clothes-influence-our-performance/.

8. Dennis Green, "It Turns Out That Dressing Well Can Actually Make You More Successful," *Business Insider*, August 5, 2017, https://www.businessinsider.com/dressing-for-success-actually-works-2017-7.

Chapter 7

1. Megan Dalla-Camina, "The Reality of Imposter Syndrome," *Psychology Today*, September 3, 2018, https://www.psychologytoday.com/us/blog/real-women/201809/the-reality-imposter-syndrome.

2. Rebecca Burn-Callander, "Imposter Syndrome: Women's Career Killer," *Telegraph*, May 16, 2019, https://www.telegraph.co.uk/business/women-entrepreneurs/imposter-syndrome-women-careers/.

3. Katty Kay and Claire Shipman, "The Confidence Gap," *The Atlantic*, May 2014, https://www.theatlantic.com/magazine/archive/2014/05/the-confidence-gap/359815/.

4. Kay and Shipman, "The Confidence Gap."

5. Burn-Callander, "Imposter Syndrome: Women's Career Killer."

6. Jessica Bennett, "How to Overcome 'Imposter Syndrome,'" *The New York Times*, ND, https://www.nytimes.com/guides/working-womans-handbook/overcome-impostor-syndrome.

7. Rebecca Hinds, "The 1 Trait 94 Percent of C-Suite Women Share (And How to Get It)," *Inc.*, February 8, 2018, https://www.inc.com/rebecca-hinds/the-1-trait-94-percent-of-c-suite-women-share-and-how-to-get-it.html.

Chapter 8

1. Megan Leonhardt, "60% of Women Say They've Never Negotiated Their Salary—and Many Quit Their Job Instead," CNBC, January 31, 2020, https://www.cnbc.com/2020/01/31/women-more-likely-to-change-jobs-to-get-pay-increase.html.

2. Taylor Lewis, "The 10 Not-So-Publicized Times Jay Z and Beyonce Gave Back," *Essence*, February 1, 2017, https://www.essence.com/lifestyle/do-good-brothers/10-not-so-publicized-times-jay-z-and-beyonce-gave-back/#144744.

3. Phoenix House, "Beyoncé Opens Cosmetology Center at Phoenix House," March 16, 2010, https://www.phoenixhouse.org/news-and-views/news-and-events/beyonc-opens-cosmetology-center-phoenix-house/.

4. Rachael Schultz, "8 of Our Favorite Philanthropic Female Celebrities," *Shape*, December 18, 2014, https://www.shape.com/celebrities/celebrity-photos/8-our-favorite-philanthropic-female-celebrities.

5. "Investing in Women and Girls," Organisation for Economic Co-operation and Development webpage, https://www.oecd.org/dac/gender-development/investinginwomenandgirls.htm.

6. "Empowering Girls & Women," Clinton Global Initiative webpage, https://www.un.org/en/ecosoc/phlntrpy/notes/clinton.pdf.

7. David Harrison and Soo Oh, "Women Working Longer Hours, Sleeping Less, as They Juggle Commitments," *The Wall Street Journal*, June 19, 2019, https://www.wsj.com/articles/women-working-longer-hours-sleeping-less-labor-department-finds-11560980344.

8. Drew Weisholtz, "Women Do 2 More Hours of Housework Daily Than Men, Study Says," Today, January 22, 2020, https://www.today.com/news/women-do-2-more-hours-housework-daily-men-study-says-t172272.

9. Alisa Wolfson, "Why Women Give So Much More to Charities Than Men," MarketWatch, October 26, 2018, https://www.marketwatch.com/story/why-women-give-so-much-more-to-charity-than-men-2018-10-26.

10. Wolfson, "Why Women Give So Much More to Charities Than Men."

Chapter 9

1. Joseph P. Lash, *Helen and Teacher: The Story of Helen Keller and Anne Sullivan Macy* (New York: Delacorte Press, 1980), p. 489.

2. Claudia Harmata, "Chrissy Teigen Gets Real About Home Life as a Celebrity: 'We Have a House Manager,'" *People*, December 10, 2019, https://people.com/home/chrissy-teigen-and-john-legend-have-a-house-manager/.

3. Ashley V. Whillans, Elizabeth W. Dunn, Paul Smeets, Rene Bekkers, and Michael I. Norton, "Buying Time Promotes Happiness," *Proceedings of the National Academy of Sciences* 114, no. 32 (August, 2017) 8523–8527; DOI:10.1073/pnas.1706541114.

4. Niraj Chokshi, "Want to Be Happy? Buy More Takeout and Hire a Maid, Study Suggests," *The New York Times*, July 27, 2017, https://www.nytimes.com/2017/07/27/science/study-happy-save-money-time.html.

5. Dina Gerdeman, "Want To Be Happier? Spend Money On Avoiding Household Chores," *Forbes*, November 14, 2017, https://www.forbes.com/sites/hbsworkingknowledge/2017/11/14/want-to-be-happier-spend-money-on-avoiding-household-chores/#6e2cd36e2553.

6. Karen Langley, "For Beyoncé, Creativity Is the Ultimate Power," *Elle*, December 9, 2019, https://www.elle.com/culture/celebrities/a29999871/beyonce-ivy-park-adidas-interview/.

7. Adam Grundy, "Nonemployer Statistics and County Business Patterns Data Tell the Full Story," United States Census Bureau, September 18, 2018, https://www.census.gov/library/stories/2018/09/three-fourths-nations-businesses-do-not-have-paid-employees.html.

8. Michael T. Deane, "Top 6 Reasons New Businesses Fail," Investopedia, February 28, 2020, https://www.investopedia.com/financial-edge/1010/top-6-reasons-new-businesses-fail.aspx#.

9. "Office Workers Lose a Third of Their Work Time to Admin According to Independent Research," BusinessWire, June 28, 2017, https://www

.businesswire.com/news/home/20170628005817/en/Office-workers-lose
-work-time-admin-independent.

Chapter 10

1. Tracy Jan, "White Families Have Nearly 10 Times the Net Worth of Black Families. And the Gap Is Growing," *The Washington Post*, September 28, 2017, https://www.washingtonpost.com/news/wonk/wp/2017/09/28/black-and -hispanic-families-are-making-more-money-but-they-still-lag-far-behind-whites/.
2. Courtney E. Martin, "Closing the Racial Wealth Gap," *The New York Times*, April 23, 2019, https://www.nytimes.com/2019/04/23/opinion/closing-the-racial -wealth-gap.html.
3. Inequality.org, "Economic Inequality Across Gender Diversity," ND, https:// inequality.org/gender-inequality/.
4. Thomas C. Corley, "After Asking Nearly 200 Self-made Millionaires, I Can Tell You There Are 3 Primary Ways They Got Rich," *Business Insider*, December 1, 2017, https://www.businessinsider.com/types-of-self-made-millionaires -2017-11.
5. Thomas C. Corley, "After Asking Nearly 200 Self-made Millionaires, I Can Tell You There Are 3 Primary Ways They Got Rich."

INDEX

ABOUT THE AUTHOR

Rachel Rodgers is a business coach, attorney, wife, mother, and founder of Hello Seven, a multimillion dollar company.

Her mission is to teach women, especially women of color, how to make more money and build wealth—without sacrificing their family, health, or sanity in the process.

Rachel started her career working for state and federal judges, nonprofits, and even Hillary Clinton. Today, she's a CEO and visionary featured in publications like *Time, Forbes, Entrepreneur, Women's Health, Fast Company*, and the *Washington Post*.

When she's not coaching, speaking, podcasting, or writing, you can find Rachel on her fifty-seven-acre ranch that she bought with her own damn money, doing horse girl shit and chasing her kids around in nature.

Learn more about Rachel and how you can grow your business and bank account at helloseven.co or by subscribing to the *Hello Seven Podcast*.

READY TO MAKE YOUR MILLION?
JOIN THE CLUB.

We Should All Be Millionaires: The Club is an online community and make-that-money classroom for women, men, and nonbinary folks who are ready to build wealth. No matter what is getting in the way of you making serious coin—whether it's shaky confidence, lack of community, knowledge gaps when it comes to marketing/sales/systems/intellectual property, or a janky mindset about money *(it's okay, we've been there!)*—The Club has got what you need. It's the perfect next step after reading this book.

We are determined to help you win.

- Ready to slay imposter syndrome and get your mindset right? We have an entire suite of resources and live weekly coaching dedicated to helping you drop Broke-Ass Thoughts and step up as the capable, qualified badass you are.
- Need to raise your prices, market your business, or expand your audience? The Club offers exclusive training and education to

show you exactly how you can grow your business or bring in more income.

- Looking for your Million Dollar Squad? They're right here—in our thriving community full of ambitious millionaire or millionaire-in-the-making folks just like you.

Ready to make Million Dollar Decisions? Join The Club. This will be your first Million Dollar Decision, but it won't be your last. Head to helloseven.co/club to join us now.